T0294860

International Business Research

Strategies and Resources

Esther L. Gil
Awilda Reyes

THE SCARECROW PRESS, INC.
Lanham • Toronto • Plymouth, UK
2013

Published by Scarecrow Press, Inc.
A wholly owned subsidiary of The Rowman & Littlefield Publishing Group, Inc.
4501 Forbes Boulevard, Suite 200, Lanham, Maryland 20706
http://www.scarecrowpress.com

Estover Road, Plymouth PL6 7PY, United Kingdom

British Library Cataloguing in Publication Information Available

Library of Congress Cataloging-in-Publication Data

Gil, Esther L., 1952-
International business research : strategies and resources / Esther L. Gil, Awilda Reyes. p. cm
Includes bibliographical references and index.
ISBN 978-0-8108-8726-8 (pbk. : alk. paper) -- ISBN 978-0-8108-8727-5 (ebook) 1. International business enterprises--Research. 2. Business--Research. 3. International trade--Research. I. Reyes, Awilda, 1952- II. Title.
HD2755.5.G535 2013
338.8'8072--dc23
2012032337

Printed in the United States of America

Contents

Introduction

For thousands of years, the human race has engaged in the exchange of goods and services across country borders, using the transportation systems available, such as roads or the sea. Often these transactions were made because the resources to manufacture or grow even the bare necessities were not available locally. For instance, the land in a particular area might not have been suitable for agriculture, so staples like fruits and vegetables had to be acquired elsewhere. This could involve traveling long distances, even crossing the borders of other territories and countries. Unfortunately, sometimes contact led to acts of war, as well.

This interaction across societies is part of globalization. Globalization is very complex and can be viewed and defined from a wide range of viewpoints, including environmental, political, sociological, philosophical, cultural, and scientific. From a social science perspective, researchers can easily see how globalization correlates with international business activity.

Beckfield and Brady refer to "the increasing intensity of international economic exchange, the rising prominence and influence of international organizations, the diffusion of cultural products across national boundaries, the spanning of social ties across international borders, and global environmental problems"[1] as elements of globalization. These specific features are evident when one looks at how international business evolves. Globalization is also defined as a process by which different parts of the globe become interconnected by economic, social, cultural, and political means.[2] As this integration develops, it is clear that companies and businesses need to rethink their approach to international trade and investment in order to develop business models that address major trade- and investment-related issues within a global context.

Advances in technology are intensifying the speed in which globalization is developing and expanding global markets. For example, the World Wide Web allows people to communicate with anybody around the world in an instant. In addition, it allows someone to buy almost anything from around the world through online storefronts. Not only is a consumer able to select products, but there are systems in place that streamline the exchange of currency needed for this to happen effectively. As a result, hundreds of shoppers around the world can engage in this activity in minutes. International trade has increased not only in speed, but also in terms of volume. Furthermore, it opens up the markets for entrepreneurs with ideas and products that can fill and satisfy their needs.

The progression of globalization and advances in technology underscore the importance of developing thorough global community understanding. In order for this to happen, a business should understand the demographics of a country, examine foreign market trends, learn about the social issues within a country, and become aware of the makeup of its religion, politics, economy, laws and regulations, language, communication, and culture. Developing countries face particular problems in dealing with technical procedures. Such difficulties arise because these countries often lack human and financial resources, scientific infrastructure, awareness of international obligations, and technical expertise to frame and develop necessary standards.[3] Being aware of issues like these is very important when conducting international business transactions.

Researchers will always face challenges when seeking international business information. This book provides an overview of strategies, based on a combination of research in the literature and the authors' own practical experiences, as well as descriptions of the sources available to meet these needs. This book will guide readers through the research process for different elements of international business research and provide information for some of the major sources for international business.

Our approach to researching international business is to look at the overall process rather than focusing on specific sources. It is somewhat geared to the academic environment, but several sources presented are available to anybody in the world with access to the Internet.

Chapter 1 introduces the reader to some basic tools and sources that should be considered when starting an international business project.

Chapter 2 presents the role of money, the international monetary system, and financial markets in international business transactions; the last two topics consist of trade and foreign direct investment. Appropriate resources for finding relevant data are presented.

Chapter 3 identifies major organizations and information providers who have resources that cover a wide range of countries. The sources from these entities are presented and descriptions given. Special attention was given to select resources that focus on major environmental, legal, political, and cultural issues within the context of globalization.

Chapter 4 gives an overview of the most relevant regional economic organizations and trading blocs of the world. This includes information about what they provide on their websites.

Chapter 5 discusses strategies and resources for conducting international company research. This includes identifying sources from database providers of company information, as well as those that can be found on the World Wide Web.

Chapter 6 reviews different classifications worldwide that are relevant when conducting industry research.

Chapter 7 and chapter 8 both identify strategies and resources for finding relevant information from a global perspective for each of its topics. Chapter 7 focuses on industry research and provides sources that help in analyzing the industry. Chapter 8 focuses on market research. It deals with the various components that embody this activity, such as the 4Ps, and identifies resources that address each one.

Chapter 9 offers ways that investors can diversity their portfolios, focusing on four specific financial instruments and the sources available for finding information about them. Trading directly in global stock markets is also addressed.

There is some overlap in the sources that have been selected for different chapters because many of the major providers of information, such as the United Nations and the Organisation for Economic Co-operation and Development, are disseminating their data through a portal. As a result, some of the data and information in a system may work for one area of research, and other facts for a different one.

Some of the websites identified in this book provide global information while others focus on regions of the world. The information and language available varies from country to country and region to region and this is noted in the description.

Links were verified prior to submitting the manuscript, but as anyone who has ever used the World Wide Web knows, web addresses and sites disappear without notice.

From an academic perspective, as globalization continues to grow, and international projects are further integrated into the curriculum of business schools and the research of its faculty, business librarians strive to identify the appropriate resources and databases to meet these needs. It is important for its academic community to be able to access not only sources that are fee-based, but those that are publicly available as well. This book offers some strategies and identifies resources on how to go about finding this information. The authors hope it offers helpful guidance into the research process when doing international business research.

NOTES

1. Jason Beckfield and David Brady, "Social and Economic Aspects of Globalization," *Social and Economic Aspects of International Encyclopedia of the Social Sciences* Vol. 3. 2nd ed. William A. Darity, Jr. (Detroit: Macmillan Reference USA, 2008), 332.

2. "Globalization." *The Hutchinson Unabridged Encyclopedia with Atlas and Weather guide*. Abington, UK: Helicon, 2010. *Credo Reference*. Web (14 June 2012).

3. "Technical Barriers to Trade." *Globalization: Encyclopedia of Trade, Labor, and Politics*. Santa Barbara, CA: ABC-CLIO, 2005. Credo Reference. Web (14 June 2012).

ONE

Basic Tools and Sources for International Business Research

An individual can begin an international business research project in different ways. Whatever the case may be, it is worth understanding the type of information and tools that are available locally, nationally, and around the world. In this chapter, we will begin by discussing in general what is available in a library and the tools to access this material (i.e., the library catalog), commercial databases, publishers of international content, search engines, browsers, research guides, and a little about Web 2.0.

LIBRARY CATALOG

In the world of information and the omnipresence of the World Wide Web, it is very easy to overlook the rich source of information provided by a library. If one has the good fortune to be a patron of such an institution, the individual should be sure to include a visit to it or go to its website and discover what is available.

US academic libraries purchase materials that meet the needs of their patrons. Their collections will reflect the curricular and research needs of the university. In response to the international courses offered in business schools and international studies programs, as well as faculty researching international issues and topics, academic libraries purchase relevant books and subscribe to appropriate online databases that cover this area. There are also individuals who may be interested in doing research for other business activities such as the globalization of investment portfolios. As such, a library's collection will reflect these needs.

The library catalog is the tool used to identify and inventory the material that a library owns. It has records for items such as print and digital books, DVDs, journals, newspapers, computer files, cartographic materials, and so forth. Some libraries also have catalog records for the databases to which they subscribe, providing an additional way that a patron can find them on a library's website. Taking this a step further, there are often library records for some of the research reports that are provided in databases such as ABI/Inform Complete and Business Source Complete. This includes Business Monitor and MarketLine (previously called Datamonitor) market reports, and Economist Intelligence Unit's (EIU) Country reports.

Library catalogs are web based and have a search interface that allows a user to find books using different options. Starting with a keyword or keywords is an effective way for the researcher to begin because generally he or she does not know what the authoritative subject heading is for the topic of interest. Once the results are presented for the keyword search, the individual can click on the title of an item and identify relevant subject headings.

The catalog interface also has features for searching in specific fields of a bibliographic record, including title, author, subject, and call number. In an academic library, bibliographic records have subject headings established by the Library of Congress. In addition, a specific call number representing a heading is assigned to the book and the record. After identifying a subject heading from the results of a keyword search, another search can be done by entering it in the subject heading field of the online catalog. Because a subject search groups material with a similar topic, it is a way to find relevant items. For example, if the individual wants to find books about multinational corporations, the Library of Congress subject heading that should be used in the subject field is "international business enterprises." If needed, results can be limited, adding additional subjects or keywords. If the user can't find what is needed in the catalog, he or she should consult with a reference librarian.

There are several advantages to using the library and its catalog. A researcher is to identify material that is only available digitally. For example, it would be possible to find scholarly books on topics related to global finance or practical books on how to diversify a portfolio using any number of financial instruments that may be provided only in electronic format. This is very important as libraries purchase fewer print material and move toward electronic versions. Specific international business-related journals, magazines, and newspapers (i.e., the *Economist*) might also be available online through the catalog. In addition, a library may subscribe to aggregated systems like Credo Reference and Gale Virtual Reference Library to provide digital access to encyclopedias and dictionaries that have background information about a topic or a definition to a term. It can also provide access to market and country reports that are published by Business Monitor, Datamonitor, and the EIU that are available through databases like ABI/Inform Complete and Business Source Complete. This is possible if the library has cataloged these items. In addition, the library may have sources available only in some form of hard copy, such as reference books, microform, and DVDs, and one would be able to identify this with the catalog. Furthermore, as a library moves more and more of its print collection to offsite facilities, the ability to browse the collection is diminished, and browsing the catalog via a call number is the only way to do this.

Despite the importance of using the catalog to find sources in a library's collections, there are stories from users saying that finding the titles of books using the Google search engine or through Amazon.com is easier than using a library's online catalog. This user experience has had librarians discussing the "next generation catalog" (NGC) for more than five years,[1] as well as developing or subscribing to other types of systems that a user can use to find material, such as Innovative Interfaces Inc.'s (III) Encore, Serials Solution's AquaBrowser, and VuFind. These systems have an interface wherein a user enters keywords in a search box, and can then limit the results using facets such as title, author, subject, formats, tags, dates, and languages. VuFind, developed by librarians, has a drop down menu enabling a user to search by title, author, subject, and tag. These types of solutions incorporate some Web 2.0 features as well, such as providing users a way to tag material that they find relevant; they can later use this tag in a keyword search and retrieve the same items.

More comprehensive discovery tools such as ProQuest's Summon, EBSCO's Discovery, ExLibris' Primo Central, and OCLC's WorldCat Local services provide a single entry point to a library's collection. The user can thus search not only the library's catalog records, but also a significant percentage of the full-text online content that is available in the library's collection at the article level (80 percent for the University of Denver's Penrose Library). These tools include facets that allow the individual to fine-tune the results.

FEE-BASED DATABASES

Despite the fact that there is a great deal of publicly available information on the Internet—including for companies—libraries still subscribe to databases provided by a wide range of vendors that cover different business-related areas. This includes those that provide information about companies, countries, industries, and markets. Some of the features they may have are as follows:

- Globally listed and unlisted company profiles, financial performance, and historical financial data
- Credit ratings, indices, investment research, and risk evaluations

- Mergers and acquisitions data
- Ratios and benchmark data
- Tools for portfolio performance analysis
- Tools to generate statistical reports dynamically
- Built-in charting capabilities, export to Excel functionality, and report builders
- Industry and market research reports that are not publicly available
- New trading and investment ideas
- Cross-country comparisons or the ability to create custom rankings
- Risk analysis
- Flexibility and the ability to customize results based on data requirements

For any type of research, databases to which a library subscribes usually have to be accessed through its website or catalog. This includes databases that focus on companies, such as Bureau van Dijk (BvD) databases, Hoovers Online, Morningstar Investment Research Center, Mergent Online, OneSource, S&P's NetAdvantage, and Thomson One. This is also true of databases that cover other areas of research, such as countries, markets, and industry, and that are produced by such companies as e-marketer, Euromonitor, Frost & Sullivan, Gartner, and IBISWorld.

Libraries usually have links from their home page with headings like "Databases," "Electronic Resources," "Online Research," "Research," and "Online Research Resources" that take an individual to the webpage where a user can access this information. They also offer subject-specific guides that incorporate resources that are pertinent to a topic.

AGENCIES, ORGANIZATIONS, PUBLISHERS

As one begins to do research related to international business, an individual should know about the basic producers of information and data in this area. For instance, the researcher should become familiar with government agencies in his or her country that support businesses that want to engage in global markets and that provide relevant information. In the United States, this includes the Department of State, the Central Intelligence Agency, the Census Bureau, the International Trade Association, and the Bureau of Economic Affairs. Examples of non-US agencies are Australia's Australian Trade Commission and Department of Foreign Affairs and Trade and the United Kingdom's UK Trade and Investment. Other governments will have these types of divisions as well.

Another group of providers with which to be aware are international organizations such as the International Monetary Fund (IMF), Organisation for Economic and Co-operative Development (OECD), World Bank, and the World Trade Organization (WTO); and collectives such as the Asia-Pacific Economic Cooperation (APEC) and European Union (EU).

These entities provide publicly available data that will be discussed later in the chapter. Agencies, organizations, and collectives provide publicly available data and reports about countries and regions, as well as other topics (i.e., global investment reports) that can be very valuable to the researcher. In addition to recognizing the kind of information and tools they provide, being familiar with such organizations can make the use of search engines more effective.

Some types of information that these entities provide include background information about a country, such as its history; an overview of its economic, political, and social situation; its culture; standard of living; and the potential risks that a business might face when entering a particular market. They also gather and analyze data worldwide and disseminate them through interactive portals. For example, the UN's Undata system allows the user to find data in many areas for countries around the world. This includes demographics, trade, and the economy. World Bank has the Doing Business series dealing with the ease of doing business in specific countries.

There are also commercial vendors who produce this type of material, including Business Monitor International, EIU, Emerging Markets Information Service (ISI), Euromonitor, and Informational Handling Services (IHS). Fee-based vendors such as Bureau van Dijk, Hoovers, Kompass, Mergent, infogroup, Standard & Poor's, and Thomson provide subscriptions to databases with company information worldwide and/or that have investment analysts' reports.

The researcher can then use the names of these organizations and publishers to search in library catalogs, discovery tools, and the web to find material that they provide.

PUBLICLY AVAILABLE SOURCES

An important trend that is happening as a result of the growth of the World Wide Web is that there is more and more publicly available information related to global business and economic activity from reliable sources. For example, if one doesn't have access to subscription databases in certain areas, there are freely available websites provided by reliable organizations such as those mentioned in the previous section, as well as programs sponsored by them. For instance, the UN has various programs, such as the UN Conference on Trade and Development (UNCTAD), UN Population Fund, and UN Research Institute for Social Development. Other groups include the US Trade and Development Agency, World Bank, and the World Trade Organization.

These entities provide a wide range of sources and data, some of which are referred to in several chapters in this book. Although free, they may have interfaces that are difficult to navigate and to retrieve the information they provide. Often it is necessary to dig through the website, find what is wanted, download and manipulate the data, and analyze the facts. Depending on the type of information sought, the researcher may have to obtain data from one, two or more internal links as well as other websites. In addition, the information provided may not be as current or detailed as needed and/or one may have to register or subscribe in order to obtain information that is provided at a site.

There are also comprehensive online directories that have been created at different academic institutions around the world. The gold standard is Michigan State University's GlobalEDGE (globaledge.msu.edu/).

This source was introduced a couple of years after the World Wide Web was launched in 1991. At the time it was called International Business Resources on the WWW (IBR). It was one of the many web-based directories that were created during the early period of the web as a way to find relevant information efficiently and effectively. The present version is much more comprehensive because it goes beyond being a webpage that identifies sources with links to them. Now it also has content and tools for its academic community. For instance, it has online tutorials on topics such as "Doing Business in . . . ," "Culture," "Exporting," "Market Research and Entry," and "Microfinance." Its Global Resource Directory identifies sources in four areas, "Research," "Current Topics in IB" (international business), "Trade," and "Reference Sources." Each of these areas is subdivided by relevant topics, such as "Globalization" under "Current Topics" or "Finance" under the "Reference Category." Clicking on one of them will provide a list of freely available sources, with descriptions for each. Although its URL, content, and look changed, it is a site that has endured for the last twenty or so years[2] and it has value not only for its own academic community, but for those around the world as well.

Another site that was created in the early days of the public World Wide Web for the purpose of organizing and identifying sources for international research on the web is the WWW Virtual Library: International Affairs Resources (www2.etown.edu/vl/). Although focused on international affairs, it does have a link for international business and economics. There are also links to other sources that would be useful for international business research, including organizations, nongovernmental organizations, news sources, and country and regional sources.

SEARCH ENGINES

There were other web-based search engines publicly available before Google entered the market in 1998, including Altavista, Excite, Lycos, and NorthernLight. However, with its PageRank system for ranking webpages[3] that quickly retrieves results that were often relevant, users gravitated toward Google as the search engine of choice. Google continues to be a top search engine, although others like Bing and Yahoo! Search compete for the same market. The entrance of these advanced search engines has improved the search experience for users and has revolutionized the way one finds information on the web. It isn't uncommon that a search engine is where researchers begin. Google (www.google.com), Yahoo! Search (search.yahoo.com), and Bing (www.bing.com) have also been launched around the world, so they are international in scope. The University of California at Berkeley also recommends Exalead (www.exalead.com/search/), pointing out that it is a very large database, has commands that allow searching by proximity, and provides numerous ways of refining a search.

Search engines generally index web pages that are static, which includes web sites that have fixed extensions, such as .html, .pdf, .doc, .xls, and .txt. These search engines will not find pages in what can be referred to as the "hidden web," and as a result, these will not be indexed. One of the reasons this occurs is because some of the pages are dynamic, which means they do not permanently exist on a server, but are generated on the fly. Another is that the owners of a website utilize a robots.txt file that blocks a search engine from indexing a page. In addition, a page may require registration or a subscription to access it. Finally, it won't be able to access those commercial databases that libraries and others subscribe to because these require a password or some other way of accessing (such as through a proxy) them. Items that are not indexed will not be found with these types of search engines. Even so, a search engine is a very good tool to use to find information. In fact, if research needs to be comprehensive, then two or more search engines should be used.

To begin using a search engine, the researcher will enter keywords in the search box provided. Thousands and millions of results are often retrieved, but they are ranked by relevancy according to a proprietary algorithm used by each search engine. Consequently, if information isn't on the first few pages, one should try a different search strategy, either using different keywords or utilizing some of the additional search features that are available. For example, most search engines allow the individual to encase a phrase with double quotations, wherein the search engine will find pages that have the desired phrase. Yahoo! Search has an advanced search option that is easily found by using the drop down menu under "More." One can then search for words or exact phrases in the title of a page, or search by site/domain names or file type. To find information from a particular country or organization, the first step is to find the domain name for the relevant country. Top-level domains, such as organization as well as country code domain names, can be found on Norid's "Domain name registries around the world" webpage (www.norid.no/domenenavnbaser/domreg.html). The domain name for websites from Australia is .au. The researcher can then use the advanced search in Yahoo! Search or use the following keywords in any of the three search engines mentioned:

International business site:au

Another strategy would be to find the Australian version of a search engine and redo the search there (www.google.com.au, au.yahoo.com).

Usually a search engine has a "Help" link to find out about other features, such as searching the title of a page or the author, and information about using Boolean operators like *and* as well as *or*. Unfortunately, at this point in time the Google and Bing websites do not feature Help on their pages. In addition, if they have an advanced search interface it is not readily available. Fortunately, the University of California at Berkeley[4] does provide a tutorial that has the commands for limiting fields in Google, Yahoo! Search, and Exalead. It also links to Google's advanced interface. As with other sites and tools on the web, these search engines are adding or deleting features.

A common phenomenon that occurs when researchers are navigating the web is that they will come upon a broken link. This happens for different reasons. For example, a website might have been moved to a different server resulting in a different URL; a webpage might have been deleted from the server; or the webpage has been generated with new software that gives it a different stem (.cfm, .asp), and the referring page has not been corrected in any of these cases. In addition, the previous web address may continue to be in a search engine's cache so that it will still appear in the results. Another reason that might cause a broken link is that a page is moved behind a firewall, requiring a password to access it.

When faced with a broken link, entering the name of the page that the referral site used in a search engine might reveal the new website. If it still exists the researcher will often find it and its new web address. Another strategy is to enter the broken link's URL in the Wayback Machine (archive.org/web/web.php) to get some insight on the type of content available and then use a search engine to potentially find an updated URL and webpage.

BROWSERS

Commonly used browsers are Microsoft Internet Explorer, Firefox, Apple's Safari, and Google Chrome. Browsers are an important consideration when navigating the web and trying to access documents, data, and other types of files. This is because one browser may not download the information while another one does. Consequently, if the individual has trouble downloading the information in one browser, another can be used. Sometimes, however, there is no choice. For example, Thomson Reuters only supports Internet Explorer.

RESEARCH GUIDES

Another strategy for finding international business information is to use the many wonderful and relevant research guides that librarians around the world have created. Research guides will identify resources that are in a library's collection (print, digital, or some other format), relevant subscription databases, and free web sources on a wide array of topics.

Many librarians are using springshare's LibGuide software to create these guides. This software provides widgets and applications that librarians can use to embed chat boxes, online tutorials, videos, podcasts, images, and RSS feeds into any guide. These features enhance the guides, not only by making them more attractive and appealing, but by providing tools that help the user develop research strategies, identify appropriate resources, receive news feeds from sources that cover the topic of the research guide, and provide a means to ask a question as the researcher is using the guide.

Many of these guides will have "LibGuides" as part of the URL. Consequently, a researcher could use the follow keyword strategy in a search engine to find one of these guides:

international business LibGuides site:edu

This search produces more than 3.5 million results from webpages that have the .edu extension. However, it isn't necessary to go beyond the first page because some of the guides that appear have been created by librarians from Rutgers University Libraries, the University of Central Florida Libraries, and the Thomas J. Long Business Library at the University of California Berkeley. However, if the researcher is not retrieving any relevant results after browsing several pages of results, he or she can revise the search strategy to include other information, such as the name of a business librarian.

To find a guide for a very specific topic, for example, information about foreign direct investment, entering the following keywords in a search engine, with or without quotes around the topic,

foreign direct investment libguides site:edu

should yield potential leads.

There are universities that don't use the LibGuides software to create these pathfinders, so the strategy could be revised as follows:

foreign direct investment research guide site:edu

This search will find guides that identify appropriate sources of information, such as the UNCTAD's *Foreign Direct Investment Database*. One can always click on the link provided within a research guide and, if it's free, the individual will be able to access it.

These guides also identify commercial databases as a source, including Business Monitor International and Passport GMID (Global Market Information Database). In such cases, the researcher will not be able to access these resources. The individual should check with his or her library and find out whether it has access and proceed from there. Print sources may also be identified in a guide. Again, the researcher should check his or her library to find out if it has the item.

WEB 2.0

Finding information does not end with databases, free websites, search engines, or library catalogs. The latest trend is Web 2.0, a technology that has a social connotation to it. The organizations and publishers mentioned in this chapter, as well as those referred to in other chapters, have some type of Web 2.0 presence on their website. This is noticeable on the US Department of State's Background Notes landing page (www.state.gov/r/pa/ei/bgn/). The site has a link to a QR code, which is used to access the page with a handheld device, as well as other methods of keeping up with what is happening at the site. It also has the Dipnote blog, Twitter, Tumblr, RSS Feeds, Facebook, Flickr, and YouTube. There are also videos of daily state briefings and remarks made by the Secretary of State on various topics. If one needs to keep updated, signing up to receive RSS feeds may be worthwhile.

SUMMARY

This chapter identified some of the types of tools and sources that exist to find international business information. This included tools like the library catalog, discovery portals, search engines, and research guides. It also identified some of the international organizations that are major producers of international information, and database providers. Where to find information was also addressed, including those sources that are publicly available and those that are provided by commercial vendors.

There will undoubtedly be something else in the future that will make the tools mentioned out of date, but as long as reliable and relevant content continues to be produced, the mechanisms by which it is delivered shouldn't be an issue as long as it is available to all users. The researcher should be aware of key content providers and keep up with the new ways of discovering information in whatever method is used to deliver it, without losing sight of the library collections. Librarians and other information professionals are already doing this.

NOTES

1. Melissa A. Hofmann and Sharon Q. Yang, "Discovering What's Changed: A Revisit of the OPACs of 260 Academic Libraries," *Library HiTech*, 30 no. 2 (2012): 253–74.

2. Anyone who is interested in seeing different iterations of the site since 1997 should enter the following URL: http://ciber.bus.msu.edu/busres.htm in the Wayback Machine (web.archive.org).

3. Rupert Goodwin, "Fast Forward," *PC Magazine* (UK), 78 no. 9 (Sept. 1999): 32.

4. "Recommended Search Engines," www.lib.berkeley.edu/TeachingLib/Guides/Internet/SearchEngines.html (30 June 2012).

TWO

International Monetary System and Financial Markets

Engaging in international business can take shape in several ways, from a small business exporting its goods to another country, to a multinational company establishing a location in a foreign country or setting up a joint venture, to an individual investing in the global financial markets. Whatever the business activity involved, it requires a system where the seller or service provider will receive the appropriate value from what it sells to the buyer. It also requires a structure that enables a business to make any investments it needs so as to export or sell a product, increase the size of its manufacturing facility, extend its services, or locate a branch of its business in another country. The international monetary system and the international and domestic financial markets provide the foundations that allow these type of business endeavors to take place. At the core of this is money. It is required to complete a trade transaction, and it is needed for investment. There are also international and domestic agencies and processes in place to fill these needs and ensure that global trade and investment run as smoothly as possible. In order to do this, they gather and disseminate the data generated by this activity, which are usually available to anyone doing research in these areas. There are also commercial vendors that provide information for a fee. Some of the sources presented later in this chapter provide information for more than one type of data element that one might be pursuing. This is true for some of the databases that are identified. For example, one might be looking for foreign direct investment and find it in a database, but that database may also provide data for the amount of investment that is obtained from the capital or bond markets.

INTERNATIONAL MONETARY SYSTEM

Money is a symbolic term that has had different physical forms throughout history. For example, "the basic monetary unit during the Shang Dynasty (c. 1500–1000 B.C.) . . . were strings of cowry shells."[1] In Mesopotamia it was clay tablets. When civilization began producing precious metals such as bronze, copper, gold, and silver, they were used to manufacture coins. These coins had different features such as images, weight, and information engraved that communicated their value. Even figures were used, as was the case in the Chou Dynasty in China (700 B.C.) where coins had the shapes of axes and knives.[2] Coins are still being used for purchasing items, but they are not made from precious metal. Paper was later used to symbolize money. These were first promissory and bank notes that promised an individual a certain value of gold when they were presented to a bank. Today money is shedding its physical form as banks, businesses, and individuals increasingly use electronic transfers for purchases and financial transactions. This virtual money is possible because buyers and sellers trust that the appropriate institutions will be able to honor the value that is set upon it.

Globally, money in every country is represented by its own currency, each of which has a different value compared to another. This is because countries are independent, and the worth of any country's currency is affected by a wide range of variables, including its culture, customs, politics, monetary and economic policies, and pride. Because of the differences in the value of each country's currency, there are and have historically been different types of currency exchange regimes that provide a method to compare the worth of one country's currency to that of another. For example, after World War II, the Bretton Woods Agreement was implemented to stabilize exchange rates and rebuild the economies of Europe and Japan. This was a fixed system whereby the anchor currency was the dollar.[3] This agreement also created the International Monetary Fund (IMF)—whose role today includes ensuring stable exchange rates—and the International Bank for Reconstruction and Development (IBRD). The latter is now one of five organizations that form the World Bank Group, and it provides loans, advisory services, and risk management products to reduce worldwide poverty in poor countries.[4]

The fixed system that Bretton Woods represented was known as a *pegged rate*, which ended in the early 1970s. A floating system of exchange rates was later implemented, which "allows each nation to use market forces to determine the value of its currency."[5] Durrucci and McKay describe the exchange system that exists today as a mixed system, having both floating and fixed currency systems.[6]

In addition to having a currency exchange regime for buying and selling globally, there are also mechanisms and institutions that ensure stable exchange rates. The IMF, the Bank of International Settlements

(BIS), and central banks work to ensure stable exchange rates by monitoring the foreign exchange market and applying selected monetary and economic policy changes when needed. The Bank of International Settlements refers to itself as the central bank of central banks. This institution not only supports these banks and oversees that exchange rates are stable, but every three years it gathers data on the amount of currency exchange activity that has occurred in the world.

Two terms that are used when discussing exchange rates are "purchasing power parity" (PPP) and the Big Mac Index. PPP means that when the currencies of two countries are exchanged to a common currency, a basket of goods and services in those nations (excluding taxes and other factors) should have the same price in the long run.[7] It is also referred to as the *Law of One Price*. However, this theory doesn't hold when currencies are *overvalued* or *undervalued*. The former refers to a currency that is worth more than would be predicted by an economic model, while the latter means the currency is worth less. For twenty-five years, the *Economist* has used the PPP to produce its Big Mac Index, which is an index representing the overvaluation or undervaluation of currency based on the price of McDonald's Big Mac in each country. Based on PPP, its price should be the same worldwide when the exchange rates are applied.

INTERNATIONAL FINANCIAL MARKETS

In addition to having a monetary infrastructure that makes possible the selling and buying of goods and services worldwide, there are international financial markets that enable foreign direct investment, individual investment, and the lending activities of banks, governments, and international financial institutions to take place. The major financial markets include domestic and global capital markets and the foreign exchange markets.[8] The capital market includes commercial banks worldwide, domestic and international bond markets, and the domestic and global stock (equity) market. Businesses use banks to borrow money, usually short term. If a company or individual borrows money in a currency that is not the lending bank's currency, this is referred to as *Eurocurrency*. When it borrows US dollars in banks outside of the United States it is obtaining a loan in *Eurodollars*. If a US company borrows dollars in a Hong Kong bank, it is borrowing Eurodollars.[9]

Companies may issue debt for long-term investment through the domestic and global bond markets; in essence, obtain loans. When companies issue a bond in a currency different from the local one, it is called a *Eurobond*. If a foreign company issues a bond in the local currency, it is a *foreign bond*. There are also global bonds, which is when bonds are issued simultaneously in multiple currencies, including the local one.

Companies may issue stock in domestic and global stock/equity markets to raise capital for expansion in and out of a country. This includes issuing stock directly on an exchange or using depositary receipts (DRs) as a way to generate capital in markets not their own. DRs are certificates that represent a group of a foreign company's trading equity and that trade on the local exchange rather than the home exchange. There are American DRs, known as ADRs, specific country DRs, and global DRs. For example, Toyota has company stock in the form of ADR certificates that are trading on the New York Stock Exchange. ZDRs are Zambian DRs, which are certificates used by foreign companies to trade on the Lusaka Stock Exchange. More about depositary receipts is covered in the chapter on global investing.

The foreign exchange market facilitates the transfer of currency from one country to that of another. For instance, exporters, importers, investors, and individuals use commercial and private banks to process and apply the appropriate exchange rates on their transactions. When the exchange is done immediately at a specific rate, it is referred to as a *spot transaction*.[10] There are also *forward transactions*, which occur when a business or individual agrees on an exchange rate that will be paid or received on a specific date in the future. *Currency swaps* is a third form of a currency transaction. Investors, including the individual and institutions, can diversify their portfolios by engaging in foreign exchange trading. More about this is provided in the chapter dealing with global investing.

SOURCES

International organizations and other types of collectives have established systems for gathering and disseminating data and information related to the activities involved in the business transactions described in this chapter. This includes establishing classification systems that countries should use when submitting data to organizations such as the International Monetary Fund and others, as well as applying methodologies that standardize data received from around the world. The statistics that are distributed are used by economists, policy makers, businesses, and faculty, students, and staff in academia for different purposes. Economists may use the information to understand what is happening in the global and domestic macro- and micro-economic environments, and often develop different theories to explain this. Policy makers and governments may use it to gain some understanding of the effects certain policies may be having on the international monetary system, financial markets, and trade, as well as to propose and implement solutions that correct any imbalances that may be occurring. Businesses may use the information as a variable in their decision-making process for expanding abroad. Academia may use it to learn more about international trade and the factors that impact it.

The information available includes current and historical currency exchange rates and the state of the foreign exchange market; data that capture the inward and outward flow of investment of a country, including capital and foreign direct investment. There are also reports analyzing the international monetary system and the financial markets. Other sources provide import and export data. One can obtain information from organizations like the IMF, the BIS, and national central banks. Other sources of information include the United Nations Conference on Trade and Development (UNCTAD), the Organisation for Economic Cooperation and Development (OECD), individual government agencies, think tanks, stock exchange websites, and commercial databases. Search engines can also be used to follow any leads discovered as part of the research process. The following sections identify specific sources to use for finding information.

Currency Exchange Rates

It makes sense that the IMF, whose responsibilities include making sure that exchange rates are stable would have a way for a researcher to obtain currency exchange rates. It does so with "Exchange Rate Archives of the Month" and an "Exchange Rate Query Tool" (www.imf.org/external/np/fin/data/param_rms_mth.aspx).

One can obtain one of three reports from the "Archives" page, each of which is generated from the IMF rates database. In each case, an individual can retrieve daily and monthly data going back to January 1994 up to the current month. The first one, "Representative Rates for Selected Currency," provides daily and monthly currency rates for over fifty countries against the dollar. Central banks provide the IMF with the data. The second is "SDRs per Currency Unit." This report has the "official rates used by the Fund to conduct operations with member countries. The rates are derived from the currency's representative exchange rate, as reported by the issuing central bank, and the SDR value of the US dollar rounded to six significant digits."[11] The third report is "Currency Units per SDR." The data provided is the opposite of that provided in the second report, but it is not used by the IMF for transactions. (SDRs refer to "special drawing rights." It is an additional reserve asset used to supplement a country's official reserves. Currently, SDRs are made up of four major currencies: the euro, Japanese yen, pound sterling, and the US dollar. The composition of the SDR is reviewed every five years by the IMF executive board; it will be up for review in 2015.[12])

The IMF exchange rate query tool has three query parameters to obtain data. The first step is to select a country or a currency. It is possible to select from a list made up of almost seventy countries and currencies. The second step is to select the type of exchange rate that is wanted (SDRs per currency unit, representative rates, or currency units per SDR; 3). The next step is to identify the date, which can be a single date (going back to 1994), a period (i.e., last month, last 30 days), or a date range (i.e., January 1, 1994, to January 31, 1994).

Other institutions that work to ensure stable exchange rates also provide them on their websites. This includes the Bank of International Settlements (BIS) (www.bis.org) and the national central banks. The BIS serves as the bank for central banks and assists them toward achieving monetary and financial stability, as well as advancing international cooperation among them.[13]

BIS provides indices for effective exchange rates against each of sixty-one economies (referred to as "broad" indices) and indices for twenty-seven economies (referred to as "narrow" indices) from 1994 onward. Every three years, BIS also publishes the *Triennial Central Bank Survey of Foreign Exchange and Derivatives Market Activity*; the most recent is dated 2010. BIS obtains the data for this publication from central banks, who in turn obtain data from the financial institutions that report to them. The document includes information about the size and structure of the foreign exchange market, top currency pairs for the period covered, and analysis.

Central banks also provide exchange rates against their country's currency. For example, the central bank for the United Kingdom, the Bank of England, has a *Statistical Interactive Database* (www.bankofengland.co.uk/boeapps/iadb/), where in addition to other types of monetary and financial data, there is daily, monthly, quarterly, and annual spot exchange rates for about fifty world currencies based on the pound sterling and the US dollar, as well as fourteen currencies compared against the Euro. One has the potential to obtain statistics from 1963 on, if available. This site provides effective exchange rate indices (ERI) for the pound sterling and other currencies. The ERI "is a measure of the overall change in the trade-weighted exchange value of sterling, calculated by weighting together bilateral exchange rates. It is designed to measure changes in the price competitiveness of traded goods and services and so the weights reflect trade flows in manufactured goods and services."[14]

Another example is the Russian Federation's central bank, the Bank of Russia, which provides monthly exchange rates of foreign currencies against the Russian ruble back to 1999 (www.cbr.ru/eng/). To access the exchange rate section, click on the statistics link on its home page, and then select the financial markets link. Also available are exchange rates of the Gosbank, which are used by the Russian Federation on trade and credit agreements made under the USSR.

The Bank of International Settlements provides a list of central banks for over 170 countries as well as links to them at its website (www.bis.org/cbanks.htm). To find the relevant data on a bank's site, look for a link called "Statistics" and access it. The statistics level may have specific categories for exchange rates, it might be necessary to go to another level. This is the case for the Bank of Russia, where one clicks on the financial markets link from its homepage to obtain the exchange rate data.

Commercial banks may be a source for exchange rates, including Barclays (www.barclays.co.uk/), Wells Fargo (https://www.wellsfargo.com/foreignexchange/), and the Bank of New York/Mellon (https://gm.bankofny.com/FX/ErisaRates.aspx). Others like Deutsche Bank might provide exchange rates for specific countries, such as those for Belgium, Hungary, India, and Switzerland.

There are other sources that provide current exchange rates, such as Bloomberg Currency Converter (www.bloomberg.com/personal-finance/calculators/currency-converter/), Financial Times Markets Data (ft.com/marketsdata), and the *Wall Street Journal*'s Market Data Center (online.wsj.mdc). The XE Universal Currency Converter (www.xe.com/ucc/) provides an interactive tool where one can obtain not only current, but historical rates ranging from November 1995 to the present.

Depending on the research, the last set of sources may be adequate. However, if an individual is doing scholarly research or engaged in policy making, it would be wiser to use the official sites like IMFs exchange center, the BIS, and the national central banks.

Investment Flows

Worldwide business transactions generate inflow and outflow of investment and merchandise trade and services between domestic and foreign residents. These are recorded in an internationally focused accounting system referred to as the balance of payments (BoP). The International Monetary Fund gathers the relevant data from countries worldwide and publishes it annually in print and electronically in its monthly and yearly publication, *Balance of Payments*. The data is also dynamically accessible through IMF eLIBRARY, a fee-based database.

"The balance of payments accounts are compiled through the use of double-entry bookkeeping with credit and debit entries; credit items include all transactions that give rise to foreign exchange inflows whereas debit items include all transactions causing foreign exchange outflows."[15] *BoP* provides information about the supply and demand of foreign exchange for a specific time period. "The balance of payments summarizes a country's transactions that require payments to other countries and transactions that require payments from other countries."[16] The BoP provides the following insights:

- Deficits and surpluses on the current account can indicate excess or underspending, which could have an effect on inflation

- An analysis of the supply and demand of foreign currencies related to BoP items helps to explain movements in the exchange rate and identify any trends that might be affecting it
- BoP data helps to explain money supply changes, which is related to monetary policy[17]

With this type of data and analysis, as well as others not mentioned here, IMF can assist countries that have balance of payment problems as well as identify a potential financial crisis before it happens and move to prevent it.[18] A country can also use the data to compare itself with other countries in its region as well as worldwide. Historical data can also be used to identify past trends.

The print version of the *BoP Yearbook* is made up of three parts. The first part consists of country tables; part two has world and regional tables, and part three provides the sources used, methodologies, and how the data were compiled for each country table in part one.

The country tables (part 1) are made up of an analytic presentation, a standard presentation, and, if a country provided data, an international investment position table. Data is provided for the last eight years (i.e., the 2010 edition covers 2002–2009) and is presented in US dollars. The analytic presentation has five major sections: the current account, capital account, financial account, net errors and omissions, and reserves and related items.

The standard presentation chart has two parts, the current account and the capital account. The current account has four elements: (1) goods, which includes exports (credits) and imports (debits) of merchandise (f.o.b.); (2) services, made up of transportation, travel, and other services, each with a credit and debit entry; (3) income; and (4) current transfers. The capital account includes the financial accounts, which is made up of (a) direct investment, both abroad and in the country; (b) portfolio investment (which includes assets and liabilities for each of the following: equity securities, debt securities, money market instruments); (c) financial derivatives; (d) other investments, assets, and liabilities; and (e) reserve assets.

Table 3, the international investment position (IIP), rearranges the data provided in the previous chart and presents it by function under assets and liabilities. Both assets and liabilities have the same categories: direct investment abroad, portfolio investment, financial derivatives, and other investment. The asset side also has a line item named reserve assets. The bottom line of this table is a country's net international investment position.

Part 2 of the *BoP Statistics Yearbook* presents data for the major balance of payments and international investment position mentioned in part 1 of this source, for each region, as well as for each country in that region.

Part 3 consists of "Methodologies, Compilation Practices, and Data Sources." The *BoP Yearbook* advises the individual to review the BoP and IIP tables simultaneously with the notes that are provided in this section of the publication.

If focusing on a specific country, sources to use are a nation's official source for statistics or other agencies that would provide the data. For the US, the Bureau of Economic Analysis (www.bea.gov) provides BoP data from the US perspective. In Germany, BoP data is provided through its central bank on the Deutsche Bundesbank Eurosystem (www.bundesbank.de/), which also provides an English version. Of course, it is possible that the information might not be in one's own language, requiring the researcher to hire a translator. If an individual is gathering data for comparative reasons, it would probably be best to use sources that come from organizations like the IMF. This is because they have methodologies in place that standardize the data gathered, making comparability of all the nations covered possible.

Foreign Direct Investment

Foreign direct investment (FDI) can be described as a company in one country locating or acquiring a facility or partnering with a business in another country and has 10 percent or more control. It is a line item in the Balance of Payments. In the BoP source, it is referred to as "direct investment abroad." Several entities disseminate FDI statistics, but the United Nations Conference on Trade and Development (UNCTAD) (unctad.org) is the premier source not only for data, but also for current and historical reports that provide analysis and identify FDI trends. One should examine the site for potential information other than those mentioned in this section.

The UNCTADSTAT database (unctadstat.unctad.org/ReportFolders/ reportFolders.aspx) allows the individual to obtain inward and outward direct investment stocks and flows, in dollars, from 1970 to 2011. Data is available for various geographic compositions, such as individual economies, the world, regions (South Africa), major exporters of manufactured goods, trade blocs (Free Trade Area of the Americas, FTAA), and G8. There are links for each of these categories, and when accessed, inward and outward data for the individual member countries is provided.

UNCTAD's Division on Investment and Enterprise (DAIE) webpage (unctad.org/en/pages/DIAE/DIAE.aspx) provides links to FDI-related news, publications, research, and the FDI portion of the UNCTADSTAT database. A key publication available at the DAIE website is the *World Investment Report* (*WIR*). Since 1991, this report has covered and provided analysis of FDI trends globally, regionally, and by country. Each year the report focuses on a specific theme. For example, in 1991 it was *The Triad in Foreign Direct Investment*; the 2010 theme was "Non-equity Modes of

International Production and Development." It is freely available online from 1991 to present.

Yet another report from UNCTAD DAIE is its *World Investment Prospects Survey*. This publication complements UNCTAD's *WIR* and presents the results of its annual survey sent to "the largest non-financial TNCs [sic transnational corporations]; (b) national investment-promotion agencies; and (c) location experts"[19] worldwide. The results provide a global outlook for FDI growth prospects, level of optimism or pessimism of the investment environment, and TNC internationalization trends.

The World Bank also provides information about FDI through its *World Development Indicators (WDI)* publication and database and its Investing Across Borders (IAB) initiative (iab.worldbank.org/). *WDI* is freely available online and can be purchased in print. More than 400 pages in length, the 2012 edition provides tables in six different areas: the world, people, environment, economy, states and markets, and global links. Consequently, this source is not limited to providing only FDI statistics. For instance, it includes exchange rates, balance of payments current accounts, domestic credit to the private sector, market capitalization, S&P global equity indices, growth of merchandise trade, direction and growth of merchandise trade, and global private financial flows that are made up of equity and debt. The foreign direct investment data is found in the equity portion of financial flows. The equity portion also includes flows from portfolio equity, defined as "net inflows from equity securities other than those recorded as direct investment and including shares, stocks, depository receipts, and direct purchases of shares in local stock markets by foreign investors."[20] Debt flows are made up of bonds and commercial banking and other lending.

FDI data for net inflows is also included in the World Bank's World Development Indicators database (data.worldbank.org/indicator). The information covers 209 countries and is generated from IMF's Balance of Payments database as well as from UNCTAD and official national sources.

World Bank's IAB covers eighty-seven countries and provides FDI-regulation indicators for the following policy-related topics: "economies' laws, regulations, and practices affecting how foreign companies invest across sectors, start businesses, access industrial land, and arbitrate commercial disputes."[21] The full 2010 *IAB Report* is publicly available online; the data for each of these topics is also available through the IAB portal. These indicators can help a business gauge the ease of doing business in a country, and perhaps suggest areas in which to do further research.

OECD provides FDI statistics through its publicly available OECD.StatExtracts database (stats.oecd.org) as well as its fee-based service OECD iLibrary (www.oecd-ilibrary.org/statistics). Both cover 2000–2010. Data for each of the countries in the database includes inward and outward flows by broad industry sectors (i.e., construction, manufacturing); inward and outward flows by OECD partners, as well as countries outside of OECD; inward and outward positions by broad industry; and FDI inward and outward positions by partners and BoP and IIP aggregates. Both have an information tab to learn more about the data presented, including its source, the statistical population that it represented, the unit measures used, and more depending on the statistics provided.

The US Department of the Census' Bureau of Economic Analysis (www.bea.gov/iTable/iTable.cfm?ReqID=2&step=1) offers several series of data for FDI, including equity outflows from the United States and equity inflows into the United States. If FDI is needed for other countries, a strategy is to identify the official agencies that gather and disseminate data of a country, and then go to their websites and search for the data. The US Census offers a list of such agencies with links at www.census.gov/aboutus/stat_int.html. For instance, the Statistics New Zealand site (www.stats.govt.nz) has a section with quarterly releases of balance of payments and international investment positions, which includes foreign direct investment. It also has a publicly available online tool called Infoshare that provides a wide range of statistics, including direct investment data from 2001 to the previous year for selected regions and countries.

Besides scrutinizing the UNCTAD site looking for reports and data related to FDI, and the other sources mentioned here, another strategy is to use a search engine to find potential data from other sites, such as those from trade or economic blocs or even a country. For example, to find data for Vietnam, one could try a trade bloc to which it belongs, such as the Association of Southeast Asian Nations (ASEAN). A possible search strategy could be:

foreign direct investment and asean

These search engine strategies may or may not be as effective in obtaining data as compared to using the UNCTAD or OECD databases. This will be especially true if data at sites are created dynamically only or the website requires the user to register to get the information. In such cases, a search engine will not be able to find the data.

There are also fee-based databases that provide this type of data, including EIU's World Investment Prospects and Euromonitor's Passport GMID.

International Monetary System and Financial Markets

Earlier, we learned that international financial markets consist of capital markets, which include the equity and bond markets, as well as the foreign exchange market. Some of the key sources already identified in this chapter can also be used in this section. For instance, *World Development Indicators* provides information about the equity and debt markets. Furthermore, a key source for international and domestic finance, IMF's *International Financial Statistics* (*IFS*), is not limited to the financial markets, but also covers the international monetary system and trade. *IFS* is published monthly and annually in print, CD-ROM, and digitally. It is possible to purchase individual publications or set up a subscription to receive in any of these formats, as well as to the interactive database, IMF eLIBRARY (imf-elibrary-data.imf.org).

The *IFS Yearbook* covers almost 200 countries, which includes IMF members and nonmembers. It starts with world and area tables, and then presents country tables. The world and area tables present twelve full years of data in nine categories for each of the regions and countries included in the source. These include exchange rates and exchange rate arrangements; fund accounts: position to date; international liquidity; monetary statistics; interest rates; prices, production, and labor; international transactions; government finance; and national accounts and population. [22] The yearbook provides detailed descriptions and explanations of what the data presents and how it was obtained or calculated. The country tables provide detailed information for individual countries to some of the series that appeared in the world tables, as well as additional categories. In this section of the *Yearbook*, data is grouped as follows: exchange rates; fund position; international liquidity; central bank; other depository corporations; depository corps. (national residency), depository corps (EA–wide residency); interest rates; prices, production, labor; international transactions and positions, balance of payments; international investment position; government finance, operations statement, general government; balance sheet; cash flow statement, budgetary central government; national accounts; and population. Each of these groups is further divided to provide a set of relevant data. For example, under the interest rate group, information includes discount rate, money market rate, Treasury bill rate, deposit rate, lending rate, and government bond yield.

The interactive database for *IFS* provides two ways of obtaining its data. One is by data source, whereby the user can select *International Financial Statistics*. This is subdivided into thirteen data reports, including world foreign exchange and world total fund credit and loans outstanding. The system also provides a way to select specific criteria in order to build a report.

Another source is IMF's Financial Stability portal (www.imf.org/external/np/mcm/financialstability/index.htm). This site has a link to the IMF Monetary and Capital Markets Department's *Global Financial Stability Report* (*GFSR*). The publication was launched in 2002 as a quarterly, and then semiannually each year since 2003. This resource provides an assessment of the stability of financial markets for the six months after the previous release, identifies issues that could lead to a crisis, analyzes policies and their impact on the market, and offers solutions. Outside global institutions, such as commercial and investment banks, insurance companies, academic researchers, and public authorities worldwide, are engaged and consulted in the creation of this report. Information is kept up-to-date with online releases of *GFSR Market Update* between the publications of *GFSR*.

The portal also has links to multilateral organizations dealing with financial stability, including the Bank of International Settlements, the Financial Stability Board, the Banking Committee on Banking Supervision, the International Association of Insurance Supervisors, and the International Organizations of Securities Commissions. There are also links to reports, working papers, and research produced by various sources, including central banks and the BIS.

There is also a regional section that is divided into Africa, Asia and the Pacific, Europe, the Middle East, and the Western hemisphere. Clicking on any region takes the user to a list of the relevant central banks in that area. Selecting a specific bank takes one to that institution's section of its website. Once at the site there is the potential to obtain reports and information related to the individual country's financial situation.

There are several sources that provide data and/or analysis not just for international financial markets, but also for the international monetary system and trade. This includes resources that have already been mentioned, including World Bank's *World Development Indicators* and IMF's *International Financial Statistics*. This is also true for the resources mentioned in the next few paragraphs: IMF's *World Economic Outlook*, IMF's *Fiscal Monitor*, the World Economic Forum's *Global Risk Report*, as well as the *Global Competitiveness Report*.

IMF's *World Economic Outlook* has been published since 1980. It also has an update that is released between the publication dates of the regular reports. Each report follows a topic relevant to what is occurring during the time period covered. For instance, in April 2002 it was "Recessions and Recovery" and in April 2012 the focus was "Growth Resuming Dangers Remain." Using data, economic and financial indicators, and policies that have been implemented by various governments, it provides an analysis of the global economy and its financial condition, identifies problem areas, and offers advice on monetary and economic policy issues. Projections for certain indicators are given, including real GDP, consumer prices, world trade volume and prices, balances on current account, net financial flows, and projections for the rest of the year and next. IMF also provides an online archive for *WEO* where one can get reports back to April 1999 to the most current report, as well as the related data (www.imf.org/external/ns/cs.aspx?id=28).

In 2012, IMF provided the *Fiscal Monitor*. It includes an analysis of the state of the global economy as a result of policies taken by individual governments to deal with their national accounts, explains how current or future strategies and adjustments made by policy makers affect national accounts and their economic indicators, and suggests strategies for improving this. There is also a *Fiscal Monitor* database for 2012 (www.imf.org/external/pubs/ft/fm/2012/01/app/FiscalMonitoring.html) that provides the data used for the current publication. It is possible to download all the 2012 data into an Excel spreadsheet.

Search engines open up the potential to find other relevant sites and information on both the international monetary system and international financial markets. For example, there are official government departments that deal with one or both of these topics. Official government sites have certain domain names which can be used in a search engine. These domain names can be found at Norid's "Domain name registries around the world" webpage (www.norid.no/domenenavnbaser/domreg.html).

The researcher could also use the "site" feature that is available in search engines like Google and Yahoo! Search. For instance, if one wanted to get FDI data for Australia from the Australian Bureau of Statistics (www.abs.gov.au/), the following search strategy could be used:

foreign direct statistics site:abs.gov.au

This strategy will frame the way the search engine looks for and retrieves results, which should come from various webpages of the Australian Bureau of Statistics.

To find a government site that dealt with financial stability in the United States or another country, like Australia or the UK, some search strategies would be as follows:

> *financial stability site:gov*
> *financial stability site:gov.uk*
> *financial stability site:gov.au*

The US search leads to discovering that the US Treasury Department hosts the Financial Stability site (financialstability.gov). The UK search finds the Financial Stability page under the HM Treasury (www.hm-treasury.gov.uk/fin_stability_index.htm). Australia has one on the Reserve Bank of Australia website (www.rba.gov.au/fin-stability/index.html).

Think tanks are another source to consider using. One way to identify top think tanks is by using the University of Pennsylvania's Think Tank and Civil Societies Program's annual publication, "Global Go To Think Tanks Report" (www.gotothinktank.com). The institutions that are included and ranked in this report have been vetted by hundreds of experts, journalists, other think tanks, academic institutions, and intergovernmental organizations. The think tanks are grouped by Top 50

Think Tanks Worldwide (Non-US), Top 50 Think Tanks Worldwide (US and Non-US), Top Think Tanks by Region (eight regions), area of research, (two of them being domestic and international economic policy), and special achievement. Although the URLs are not provided here, the home pages for these entities are easily found with a search engine.

The top think tank in the report is the Brookings Institute, which was ranked first under domestic economic policy research and second in international economic policy research. The Brookings website (www.brookings.edu) reveals a section on Financial Markets and Services. Other institutes ranked in this research area included Chatham House in the UK (www.chathamhouse.org/research/economics) and the World Economic Forum in Switzerland (www.weforum.org). Two recent themes from Chatham House falling under its International Economics section are "Growth of Financial Centres and Financial Integration" and "Reform of the International Monetary System."

The World Economic Forum publishes the *Global Risk Report* as well as the *Global Competitiveness Report*. The *Global Risk Report* covers global financial systems, but it provides an overview of risks in other areas, such as security and illegal economic activity, such as illicit trade.

With more than 500 pages, the *Global Competitiveness Report* is a comprehensive document that analyzes the microeconomic and macroeconomic environments related to competitiveness. The report defines the term "as the set of institutions, policies, and factors that determine the level of productivity of a country."[23] These are made up of twelve "pillars," which include institutions, macroeconomic environment, goods market efficiency, and financial market development. The 2012 report covers 142 countries. In the first half of the report, areas of the twelve pillars are discussed as they relate to these countries. In the second half of the report, there are two page profiles of these nations. These present key indicators, the global competitiveness index for each pillar, ratings for problem areas for doing business in the country, and indices for each element covered in each of the twelve pillars. This report isn't limited to providing data only for the international monetary system and the international financial markets, but it does have some relevant indices for each country in these areas. This includes eight items under financial market development, ranging from availability of financial services, financing through local equity market, and soundness of banks.

If a researcher is interested in finding information from think tanks, the *CIAO Columbia International Affairs Online* database is a good choice. Working papers, policy briefs, conference proceedings, and articles produced by almost 400 think tanks, publishers, and universities worldwide are accessible with a subscription.

Another area of research could be the global system of stock exchanges. A source for an overall view is the World Federation of Exchanges (www.world-exchanges.org/statistics). This site provides monthly reports, time series, and annual market highlights on the performance and transactions of the different capital markets, including equity, bond, derivatives, and exchange traded funds. One can also get time series data going back to 1990 to relatively present (2011 at the time of review of this site) in areas that include the following categories: value of bond trading, fifty-five indexes, dividend yield, value of share trading, market capitalization, and number of listed companies. The site also has a query tool where an individual can customize the series data for all the countries within the WFE, in specific regions, for three types of financial instruments: equity, bond, or derivative. For example, it is possible to obtain the number of foreign and local listed companies on the Buenos Aires Stock Exchange, the Mexican Exchange, and NASDAQ OMX that provide equity instruments for each month from January 31, 2009, to the present.

Depending on the type of information the researcher wants, one could look for articles in newspapers, magazines, trade journals, and scholarly journals. Besides individual websites like those for the *Wall Street Journal*, *Financial Times*, the *Economist*, or other personal favorites, sources provided by aggregators are another option. These sources will provide articles from the periodical and newspaper titles and scholarly journals they cover, so they are not limited to only one publication. Standard databases that provide such content include ABI/Inform, Business Insights: Essentials, Business Source Complete, Factiva, and LexisNexis Academic. Results might lead to current articles in news and trade publications about what is currently happening in the financial markets, and/or policy decisions that are affecting the international monetary system. Scholarly journals could provide an analysis on a wide range of topics, such as the volatility of exchange rates, a review of the international monetary system, or the role of a currency in the international financial markets. To find scholarly journals, standard databases to use are ABI/Inform or Business Source Complete, as well as the Business Insights: Essentials. One can also search Google Scholar (scholar.google.com).

Flow of Goods and Services

This category refers to imports and exports that occur around the world. Imports are the goods and services that go into a country. Exports deal with goods and services that go out of a country to another. There are numerous sources for this type of data, some of which provide the data down to the commodity level. This section focuses on sources that provide statistics on a macro level; that is, those that provide aggregate data. There are several resources that do this. These include the sources already mentioned in this chapter, which are IMF's *International Financial Statistics* monthly and yearbook publications and IMF eLibrary portal, the UNCTADStats database, and OECD iLibrary. The ones identified in the next paragraphs are from the United Nations (UN), the IMF, the OECD, and the World Trade Organization (WTO). Other sources that provide data on a commodity level are located in the chapter that covers industry research.

The UN provides access to data online through its undata portal (data.un.org). From this site the individual can access the *Monthly Bulletin of Statistics*, which has total import and export data for the countries covered in the system. One can retrieve monthly, quarterly, or annual data from 2000 to the present year. This portal also provides access to data from the IMF's *International Financial Statistics* source; this has aggregate trade data from 2004–2009.

Another source for global trade statistics is the United Nations' *International Trade Statistics Yearbook*, which is available in print and online. The United Nations Statistics Division (UNSD) obtains data from more than 170 countries, which it then standardizes and disseminates through this publication[24] and via the UN comtrade portal (comtrade.un.org). Current and past publications of the *Yearbook* are also available back to 1992 through this portal. These sources also provide detailed annual trade data for commodities and the partner countries.

The United Nations Statistics Division has a database for services, referred to as the United Nations International Trade Services Database (UN Service Trade) (unstats.un.org/unsd/servicetrade/). This is a publicly available system for storing and disseminating international trade in services statistics. Data is presented using the Extended Balance of Payments System (EBOPS) and the partner country.[25] In this database one can find the trade value of a service exported or imported from one country to another.

The IMF's gold standard publication for import/export data is the *Direction of Trade Statistics* (*DOTS*), first published under the shorter title *Direction of Trade* in 1964. *DOTS* provides the value of import and export data, in US dollars, for almost 200 countries with their most important trading partners, the world, and areas (i.e., emerging and developing economies; the Middle East). The print publication is published quarterly and annually. The annual edition presents current estimates of import/export data for the last seven years, and the quarterly provides data for the previous year and the last six quarters. Approximately forty-nine countries, which make up most of the advanced economies, and around eighteen developing and emerging countries, provide monthly data "on a regular and current basis" (i.e., with a delay of four months or less from the current month).[26] "This represents about four-fifths of the value of recorded world exports and imports in recent years."[27] *DOTS* is available by subscription in print and through IMF eLibrary or CD-ROM.

The Organisation for Economic Co-operation and Development (OECD) also publishes trade data in three sources, *International Trade by Commodities Statistics*, *Monthly Statistics of International Trade*, and *OECD*

Statistics on International Trade in Services. International Trade by Commodities Statistics is a five-volume set published annually. It provides country import/export commodity data that is available for the most recent five years for each OECD member country with seventy partner countries or groupings. Statistics are presented using two levels of the SITC, rev. 3 classification system. The first level represents the section of the industry, and the second is the division (see Chapter 6, "Classification Systems for Industry," for a description of SITC). Also included in the fifth volume is trade data by OECD main country groupings, which includes OECD Total, NAFTA, OECD Asia and Pacific, OECD Europe, and EU27. The *Monthly* print publication provides "up-to-date aggregates, indices and indicators."[28] These sources are online through OECD iLibrary (covered earlier in this chapter). The online version is updated more often, and commodities are classified by SITC or the Harmonised System.

OECD Statistics on International Trade in Services is a joint publication of OECD and Eurostat, the unit that gathers statistics from the European Community. This source is made up of two volumes. Volume 1 is in three parts. Part I provides a summary of international and regional service trade trends, as well as import and export data for fourteen service categories, in addition to total services from each OECD country that was a member at the time of publication, as well as for seven economic zones, including NAFTA and the world. Part II is made up of the country tables. Each of these tables has import and export data for sub-items under the major service categories (i.e., freight insurance under the insurance services category) for each OECD country. Part III shows additional data that countries submitted using their national classification schemes. Volume 2 of this title is made up of two parts. Part I lists the top seven trading partners for each OECD reporting country, based on the value of total service imports and exports. The value of service imports/exports for each OECD reporting country to and from the world and the EU27, as well as for groupings, such as Gulf Arabian countries is given when relevant. Part II presents the value of trade for each service for each OECD country in the last five years (which in the 2011 publication covers 2004–2008), by its OECD partners, as well as non-OECD countries.

Yet another source of trade data is the World Trade Organization (WTO). The WTO provides merchandise and commercial services trade data through its print publication *International Trade Statistics* and on its International Trade and Tariff Data website (www.wto.org/english/res_e/statis_e/statis_e.htm). This website provides access to trade data from the most current print publication. It also has a link to its statistics interactive database that allows the user to obtain time series of trade data. "Trade profiles" covers more than 180 economies and "services profiles" covers telecommunications, finance and insurance, and shows "100 indicators relating to investment, market performance, production, employment, trade, as well as performance rankings," for more than ninety economies.

CONCLUSION

This chapter presented a concise overview of the infrastructure that allows international business transactions to occur. This included an introduction to the monetary system and the roles money and exchange rates play. How financial markets enable companies to engage in international business activities, whether by trade or foreign direct investment, was also covered. Sources were identified that could provide information for different elements of the international monetary system and financial markets. For instance, resources for locating data related to the two main types of international business engagement—foreign direct investment and trade—were presented. Sources for finding current and historical currency exchange rates and locating data on global investment flows that are a critical part of a system where there is an exchange of goods and services were also given. Ways to find information about the overall stability of the international monetary system and financial markets from global experts and in articles were also covered.

The sources presented in this chapter are ways that the international monetary system, financial markets, and the exchange of goods and services are monitored to keep the world economy in balance. The importance of these efforts rises as globalization becomes more and more dynamic.

LIST OF SOURCES

Databases

This is an alphabetical list of the fee-based databases mentioned in this chapter.

ABI/Inform (Ann Arbor, MI: ProQuest, 1971–), www.proquest.com/products_pq/descriptions/abi_inform.shtml.
Business Insights: Essentials (Farmington Hills, MI: Gale Cengage Learning, 2012–), www.cengagesites.com/Literature/782/gale-business-insights-global-essentials.
Business Source Complete (Ipswich, MA: EBSCO Pub., 2005–) www.ebscohost.com/public/business-source-complete.
CIAO Columbia International Affairs Online (New York: Columbia University Press, 1997–), www.ciaonet.org.
Factiva (New York: Dow Jones & Reuters, 2001–), www.dowjones.com/factiva/index.asp. IMF eLIBRARY (Washington, D.C.: International Monetary Fund, 2009–), www.elibrary.imf.org.
LexisNexis Academic (Dayton: OH: LexisNexis, Division of Reed Elsevier, 2002–) academic.lexisnexis.com/online-services/academic/academic-overview.aspx.
OECD iLibrary (Washington, D.C.: OECD, 2000–), www.oecd-ilibrary.org/statistics.
Passport GMID (London: UK; Chicago, IL: Euromonitor International, 1990s–), www.euromonitor.com/passport-gmid.

Websites

This is an alphabetical list of association, government, and publisher websites mentioned in this chapter.

Australian Bureau of Statistics, www.abs.gov.au/ (11 June 2012).
Bank of England Statistical Interactive Database, www.bankofengland.co.uk/boeapps/iadb/ (11 June 2012).
Bank of International Settlements, www.bis.org (11 June 2012).
Bank of International Settlements, List of Central Banks, www.bis.org/cbanks.htm (11 June 2012).
Bank of New York/Mellon, https://gm.bankofny.com/FX/ErisaRates.asp (11 June 2012).
Bank of Russia, www.cbr.ru/eng/ (11 June 2012).
Barclays (www.barclays.co.uk/ (11 June 2012).
Bloomberg Currency Converter, www.bloomberg.com/personal-finance/calculators/currency-converter/ (11 June 2012).
Brookings Institute, www.brookings.edu (11 June 2012).
Chatham House, www.chathamhouse.org (11 June 2012).
Deutsche Bundesbank Eurosystem, www.bundesbank.de/ (11 June 2012).
Financial Time Markets Data, Ft.com/marketsdata (11 June 2012).
Global Go To Think Tanks Report, www.gotothinktank.com (11 June 2012).
Google Scholar, scholar.google.com (11 June 2012).
HM Treasury, Financial Stability, www.hm-treasury.gov.uk/fin_stability_index.htm (11 June 2012).
IMF Exchange Rate Archives by Month, www.imf.org/external/np/fin/data/param_rms_mth.aspx (11 June 2012).
IMF Financial Stability portal, www.imf.org/external/np/mcm/financialstability/index.htm (11 June 2012).
IMF Fiscal Monitor, www.imf.org/external/pubs/ft/fm/2012/01/fmindex.htm (11 June 2012).
IMF Fiscal Monitor database, www.imf.org/external/pubs/ft/fm/2012/01/app/Fiscal-Monitoring.html (11 June 2012).
IMF Global Financial Stability Report, www.imf.org/external/pubs/ft/gfsr/index.htm (11 June 2012).
IMF World Economic Outlook databases, www.imf.org/external/ns/cs.aspx?id=28 (11 June 2012).
Norid, "Domain Name Registries Around the World," www.norid.no/domenenavnbaser/domreg.html (11 June 2012).
OECD.StatExtracts database, stats.oecd.org (11 June 2012).
Reserve Bank of Australia, "Financial Stability," www.rba.gov.au/fin-stability/index.html (11 June 2012).
Statistics New Zealand, www.stats.govt.nz (11 June 2012).
UN comtrade portal, comtrade.un.org (14 June 2012).
UNCTAD. Division on Investment and Enterprise (DAIE), unctad.org/en/pages/DIAE/DIAE.aspx (11 June 2012).
UNCTADSTAT database, unctadstat.unctad.org/ReportFolders/reportFolders.aspx (11 June 2012).
undata portal, data.un.org (11 June 2012).
UN Service Trade, unstats.un.org/unsd/servicetrade/ (11 June 2012).
US Department of Commerce. Bureau of Economic Analysis, www.bea.gov (11 June 2012).
United States Census Bureau, International Statistical Agencies, List of Official Statistical Sites, www.census.gov/aboutus/stat_int.html (11 June 2012).
United States International Trade Commission, "HTS Online Reference Tool," hts.usitc.gov/ (28 June 2012).

US Department of the Treasury, "Financial Stability," financialstability.gov (11 June 2012).

Wall Street Journal's Market Data Center (online.wsj.com/mdc) (11 June 2012).

Wells Fargo, https://www.wellsfargo.com/foreignexchange/ (11 June 2012).

World Bank, Investing Across Borders (IAB), iab.worldbank.org/ (11 June 2012).

World Bank, World Development Indicators (WDI) database, data.worldbank.org/indicator (11 June 2012).

World Economic Forum, www.weforum.org (11 June 2012).

World Economic Forum, Global Competitiveness Report, www.weforum.org/issues/global-competitiveness (11 June 2012).

World Economic Forum, Global Risk Report, www.weforum.org/issues/global-risks (11 June 2012).

World Federation of Exchanges, Statistics, www.world-exchanges.org/statistics (11 June 2012).

World Investments Prospects Survey, 2010–2012, unctad.org/en/docs/diaeia20104_en.pdf (11 June 2012).

World Investment Report Archive (WIR), archive.unctad.org/templates/Page.asp?intItemID=1465&lang=1 (11 June 2012).

WTO International Trade and Tariff Data website, www.wto.org/english/res_e/statis_e/statis_e.htm (11 June 2012).

XE Universal Currency Converter, www.xe.com/ucc/ (11 June 2012).

NOTES

1. Rajesh Iyer, *MBA Fundamentals International Business* (New York: Kaplan Publishing, 2009), 60.

2. Iyer, *MBA Fundamentals International Business*, 61.

3. Andrew Harrison, *Business Environment in a Global Context* (New York: Oxford University Press, 2010), 125.

4. World Bank. International Bank for Reconstruction and Development. "About," 2011, web.worldbank.org (3 June 2012).

5. John Cullen and K. Praveen Parboteeah, *International Business: Strategy and the Multinational Company* (New York: Routledge, 2010), 135.

6. Ettore Dorrucci and Julie McKay, *The International Monetary System after the Financial Crisis* (Germany, European Central Bank, 2011) www.ecb.int/pub/pdf/scpops/ecbocp123.pdf (3 June 2012).

7. Cullen and Parboteeah, *International Business: Strategy and the Multinational Company*, 138.

8. Harrison, *Business Environment in a Global Context*, 123.

9. Cullen and Parboteeah, *International Business: Strategy and the Multinational Company*, 160.

10. Cullen and Parboteeah, *International Business: Strategy and the Multinational Company*, 133.

11. International Monetary Fund, "Exchange Rate Archives by Month," www.imf.org/external/np/fin/data/param_rms_mth.aspx (15 June 2012).

12. International Monetary Fund, "Factsheet—Special Drawing Rights" (24 August 2012) www.imf.org/external/np/exr/facts/sdr.htm (15 June 2012).

13. Bank for International Settlements, "About BIS," www.bis.org/about/index.htm?l=2 (3 June 2012).

14. Bank of England. "Explanatory Notes—New Sterling ERI," www.bankofengland.co.uk/statistics/pages/iadb/notesiadb/neweri.aspx (3 June 2012).

15. Marios Katsioloudes and Spyros Hadjidakis, *International Business: A Global Perspective* (Hoboken, NJ: Routledge, 2012), 130, du.eblib.com (1 July 2012).

16. Katsioloudes and Hadjidakis, *International Business: A Global Perspective*, 99.

17. International Monetary Fund, Statistics Division, *Revision of the Balance of Payments Manual, Fifth Edition* (Annotated Outline), (2004), 170 www.imf.org/external/np/sta/bop/pdf/ao.pdf (27 June 2012).

18. ESDS International, "A Step-by-Step ESDS International Dataset Guide," www.esds.ac.uk/international/support/user_guides/imf/bops.asp (18 June 2012).

19. United Nations Conference on Trade and Development, *World Investment Prospects Survey, 2010–2012* (New York and Geneva, United Nations, 2010), 19, unctad.org/en/docs/diaeia20104_en.pdf (18 June 2012).

20. World Bank, *World Development Indicators* (Washington, DC, International Bank for Reconstruction and Development/THE WORLD BANK, 2012), 369, data.worldbank.org/sites/default/files/wdi-2012-ebook.pdf (13 June 2012).

21. World Bank. *Investing Across Borders* (Washington, DC, World Bank Group, 2010), 2, iab.worldbank.org/~/media/FPDKM/IAB/Documents/IAB-report.pdf (13 June 2012).

22. IMF Statistics Department, *International Financial Statistics Yearbook* (Washington, DC, International Monetary Fund, 2010), v.

23. World Economic Forum, *Global Competitiveness Report* (Geneva, World Economic Forum, 2011), 4, www3.weforum.org/docs/WEF_GCR_Report_2011-12.pdf (15 June 2012).

24. United Nations International Trade Statistics Knowledgebase, "What is UN Comtrade?," unstats.un.org/unsd/tradekb/Knowledgebase/What-is-UN-Comtrade (20 Oct. 2011).

25. EBOPS is covered in chapter 6, which deals with classification systems for industry.

26. International Monetary Fund, *Direction of Trade Statistics Yearbook* (Washington, DC: International Monetary Fund, 2009), ix.

27. *Direction of Trade Statistics Yearbook*, ix.

28. OECD, *International Trade by Commodity Statistics* (OECD Publishing, 2011), Back Cover.

THREE

Resources with World Coverage

Whenever a business is considering introducing a new product or service into a new international market it must analyze the country of interest to determine if it would be feasible to do so. The strategy for doing this can involve finding several different types of information about a country. This includes background information, history of a country, an overview of the political and economic situation, the social and political environment, facts about its culture, standard of living, and the potential risks that one might face in entering a particular market.

The resources identified in this chapter are websites and print resources that provide this type of basic information for most of the countries of the world. The information they provide may overlap but they will also have unique coverage in certain areas needed for research that is not covered in other sources. Some of the basic information that is generally included in most of the websites are general statistics, business directories, information about government officials, and financial information.

US-BASED SOURCES

An important source that is publicly available as well as in print is Country Studies/Area Handbook Series (lcweb2.loc.gov/frd/cs) from the Library of Congress (figure 3.1). It covers the history, politics, geography, and economy of individual countries. The website provides access to digital copies of 101 countries and regions that made up the 1992–1998 print copies of the *Country Studies/Area Handbook* Program sponsored by the US Department of the Army. Countries included in the series were mainly from areas that were less known or where US forces could be deployed. Consequently there are several countries not included. Although it is not updated annually (the most recent publications at the time of this writing are for Afghanistan and Yemen, which were updated August 2008), the reports provide very good background for a country.

Background Notes (www.state.gov/r/pa/ei/bgn/), which are available through the US Department of State, are updated regularly by the Office of Electronic Information and Publications of the Bureau of Public Affairs when information is received from the Department's regional bureaus.[1] It provides some general answers to a country's political situation, and economic trends, as well as information about the culture and regulations related to international trade. There are 201 countries covered. Information about a country is grouped into the following categories, with a brief summary provided for each, and then goes into more detail further in the report:

- Profile
- People
- History
- Government
- Political Conditions
- Economy
- Defense
- Foreign Relations
- US Relations
- Travel/Business

Some of the information in this source is the same as in the *CIA World Factbook*, but other elements are presented in more detail. As of May 2012, the *Background Notes* are in the process of being replaced by fact sheets that focus on US relations with each country. Notes will continue to be

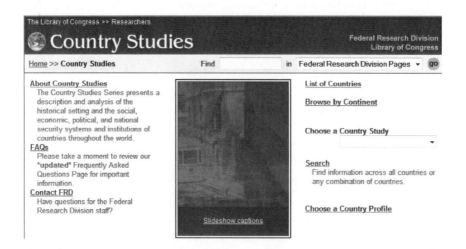

Figure 3.1. Country Studies/Area Handbook Series.

available on the Department of State's website, www.state.gov, whether they appear as background notes or are replaced by a fact sheet.[2]

Ediplomat (www.ediplomat.com/) is designed for State Department personnel stationed at embassies and consulates. This is a publicly available website that provides a list of famous diplomats, national anthems, cultural etiquette, and country briefs.

The *CIA World Factbook* (https://www.cia.gov/library/publications/the-world-factbook/) comes from the US government's Central Intelligence Agency (figure 3.2). Its website is an interactive portal that issues "information on the history, people, government, economy, geography, communications, transportation, military, and transnational issues for 267 world entities."[3] This source will enable the researcher to become oriented to the country being studied. There are nine major categories of information provided:

- Introduction: Provides background
- Geographic
- People and society
- Government
- Economy
- Communications
- Transportation
- Military
- Transnational issues

SOURCES FROM INTERNATIONAL ORGANIZATIONS

There are several international organizations that provide country information as well as socioeconomic data, including the United Nations (UN), Organization for Economic Co-operation and Development (OECD), and the World Bank. These three agencies publish print and electronic versions of titles that are very useful. They also provide interactive databases that allow users to retrieve information pulled from different types of data sets, such as demographic, economic, and social statistics.

The United Nations (www.un.org/en/members/index.shtml) is an international organization that was founded after World War II, in 1945. In addition to working on peacekeeping, peace building, conflict prevention, and humanitarian assistance, it also deals with other problems, including "sustainable development, environment and refugees protection, disaster relief, counter terrorism, disarmament and non-proliferation, to promoting democracy, human rights, gender equality and the advancement of women, governance, economic and social development and international health, clearing landmines, expanding food production."[4] There are the 192 member states of the United Nations. Through its statis-

Figure 3.2.

tical related units, the United Nations provides a wide range of data that can be used by international business researchers.

The UN publishes the *World Statistics Pocketbook* (unstats.un.org/unsd/ pocketbook/), which provides profiles for 216 countries and other global areas. It also includes "50 key indicators in the areas of population, economic activity, agriculture, industry, energy, international trade, transport, communications, gender, education and environment."[5] The data is compiled from over twenty international statistical sources.

The UN also publishes the *Monthly Bulletin of Statistics* (unstats.un.org/unsd/mbs/app/DataSearchTable.aspx). This source presents current economic and social statistics for more than 200 countries and territories of the world. It contains 55 tables, comprising over 100 indicators, of monthly, quarterly, and annual data on a variety of subjects. These tables illustrate important economic trends and developments, including population, industrial production indices, price indices, employment and earnings, energy, manufacturing, transport, construction, and international merchandise.

The World Bank (www.worldbank.org) is an organization that provides financial and technical support to developing countries across the world. Its publications cover twenty-nine subjects, including communities and human settlements, conflict and development, culture and development, education, gender, health, nutrition, population, and social development. This is an open initiative project whereby one uses a single interface to pull data from such World Bank publications as *World Development Indicators*, *Africa Development Indicators*, and *Gender Statistics*. The *World Development Indicator* database allows one to run a time series for numerous indicators (GDP, final consumption expenditure, foreign direct investment, Internet users, literacy rate, population, etc.), for different countries. One should also look at the Doing Business series for the specific country; this source is covered in the chapter related to industry research.

OECD (www.oecd.org/) is an international organization that promotes policies that support the economic and social development of the global community. It is made up of thirty-four member countries, including advanced and emerging countries. They also partner with China, India, and Brazil, as well as developing countries in Africa, Asia, Latin America, and the Caribbean. They "measure productivity and global flows of trade and investment [as well as] analyze and compare data to predict future trends." These are disseminated through a wide range of print and digital publications and through interactive databases.

FEE-BASED SOURCES

There are also commercial publishers that produce publications that provide information about countries.

The Economic Intelligence Unit (EIU) (www.eiu.com) publishes several sources for country information. These include the *Country Report* series focusing on the political and economic outlook for 190 countries; *Country Forecast*, dealing with the business environment in ninety-two countries; and *Country Risk*, providing insight to 121 countries. A researcher can purchase these and other publications as needed through the EIU Store. EIU will also conduct customized research as needed. In addition, EIU provides different library subscription packages to which many academic libraries subscribe.

These EIU publications are also available through databases produced by aggregators like Gale/Cengage, EBSCO, and ProQuest. They each provide access to EIU's Country Profiles, Country Reports, and Country Finance. EBSCOhost's Business Source Complete and Business Source Premier provide access to Country Commerce and Country Reports. ProQuest's ABI/Inform Complete has Country Commerce. The researcher should be aware that in the many cases where a publisher is permitting an aggregator to provide its content in a database, there will most likely be a limit to the content coverage, also known as an *embargo*. EIU also provides users with free limited access at its website to some of the country information after registering for an account.

Country Watch is another producer of country information. Country Watch "covers 194 independent and sovereign states in the world, including the world's newest countries, East Timor and Kosovo"[6]; the countries that are covered must be recognized as a country by the US Department of State. Its products include Country Reviews, Country Wire, Country Data, Country Maps, and Forecasts. Country Reviews includes demographic, political, economic, business, cultural, and environmental information. Country Reviews also includes indexes for political risk, political stability, economic performance, foreign investment, and human development. Country Wire provides daily news coverage for every country in the world. It offers individual, public library, corporate/government, and educational subscriptions. EBSCOHost's Business Source Complete provides CountryWatch's Forecast Brief as well as selected country reports and country reviews.

Europa World Year Book has an online version called Europa World (www.europaworld.com/). It was first published in print in 1926 by Routledge Taylor & Francis Group. It covers contemporary political history, constitution and government, demographic information, an industry overview, religion, and judicial system and economic information on more than 250 countries and territories. Subscribers can download archived information.

Political Risk Yearbook is a source that can assist the researcher in evaluating risks in a country. Updated annually, the resource is produced by the Political Risk Services (PRS) Group. The print version is an eight-volume set. Volume 1 covers North and Central America; volume 2, the Middle East and North Africa; volume 3, South America; volume 4, Sub-Saharan Africa; volume 5, East Asia and the Pacific; volume 6, West Europe; and volume 7, East Europe; and volume 8, Central and South Asia. These volumes cover 100 countries. Each report has a country ranking by the Global PRS Risk Index, as well as a rank by region. Risk factors covered are turmoil, investment (equity, operations, taxation, repatriation, exchange), trade (tariffs, other barriers, payment delays), and economic (expansion, labor costs, foreign debts). A report also identifies and provides a brief description of political players to watch, and the climate for investment and trade. The online version duplicates the print volumes. A monthly newsletter that summarizes PRS's latest forecasts for economic and political changes is available by subscription.

COUNTRY INFORMATION WEBSITES

BBC Country Profiles (news.bbc.co.uk/2/hi/country_profiles/default.stm) Provides guides to the history, politics, and economic background of countries and territories, and background on key institutions.

Country Briefings (www.countrybriefings.com/) provides information only on leading countries' economies. Each *Country Briefing* comprises the country's economy, economic indicators, stock market, politics, international relations, corporate news, mergers and acquisitions, results together with editorial comment and analysis, and basic economic statistics. It covers thirty-two major world economies.

Country Profiles ELDIS (www.eldis.org/) covers developing countries in Africa, Asia, Latin America, and the Middle East. Links are provided to news, statistics, organizations, and reports on sectoral information such as agriculture, environment, education, gender, health, trade, and governance.

Embassy World (www.embassyworld.com/embassy/dircctory.htm) provides a comprehensive list of contact resources for all of the world's diplomatic offices. Geography IQ (www.geographyiq.com/) includes facts and figures about each country's geography, demographics, economy, government, and political system. This website also offers historical, cultural, and political background information. GlobalEdge (globaledge.msu.edu/) is funded in part by the US Department of Education Title VIB grant; GlobalEDGE delivers a comprehensive research tool for academics, students, and businesspeople. Economic and political risk ratings are featured along with culture, statistical data, and more.

Cofacc (www.coface.com/), whose headquarters is located in France with branches around the world, offers information about country risk and economic research. Country analysis and forecasts assess overall business environment quality in a country. Users can also find information on business climate by selecting "country" to find information. It includes country risk ratings for 154 countries.

SOURCES FOR INTERNATIONAL FINANCE AND INVESTMENT

Other examples of free resources available on the Internet that provide multiple country coverage as well as financial information are the Bank for International Settlements (BIS) (www.bis.org/cbanks.htm), the African, Caribbean and Pacific Group of States (ACP) (www.acp.int/), and the World Association of Investment Promotion Agencies. These websites are non-US based.

The Bank for International Settlements (www.bis.org) was established on May 17, 1930. It is the world's oldest international financial organization. This site offers a wide range of financial services specifically designed to assist central banks and other official monetary institutions in the management of their foreign exchange reserves. There are 140 customers, including various international financial institutions. It serves central banks in the pursuit of monetary and financial stability and fosters international cooperation.

The African, Caribbean and Pacific Group of States (ACP) (www.acp.int/) is composed of seventy-nine African, Caribbean, and Pacific states. There are forty-eight countries from Sub-Saharan Africa, sixteen from the Caribbean, and fifteen from the Pacific. One of the ACP group's main objectives is the sustainable development of its member states and their gradual integration into the global economy. This site brings together facts, figures, reports, and financial information.

The World Association of Investment Promotion Agencies (WAIPA) is a nongovernmental organization (NGO). The Association has 249 member agencies from 157 countries. WAIPA acts as a forum for investment promotion agencies (IPAs) to provide networking opportunities and facilitate the exchange of best practices in capacity building and investment promotion. WAIPA's Consultative Committee consists of the following international governmental and nongovernmental organizations:

- Foreign Investment Advisory Services (FIAS) of the World Bank Group; International Economic Development Council (IEDC)
- Organisation for Economic Co-operation and Development (OECD)
- ProInvest
- United Nations Conference on Trade and Development (UNCTAD)
- United Nations Industrial Development Organization (UNIDO)

Clicking on the membership link, the researcher will find a list of the members, as well as their web addresses (with some variation in topics and languages from country to country).

WAIPA's IPA Tool allows the researcher to access several links to information, including Investor Targeting Toolkit, Investment Gateway, FDI Promotion Center, Investment Map, Investment Promotion Tool, and UNCTAD's *World Investment Report*, the work program on international investment agreements and more.

The US Chamber of Commerce (www.uschamber.com/) is the world's largest business organization representing the interests of more than 3 million businesses of all sizes, sectors, and regions. It provides contact information and country business information.

The International Chamber of Commerce (www.iccwbo.org/) has direct access to national governments all over the world through its national committees. The organization's Paris-based international secretariat feeds business views into intergovernmental organizations on issues that directly affect business operations. Their websites provides links to a selection of thousands of company members' websites of every size from over 120 countries.

Numerous other sources that provide country information have not been covered here. These include free websites that might have been created by a country's government and international organizations like the International Monetary Fund (IMF), United Nations Conference on Trade and Development (UNCTAD), and the World Trade Organization (WTO). Material published by these types of organizations focus on specific topics and thus are very useful when doing research in those areas. For example, one would use IMF sources for information related to the international monetary system and financial markets. For trade, one would look for information from both the UNCTAD and WTO would be used for trade.

CONCLUSION

This chapter presented a general overview and a starting point for international business research. The sources selected covered multiple countries and featured various types of information. If a user needs resources that focus on a region or country, the next chapter will provide an overview of major regional trade blocs and economic organizations.

LIST OF SOURCES

This is an alphabetical list of the websites mentioned in this chapter.

African, Caribbean and Pacific Group of States (ACP), www.acp.int/ (7 June 2012).
Background Notes, www.state.gov/r/pa/ei/bgn/ (4 June 2012).
The Bank for International Settlements (BIS), www.bis.org/cbanks.htm (4 June 2012).
BBC Country Profiles, news.bbc.co.uk/2/hi/country_profiles/default.stm (1 June 2012).
Country Briefings, www.countrybriefings.com/ (14 June 2012).
Country Profiles ELDIS, www.eldis.org/ (10 June 2012).
Country Studies/Area Handbook Series, lcweb2.loc.gov/frd/cs (10 June 2012).
Country Watch, "Frequently Asked Questions," www.countrywatch.com/help/faqs.aspx (5 June 2012).
Ease of Doing Business Rankings, www.doingbusiness.org/economyrankings/ (31 May 2012).
Ediplomat, www.ediplomat.com/ (14 June 2012).
EIU, www.eiu.com (14 June 2012).
Embassy World, www.embassyworld.com/embassy/directory.htm (18 June 2012).
Europa World, www.europaworld.com/ (18 June 2012).
GlobalEdge, globaledge.msu.edu/ (29 June 2012).
Geography IQ, www.geographyiq.com/ (12 June 2012).
International Chamber of Commerce, www.iccwbo.org/ (19 June 2012).
Monthly Bulletin of Statistics, unstats.un.org/unsd/mbs/app/DataSearchTable.aspx (19 June 2012).
US Chamber of Commerce, www.uschamber.com/ (19 June 2012).

World Association of Investment Promotion Agencies (WAIPA), www.waipa.org (29 June 2012).

World Factbook, https://www.cia.gov/library/publications/the-world-factbook/ (1 June 2012).

NOTES

1. US Department of State, "Background Notes," www.state.gov/r/pa/ei/bgn/ (5 June 2012).

2. *Background Notes*, www.state.gov/r/pa/ei/bgn/ (24 June 2012).

3. Central Intelligence Agency. Publications. *World Factbook*, https://www.cia.gov/library/publications/the-world-factbook/index.html (5 June 2012).

4. United Nations. "UN at a Glance," www.un.org/en/aboutun/index.shtml (29 June 2012).

5. United Nations Publications, "Product Details," https://unp.un.org/Details.aspx?pid=21306 (29 June 2012).

6. Country Watch, "Frequently Asked Questions," www.countrywatch.com/help/faqs.aspx (30 June 2012).

FOUR

Regional Economic Organizations and Trade Blocs

The environment in which businesses engage today is one that is increasingly global. This means that a company located anywhere in the world may decide to go outside its borders in order to reach new markets. This will require the business to find information about a country, industries, products, and consumers to be successful. There are a number of strategies and sources that one can use to do this analysis.[1] For instance, there are many sources such as databases and websites that provide news, reports, documents, and other information for other countries in English, but it is also a fact that even those sources do not cover everything available in the original languages.[2] A strategy the researcher can take to find relevant business information is to use regional economic organizations and trade or trading blocs. "Some countries form alliances, or trading blocs, which give companies easier access to foreign markets and make it more profitable for them to trade with countries that are also members of the bloc."[3] Almost every country in the world belongs to at least one of these. A trade bloc refers to "groups of countries that have established preferential trade arrangements aiming at increasing trade among each other. Trade blocs have been formed along geographical lines leading to the emergence of regional bloc trading."[4] Below is a list of the main trade blocs in the world:

Europe

- European Union (EU)
- European Free Trade Agreement (EFTA)
- European Agreements

45

- European Economic Area (EEA)

United States and Canada

- North American Free Trade Agreement (NAFTA)
- Canada–US Free Trade Agreement (CUSTA)
- US–Israel Free Trade Agreement

Latin America

- Common Market of the South (MERCOSUR)
- Central American Common Market (CACM)
- Andean Pact
- Latin American Integration Association (LAIA)
- Caribbean Community and Common Market (CARICOM)

Africa

- Communauté Economique de l'Afrique Occidentale (CEAO)
- Union Economique et Monétaire de l'Afrique Occidentale (UE-MOA)
- Union Douanière et Economique d'Afrique Centrale (UDEAC)
- Common Market of Eastern and Southern Africa (COMESA)
- Preferential Trade Area for Easternand Southern African States (PTA)
- Southern African Customs Union (SACU)

Asia

- Association of Southeast Nations (ASEAN)
- ASEAN Free Trade Area (AFTA)
- Australia–New Zealand Closer Economic Relations Trade Agreement (ANZCERTA).

The information sources users can find from these economic organizations and trade blocs is remarkable and very diverse. Some of the websites identified for these groups may contain the same or similar information; others may include unique coverage of certain topics. The information available includes general statistics on the economy, business directories, information about government officials, and cultural and investment information.

The United States government publishes a great amount of country information that they disseminate through the websites. Consequently, finding information from the United States' perspective and other business sources can be easier than trying to get it from the country itself. For example, the US State Department has commercial trade experts in most countries, and they collect and produce a vast amount of materials. This information is produced in English. On the other hand, other trade blocs or economic organizations may use languages other than English.

Instead of searching country by country for business information, a good alternative is to access regional economic organizations' and treaties' websites. Most of these sites have useful business information covering multiple countries in one stop. The selected resources identified below are websites that provide information for individual country members in the economic regions.

ASIA–PACIFIC ECONOMIC ORGANIZATIONS

There are several treaties in Asia and the Pacific, but not all countries are members of the treaties. On the websites of Asian and Pacific blocs, information is mostly in English. Asia: the Pacific Economic Cooperation APEC (www.apec.org/) is the premier forum for facilitating economic growth, cooperation, trade, and investment in the Asia–Pacific Region. APEC's twenty-one member economies are the United States, Australia, Brunei Darussalam, Canada, Chile, China, Hong Kong, Indonesia, Japan, Malaysia, Mexico, New Zealand, Papua New Guinea, Peru, the Philippines, Russia, Singapore, South Korea, Taiwan, Thailand, and Vietnam. Information available includes news, information about the economies of the twenty-one member countries, a business center, publications, a virtual library, and a database of useful links. Some interesting resources from the APEC website are

- *Business Travel Handbook*: This *APEC Business Travel Handbook* is intended to assist business people who travel in the Asia–Pacific region by providing a quick reference guide to the visa and entry requirements of APEC member economies. The electronic *Handbook* also provides contact details for the embassies, consulates, and other visa-issuing agencies of each member economy. The information in this book remains the sole responsibility of the respective APEC member economy that publishes the handbook. Researchers can find more detailed information on individual economies, visa laws, and regulations at this website: www.businessmobility.org/travel/index.asp.
- *Investing Across Borders*: This report presents facts and data on laws and regulations in selected policy areas affecting entry and operations of foreign direct investors for each APEC member. The data is based on surveys and interviews with private sector intermediaries, such as investment lawyers, accountants, and investment promo-

tion specialists, working with foreign investors in each of the benchmarked economies. Chapter 5 of the report profiles the APEC member economies (publications.apec.org/publication-detail.php?pub_id=1149).

The Association of Southeast Asian Nations ASEAN (www.aseansec.org) is comprised of three pillars: the Political-Security Community, Economic Community, and Socio-Cultural Community (figure 4.1). Members are Brunei Darussalam, Cambodia, Indonesia, Lao PDR, Malaysia, Myanmar, the Philippines, Singapore, Thailand, and Vietnam. When on the site, select ASEAN *Members States* to find the official government website of each.

The Asian Development Bank ADB (www.adb.org/) has sixty-seven members, of whom forty-eight are from within Asia and the Pacific and nineteen are from outside the region. The *ADB Factsheets* provide concise information on the Bank's member economies, its operations, and contact information. ADB, in partnership with member governments, independent specialists, and other financial institutions, is focused on delivering projects that create economic and developmental impacts. By selecting a country, one will be able to find the *Country Operations Business Plan*

Figure 4.1.

(COBP), which describes the consistency of the business plan with the country partnership strategy. Reports are available in English.

The Cooperation Council for the Arab States of the Gulf GCC (www.gcc-sg.org/eng/) formulates regulations in various fields such as economy, finance, trade, customs, tourism, legislation, and administration, as well as fostering scientific and technical progress in industry, mining, agriculture, water, and animal resources; setting up joint ventures; and encouraging cooperation of the private sector. Members include the United Arab Emirates, the State of Bahrain, the Kingdom of Saudi Arabia, the Sultanate of Oman, the State of Qatar, and the State of Kuwait. On the website, select Recent Publications in the menu bar for statistics, demographics, and business information (see figure 4.2). Some examples of resources for member countries are the Statistical Bulletin, Consumer Price Index, and National Accounts Bulletin.

The Colombo Plan for Cooperative Economic and Social Development in Asia and the Pacific CPS (www.colombo-plan.org/) promotes interest in and support for the economic and social development of Asia and the Pacific and facilitates the transfer and sharing of the developmental experience among member countries within the region with emphasis on the concept of South-South cooperation.

Figure 4.2.

The Asian Association for Regional Cooperation SAAR (saarc-sic.org/beta/index.asp/) is an organization of South Asian nations dedicated to economic, technological, social, and cultural development that emphasizes collective self-reliance. Some areas of cooperation are biotechnology, culture, energy, environment, economy and trade, finance, human resource development, people-to-people contact, science and technology, communications, and tourism. Country members are Afghanistan, Bhutan, Bangladesh, Pakistan, India, Maldives, Nepal, and Sri Lanka.

Although not an organization, The Asian Banker (main.theasianbanker.com/) provides good coverage for the region.

LATIN AMERICA AND THE CARIBBEAN ECONOMIC ORGANIZATIONS

The language for the majority of the countries in Latin America and the Caribbean is Spanish; other languages spoken are Portuguese, English, French, and some Indian dialects. When searching for Latin America resources, it is important to know that it includes countries in South America, Central America, Mexico, and Spanish-speaking countries in the Caribbean.

Andean Community—Comunidad Andina (CAN; Spanish acronym) (www.comunidadandina.org/) is a trade bloc of four countries that voluntarily decided to join together for the purpose of achieving more rapid and autonomous development through Andean, South American, and Latin American integration. Members countries are Bolivia, Colombia, Ecuador, and Perú.

The Association of Caribbean States—Asociación de Estados del Caribe (AEC; Spanish acronym) (www.acs-aec.org/) is a union of nations centered on the Caribbean Basin. The primary purpose of the ACS is to develop greater trade between the nations, enhance transportation, develop sustainable tourism, and facilitate greater and more effective responses to local natural disasters.

The Caribbean Community CARICOM's (www.caricom.org/) member states are Antigua and Barbuda, the Bahamas, Barbados, Belize, Dominica, Grenada, Guyana, Haiti, Jamaica, Montserrat, Saint Lucia, St. Kitts and Nevis, St. Vincent and the Grenadines, Suriname, and Trinidad and Tobago. CARICOM produces a number of statistical reports on the member countries and has free access to selected datasets. Some of the datasets included are National Accounts, Balance of Payments, and Trade in Services.

The Dominican Republic–Central America–United States Free Trade Agreement—CAFTA-DR (www.caftadr.net/) is a US agreement with five Central American countries: Costa Rica, El Salvador, Guatemala, Honduras, Nicaragua, and the Dominican Republic. It is a free trade area, similar to the North American Free Trade Agreement (NAFTA). CAFTA-DR facilitates trade and investment among the members. Choose a country to find financial information.

The Economic Commission for Latin America ECLA — Comisión Económica para América Latina y el Caribe (CEPAL; Spanish acronym) (www.cepal.org/comercio/) is one of the five regional commissions of the United Nations. It was founded in 1948 with the purpose of contributing to the economic development of Latin America. ECLA coordinates actions directed toward this end and reinforces economic ties among countries and with other nations of the world. It also promotes the region's social development.

Ibero–American Association of Chambers of Commerce — Asociación Iberoamericana de Cámaras de Comercio (AICO; Spanish acronyms) (www.aico.org/) is a nonprofit, independent association that brings together and represents all major chambers of commerce, associations, corporations, and entities of Spanish and Portuguese speakers from twenty-three countries of Latin America, the Caribbean, the Iberian Peninsula, and Spanish Communities in the United States. The website links to business information issues from the region, business directories, embassies, and customs information. Most of the links are in Spanish.

The Inter-American Development Bank IDB (www.iadb.org/en/inter-american-development-bank,2837.html) is the largest source of development financing for Latin America and the Caribbean. Its website provides links to the twenty-six country members' economy and financial information. The Bank has compiled and organized over 1,000 searchable statistics and indicators for countries in Latin America and the Caribbean, as well as other world regions, thereby creating a comprehensive dataset for the region. The following are some of the statistics and databases available on the website:

- DataGov: governance indicators from key public databases consolidated for all countries in the world (www.iadb.org/datagob/index.html)
- DataIntal: trade statistics of countries in the Americas developed by the Institute for the Integration of Latin America (INTAL) (www.iadb.org/dataintal/)
- Latin America and Caribbean Macro Watch Data Tool (www.iadb.org/Research/LatinMacroWatch/lmw.cfm): features 500 indicators that consolidate data on macroeconomics, social issues, trade, capital flows, markets, and governance
- INTradeBID: provides public access to data, statistics, and legal information (www.iadb.org/int/intradebid/?lang=ing)

The Latin American and the Caribbean Economic System, officially known as Sistema Económico Latinoamericano y del Caribe SELA (Spanish acronym) (www.sela.org/) is an organization that promotes economic cooperation and social development between Latin America and the Caribbean countries. Its representatives consist of members from twenty-eight countries that took part in the General Agreement on Tariffs and Trade (GATT) negotiations, which led to a new global agreement on restrictions on trade and established the World Trade Organization (WTO). The website contains the profiles of each of the twenty-eight member states of SELA, with information on geography and climate, population, human development indicators, education, health, poverty, government, and economy. Essentially, the information comes from each member's official website and the websites of relevant national authorities such as the International Monetary Fund and the United Nations Population Fund—UNFPA. For country information, select the name of the country. Current SELA membership states include Argentina, Bahamas, Barbados, Belize, Bolivia, Brazil, Colombia, Costa Rica, Cuba, Chile, Ecuador, El Salvador, Grenada, Guatemala, Guyana, Haiti, Honduras, Jamaica, Mexico, Nicaragua, Panama, Paraguay, Perú, the Dominican Republic, Suriname, Trinidad and Tobago, Uruguay, and Venezuela.

MERCOSUR is South America's leading trading bloc. Known as the Common Market of the South, it aims to bring about the free movement of goods, capital, services, and people among its member states. MERCOSUR members are Bolivia, Chile, Colombia, Ecuador, Perú, and Venezuela. Official documentation and links in this website are in Spanish and Portuguese at www.mercosur.int. The website offers useful links to all the official members' governmental departments, including statistics and business information.

The North American Free Trade Agreement NAFTA (www.nafta-sec-alena.org/en/view.aspx) is a regional agreement among the government of Canada, the government of the United Mexican States, and the government of the United States of America to implement free trade in the area. This is the world's largest trade bloc. Links to government organizations, regional and international organizations, and harmonized tariff are found on the website.

Organization of American States—Organización de los Estados Americanos OEA (Spanish acronym) (www.oas.org/) is the world's oldest regional organization made up of 35 independent states of the Americas and constitutes the main political, judicial, and social governmental forum in the hemisphere. Related to OEA is a network of e-Government leaders of Latin America and the Caribbean (figure 4.3) (Red GEALC). This network puts in operation a series of mechanisms that facilitate the generation and dissemination of knowledge in the area of e-Government, as well as the cooperation in e-Government of all the countries in the region.

The Association of American Chambers of Commerce in Latin America AACCLA (www.aaccla.org/) is comprised of twenty-three American Chambers of Commerce divisions. AACCLA represent more than 20,000

Figure 4.3.   Trinidad and Tobago: e-Government leaders of Latin America and the Caribbean.

companies and over 80 percent of US investment in the region. It has become the premier advocate for US businesses in the Americas. It promotes trade and investment between the United States and the countries of the region through free trade, free markets, and free enterprise.

CAMACOL (www.camacol.org/) is the largest Hispanic business organization in the State of Florida and one of the most influential minority business groups in the United States. Select *Links* for statistics and financial information.

The Latin American Banking Federation—Federación de Bancos Latinomericanos FELEBAN (Spanish Acronym) (www.felaban.com/) is a non-profit organization that is made up of banking associations and other agencies from 19 Latin American countries encompassing more than 500 regional banks. Most of the information is in Spanish. FELEBAN promotes and facilitates contact and understands and directs relationships between the financial entities in Latin America. Its website provides links to numerous publications, both regional and country-specific.

LANIC (lanic.utexas.edu/), Latin American Network Information Center, is affiliated with the Lozano Long Institute of Latin American Studies (LLILAS) at the University of Texas at Austin. LANIC's directory provides information for thirty-five countries on forty-nine subjects. The website's structure is arranged by country and by subject. The information is available in English, Spanish, and Portuguese.

AFRICA ECONOMIC ORGANIZATIONS

The continent of Africa is diverse culturally, geographically, ethnically, and linguistically. The biggest challenge for doing business in Africa is the lack of current information for some of the countries in the continent. Other challenges of doing business in Africa are fluctuating currencies, lack of local capital, monopolies such as marketing boards, foreign exchange restrictions, nepotism, and lack of infrastructure.

The African Union (www.au.int/en/) is home to a wide range of information for the continent. It is a starting point to find country profiles, currency type, government information, and news. The African Union has also created three financial institutions to attempt to facilitate trade within the countries in the continent. They are the African Investment Bank (AIB) (www.afrikainvestmentbank.com/), the African Monetary Fund (AMF), and the African Central Bank (ACB) (www.aacb.org/).

The Common Market for Eastern and Southern Africa (COMESA) (www.comesa.int/) is a free trade area that encompasses twenty countries: Angola, Burundi, Comoros, the Democratic Republic of Congo, Djibouti, Egypt, Eritrea, Ethiopia, Kenya, Libya, Madagascar, Malawi, Mauritius, Rwanda, Seychelles, Sudan, Swaziland, Uganda, Zambia, and Zimbabwe.

The COMESA treaty clearly highlights the role of statistics in the integration monitoring process. In the treaty's vision for a "Common Market Information System," it states, "the Member States undertake to co-operate in the field of statistics in order to create an enabling environment for the regular flow of up-to-date, reliable, harmonized and comparable statistical data on various sectors of economic activity, required for an efficient implementation of the objectives of the Common Market."[5] Its website also provides the database COMSTAT. The statistical information covered in COMSTAT includes merchandise trade statistics, trade integration indicators, and trade flow analysis. New users need to register.

The mission of the Southern African Development Community (SADC) (www.sadc.int/) is to promote sustainable and equitable economic growth and socioeconomic development through efficient productive systems, deeper cooperation and integration, good governance, and durable peace and security, so that the region emerges as a competitive and effective player in international relations and the world economy. Members are Angola, Botswana, Democratic Republic of Congo, Lesotho, Madagascar, Malawi, Mauritius, Mozambique, Namibia, the Seychelles, South Africa, Swaziland, United Republic of Tanzania, Zambia, and Zimbabwe. Search the investment portal to find business and financial data for member countries.

Southern African Customs Union's (SACU) (www.sacu.int/) mission is to serve as an engine for regional integration and development, industrial and economic diversification, the expansion of intra-regional trade and investment, and global competitiveness. SACU consists of Botswana, Lesotho, Namibia, South Africa, and Swaziland. SACU was established in 1910, making it the world's oldest customs union. Its website provides links to official government websites, statistics, and trade organizations.

The Nile Basin Initiative (NBI) (www.nilebasin.org/newsite/) pursues cooperative development, shares substantial socioeconomic benefits, and promotes regional integration. Its basin includes nine African countries. Country members are Burundi, the Democratic Republic of Congo,

Egypt, Kenya, Rwanda, South Sudan, Sudan, Tanzania, and Uganda. The website provides links to country profiles, country news, and information on investment programs.

The Communauté Economique et Monétaire de l'Afrique Centrale (CEMAC) (www.cemac.int/) is an economic community of the African Union for the promotion of regional economic cooperation in Central Africa. The members of CEMAC include Cameroon, Congo, Gabon, Guinea Equatorial, Central African Republic, and Chad. Sources for data and information are from the economic union (UEAC) (Union économique de l'Afrique Centrale) and a monetary union (UMAC) (Union monétaire de l'Afrique Centrale). Member countries include Angola, Burundi, Cameroon, Central Africa, Congo, Republic of Congo, Gabon, Equatorial Guinea, Sao Tome et Principe, and Chad.

The Economic Community of West African States (ECOWAS) (www.ecowas.int/) is a regional organization of sixteen West African nations. The main objective of forming ECOWAS was to achieve economic integration and shared development so as to form a unified economic zone in West Africa. Later on, the scope was increased to include sociopolitical interactions and mutual development in related spheres. Currently, there are fifteen member countries in the organization. The membership list includes Benin, Burkina Faso, Cape Verde, Côte d'Ivoire, Gambia, Ghana, Guinea, Guinea-Bissau, Liberia, Mali, Niger, Nigeria, Senegal, Sierra Leone, and Togo. Documents are available in English, French, and Portuguese.

West African Economic and Monetary Union (UEMOA) (www.uemoa.int/Pages/Home.aspx) members are Benin, Burkina Faso, Côte d'Ivoire, Guinea-Bissau, Mali, Niger, Senegal, and Togo. UEMOA has established a common accounting system periodic reviews of member countries' macroeconomic policies based on convergence criteria, a regional stock exchange, and the legal and regulatory framework for a regional banking system. This website is in French.

French is the official working language of Banque Centrale des Etats de l'Afrique de l'Ouest (BCEAO) (www.bceao.int). However, its website includes a limited selection of documents in English. Country profile and financial information is available in French only.

Banque Ouest Africaine de Développement (BOAD) (www.boad.org/) is an international multilateral development bank serving the nation's Francophone and Lusophone speakers. Its main objective is to focus on the development of the economy of West Africa. Its mission is poverty reduction, economic integration, and promotion of private sector activity. Member countries are Benin, Burkina-Faso, Côte d'Ivoire, Guinea Bissau, Mali, Niger, Senegal, and Togo. Most of the information on the website is in French.

East African Community's (EAC) (www.eac.int/) main objective is set out in its treaty. Its goal is to enhance the region's competitiveness through integration, starting with a customs union, followed by a common market, a monetary union, and ultimately, a political federation of East African states.

Indian Ocean Commission (IOC) (www.coi-ioc.org/ndian) is an intergovernmental organization of regional cooperation. Country members are Maurtius, Seychelles, Comoros, Madagascar, and Reunion. Their website includes information about members' economies. Most of the information available is in French.

EUROPE ECONOMIC ORGANIZATIONS

European Union (EU) (europa.eu/) is a unique economic and political partnership between twenty-seven European countries. The first purpose for its creation was to foster economic cooperation. The idea was that countries that trade with one another become economically interdependent and are, therefore, more likely to avoid conflict. This is based on a single market money and freedom of movement of goods, persons, services, and capital.

The European Economic Area (EEA) (eeas.europa.eu/eea/) brings together the EU member states bilateral relations with countries and regions. This website links to all the European country members and to regions of the world. It also links to international organizations like the International Monetary Fund (IMF). Information is available in twenty-three languages.

The European Investment Bank (EIB) (www.eib.org/) consists of shareholders in twenty-seven member states of the union. The EIB aims to provide users with the information in the member's own language. Official documents are frequently published in English, French, and German. The EIB publishes a wide range of brochures aimed at both professionals and the general public. Information published in these documents and on the websites can be freely reproduced.

The European Bank for Reconstruction and Development (EBRD) (www.ebrd.com) provides project financing for banks, industries, and businesses, both new ventures and investments in existing companies. The EBRD also works with publicly owned companies. Its website provides links to research and publications, country overviews, news, publications by country and by theme, financial institutions, and legal reform. EBRD develops partnerships with local and international businesses and investment communities. It acts in close cooperation with all members, both public and private, and all multilateral institutions concerned with the economic development of and investment in countries from central Europe to Central Asia. These include the European Union, the European Investment Bank, the World Bank Group, the International Monetary Fund, and the United Nations and its specialized agencies.

Australia New Zealand Closer Economic Agreement (ANZCERTA; www.austrade.gov.au/ANZCERTA/default.aspx) is a bilateral agreement. Its website covers a wide range of trade issues including agricultural products and services. The main page links to useful information for those interested in learning about exporting, buying, and investing with Australia and New Zealand or with other countries around the world. ANZCERTA's website also provides tips on their "Doing Business" page, which includes social etiquette, business tips, and other documents required for doing business abroad.

Franc Zone (www.banque-france.fr/en/home.html) includes fourteen Sub-Saharan countries, the Comoros, and France. It manages a company's database denominated FIBEN for "Fichier Bancaire des Entreprises." It was set up to facilitate the implementation of monetary policy.

CONCLUSION

Throughout this chapter, sources were provided that could help find information for multiples countries in one stop. The available information could include: country background, financial information, statistical sources, and investment resources. While this list is not exhaustive it is a good starting point for country information research.

LIST OF SOURCES

This is an alphabetical list of Internet websites mentioned throughout the chapter.

Andean Community—Comunidad Andina (CAN), www.comunidadandina.org/ (4 June 2012).
The African Central Bank (ACB), www.aacb.org/ (4 June 2012).
African Investment Bank (AIB), www.afrikainvestmentbank.com/ (4 June 2012).
African Union, www.au.int/en/ (4 June 2012).
Asian Association for Regional Cooperation (SAAR), saarc-sic.org/beta/index.asp/ (5 June 2012).
The Asian Banker, main.theasianbanker.com/ (11 June 2012).
Asian Development Bank (ADB), www.adb.org/ (12 June 2012).
Association of American Chambers of Commerce in Latin America (AmChams), www.aaccla.org/ (6 June 2012).
Association of Caribbean States—Asociación de Estados del Caribe AEC, www.acsaec.org/ (18 June 2012).
Association of Southeast Asian Nations (ASEAN), www.aseansec.org/ (6 June 2012).
Banque Centrale des Etats de l'Afrique de l'Ouest (BCEAO), www.bceao.int (14 June 2012).
Banque Ouest Africaine de Développement (BOAD), www.boad.org/ (14 June 2012).
Business Travel Handbook, www.businessmobility.org/travel/index.asp (4 June 2012).
CAMACOL, www.camacol.org/ (13 June 2012).
The Colombo Plan for Cooperative Economic and Social Development in Asia and the Pacific, www.colombo-plan.org/ (12 June 2012).

The Common Market for Eastern and Southern Africa (COMESA), www.comesa.int/ (31 May 2012).

Communauté Economique et Monétaire de l'Afrique Centrale (CEMAC), www.cemac.int/ (31 May 2012).

The Cooperation Council Gulf for the Arab States of the Gulf (GCC), www.gcc-sg.org/eng/ (11 June 2012).

CPS Caribbean Community (CARICOM), www.caricom.org/ (29 June 2012).

DataGov, www.iadb.org/datagob/index.html (18 June 2012).

DataIntal, www.iadb.org/dataintal/ (18 June 2012).

Dominican Republic-Central America-United States Free Trade Agreement (CAFTA-DR), www.caftadr.net/ (19 June 2012).

The Economic Commission for Latin America (ECLA), Comisión Económica para América Latina y el Caribe (CEPAL), www.cepal.org/comercio/ (1 June 2012).

The Economic Community of West African States (ECOWAS), www.ecowas.int/ (1 June 2012).

East African Community (EAC), www.eac.int/ (1 June 2012).

Ediplomat, www.ediplomat.com/ (1 June 2012).

European Bank for Reconstruction and Development (EBRD), www.ebrd.com (19 June 2012).

European Investment Bank (EIB), www.eib.org/ (19 June 2012).

European Economic Area (EEA), eeas.europa.eu/eea/ (19 June 2012).

European Union, europa.eu/ (19 June 2012).

Franc Zone, www.banque-france.fr/en/home.html (19 June 2012).

Ibero-American Association of Chambers of Commerce   Asociación Iberoamericana de Cámaras de Comercio (AICO), www.aico.org/ (19 June 2012).

Indian Ocean Commission (IOC), www.coi-ioc.org/ndian (31 May 2012).

Inter-American Development Bank (IDB), www.iadb.org/en/inter-american-development bank,2837.html (31 May 2012).

INTradeBID, www.iadb.org/int/intradebid/?lang=ing (31 May 2012).

Investing Across Borders, publications.apec.org/publication-detail.php?pub_id=1149 (13 June 2012).

LANIC, Latin American Network Information Center, lanic.utexas.edu/ (13 June 2012).

Latin America and Caribbean Macro Watch Data Tool, www.iadb.org/Research/Latin-MacroWatch/lmw.cfm (18 June 2012).

Latin American and the Caribbean Economic System, Sistema Económico Latinoamericano y del Caribe (SELA), www.sela.org/ (1 June 2012).

Latin American Banking Federation, Federación de Bancos Latinomericanos (FELEBAN), www.felaban.com/ (19 June 2012).

Library of Congress, Country Studies/Area Handbook Series, lcweb2.loc.gov/frd/cs (31 May 2012).

MERCOSUR, www.mercosur.int/ (15 October 2012).

The Nile Basin Initiative (NBI), www.nilebasin.org/newsite/ (19 June 2012).

North American Free Trade Agreement (NAFTA), www.nafta-sec-alena.org/en/view.aspx (14 May 2012).

Organización de los Estados Americanos (OEA), www.oas.org/ (19 June 2012).

Southern African Customs Union (SACU), www.sacu.int/ (15 June 2012).

Southern African Development Community (SADC), www.sadc.int/ (15 June 2012).

West African Economic and Monetary Union (UEMOA), www.uemoa.int/Pages/Home.aspx (11 June 2012).

US Department of State, *Background Notes,* www.state.gov/r/pa/ei/bgn/ (31 May 2012).

The World Association of Investment Promotion Agencies, www2.waipa.org/cms/Waipa (31 May 2012).

The Word Factbook, www.cia.gov/library/publications/the-world-factbook/ (1 June 2012).

Bank for International Settlements, Central Bank and Monetary Authority Websites, www.bis.org/cbanks.htm (1 June 2012).

NOTES

1. Marydee Ojala, "The Small World of International Business Research," *Online* 31, no. 6 (Nov. 2007): 47–49.

2. Eiko Shaul, "Business Research Beyond Borders," *Bulletin of the American Society for Information Science & Technology* 37, no. 1 (2010): 35–36. *Library, Information Science & Technology Abstracts.* Web. (11 June 2012).

3. "World Trade," *Geography of the World* (London: Dorling Kindersley Publishing, Inc., 2009), *Credo Reference*, web (12 June 2012).

4. "Trade Bloc," *Encyclopedia of Business in Today's World* (Thousand Oaks, CA: Sage Publications 2009), *Credo Reference*, web (7 June 2012).

5. About COMESA, www.comesa.int/ (14 October 2012).

FIVE

International Company Research

Company research is an essential part of business research. There are different reasons why one might be trying to find company information. It could be that an individual wants to evaluate the performance of a company for investment purposes; a businessperson might be trying to find information about a competitor for market research; or it could be a student who is learning about a company's strategy, human resource practices, leadership, or organizational culture for a management class.

As a researcher engages in this activity, he or she will encounter different types of companies in terms of their size and structure. They could be multinational corporations (MNC), multinational enterprises, multinational organizations, transnational corporations, and increasingly, those that are micro-, small-, and medium-sized enterprises.

There are many companies that one might describe as an MNC. Traditionally, these companies have the resources to enter markets outside their country of origin. These entities also own and control foreign assets, produce goods and/or services outside the local country, and make them available worldwide. "MNC's generally coordinate their activities from a central headquarters but may also allow their affiliates or subsidiaries in foreign markets considerable latitude in adjusting their operations to local circumstances."[1] Sometimes these may be referred to as international business enterprises. This term, however, covers more than just the MNC, in that it could also cover the small and medium-sized enterprises (SME).

Other types of large entities that are not corporations may be referred to as multinational enterprises, such as Lloyd's of London. There are also multinational organizations that are made up of nonprofit organizations, such as the International Red Cross.[2]

The United Nations Conference on Trade and Development (UNC-TAD) has another category for very large companies with overseas operations, transnational with corporations (TNC). These are defined to be "incorporated or unincorporated enterprises comprising parent enterprises and their foreign affiliates. A parent enterprise is defined as an enterprise that controls assets of other entities in countries other than its home country, usually by owning a certain equity capital stake."[3]

A trend is the increase in the number of micro-, small-, and medium-sized enterprises worldwide, which is having a major impact on local, national, regional, and global economies. The European Commission describes a micro entity as having less than ten employees and fewer than 2 million Euros in turnover or annual balance sheet total. Small enterprises have fewer than 50 staff, and less than 10 million Euros in turnover or balance sheet total.[4] Medium enterprises are defined to have less than 250 staff, less than 50 million euros in annual turnover, and less than 43 million euros in annual balance sheet total.

The researcher will invariably run across any of these types of "enterprises" as he or she goes through the process, discovering that there are different amounts of information for these different types of businesses. It will generally be easier to find information for the large companies, and more difficult for SMEs. In addition, one will also learn that the nature of regulations that apply for incorporation, as well as geographic location worldwide, will influence the type of information to which the researcher has access.

This chapter will identify strategies and sources for companies that are listed, unlisted, and subsidiaries.

STRATEGIES FOR FINDING COMPANY INFORMATION

When doing research about US companies, the first step to take is to determine whether the company is public, private, or a subsidiary. Making this determination empowers the researcher to formulate the search strategy and identify sources to use. For example, if a US company is public, it will have to file legally required documents, including the 10-K. The 10-K is an annual report that US companies trading on a US exchange must file with the Securities Exchange Commission (SEC). It can often be lengthy. For example, Kellogg's 2012 10-K is made up of 120 pages. This document has information about the company's business, a review of the industry landscape, information about competitors, strategies it has, and financials. These documents are publicly available via the SEC Electronics Data Gathering Analysis and Retrieval (EDGAR)[5] website. What this means to the researcher is that there will be many sources in which to find information, one of them being this site. Because of the availability of these documents, commercial publishers such as BvD, Dun

& Bradstreet (D&B), Mergent, infogroup, Standard & Poor's, and Thomson, to name a few, are able to extract data from these records to create a range of company databases with powerful capabilities.

Unfortunately, if one identifies a US company to be private or a subsidiary, the amount of information decreases tremendously, and for some companies it won't exist. Financial information won't be available even in the commercial databases. Private companies are not traded. A company is a subsidiary when another company has control of more than 50 percent of its voting stock.

When international company research is added to the process, the search strategy should be refined to incorporate other sources of information. This is because other countries have different laws of incorporation which frame the availability of information.

The terms *private* and *public* are probably more of a North American concept in describing a company's legal status.[6] In addition, many unlisted companies are in the "public" sector, being either nationalized or owned by the state.[7] Using "listed" and "unlisted" is more characteristic of the type of companies they represent. That is, the former refers to companies that are listed and trading on a stock exchange, those that are unlisted aren't. There are also cases when reference to a "public" company may be to a government-owned entity or a nonprofit.

Like US-based company research, when researching non-US companies one can employ the basic strategy of determining whether a company is listed, unlisted, or holds some other designation, with the additional step of determining its country of origin. Despite the popularity of search engines, and recognizing that there are times when these can yield adequate results, a good place to start is often with directories or databases that include companies from around the world, both listed and unlisted. These sources can be either online or in print.

Online databases are ideal in several ways. For example, a user may be able to access them remotely, they are often updated regularly, and they may have additional features that provide more than basic information, which usually consists of address, contact information (i.e., phone number, email address), and possibly an indicator of being traded, such as a ticker symbol. Furthermore, depending on the source, a database may cover nonprofits and other types of organizations. Another advantage is that a database significantly streamlines the research process.

Some online sources that may be categorized as directories, such as Hoovers Online, will also include company profiles that can be brief or extensive. Some basic features that a directory provides include the contact information described earlier, the industry or industries in which it participates, a list of competitors with links that allow the researcher to access the information for these companies, and a link to news. A directory also informs the user of the company's ownership status (public, private, subsidiary, holding company) although this may not be needed for those that are obviously trading.

A number of subscription-based databases are available for this type of research, including BvD's Mint Global, Dun & Bradstreet's Million Dollar Directory (D&B), Mergent Online, infogroup's OneSource, and Standard & Poor's (S&P)[8] NetAdvantage. Other alternatives are Lexis-Nexis' Corporate Affiliations and the Company Dossiers, and Gale/Cengage's Business Insights: Essentials. Databases from Morningstar and Thomson are also available. A system like Bloomberg and the data sets in S&P's Compustat provide added features that are not available in the other sources identified in this chapter.

Listed Companies

When using databases referred to earlier, a listed company's information will include its ticker symbol, and an indicator that represents the name of the exchange (i.e., TSX for Toronto Stock Exchange) in which it trades. It will also say it is public in the record.

When a global company is listed on a stock exchange, the amount of information that is available is deep and broad. When one finds the information in databases, such as Hoovers Online or OneSource, that identified earlier, the researcher should extract all the information possible using the many facets in which the information is organized. For example, databases will generally have links to the financials, a place to find its competitors, and key executives. Some will also have a way of making a comparative analysis by providing a list of competitors and indicators, such as sales, income, ratios, price of the share, and others, which can use to compare companies. Databases also have interactive tools for selecting specific companies and data items such as those mentioned, as well as a range of other categories. For example, Mergent Online allows customization by the comparison analysis using pricing information (i.e., dividend yield, earnings per share [EPS], closing price), income statement, balance sheet, cash flows, ratios, executives (i.e., officers, directors, insider trades), and news (i.e., recent, history).

If a foreign company such as Tata Motors is trading on a US exchange, the researcher should look for the company's 20-F. The 20-F is equivalent to the 10-K that American companies file. It is a legal form that foreign companies trading on a US stock exchange must file with the SEC. Like the 10-K, it is also available through the SEC EDGAR search interface.[9] Database providers will have a link to these and any other SEC required documents in their systems.

On the other hand, if the foreign company is not trading on a US exchange, there may be some summary information about the financials of the company, such as Bombardier, but there will not be any links to annual reports.

This section has dealt with the research process using fee-based data-bases. The next section will present some ways of obtaining information about listed companies if one doesn't have access to these types of resources.

Stock Exchanges

There are several other ways of obtaining publicly available information for listed companies. For instance, a free directory like the one BvD offers may report that a company is publicly quoted (www.bvdinfo.com).

Using Tata Motors as an example, the individual discovers from the BvD site that its ticker symbol is tatamotors, but it doesn't provide the exchange. It does give its location as Mumbai, India. One can presume that it trades on a Bombay Stock Exchange and go from there.[10] To verify that this is the case, look for the company in the listings directory that an exchange provides or search for it in the system. A search on the Bombay Stock Exchange revealed that there were two types of stocks in which it was trading, tatamotors and tatamotors-dvr-a-ordy. The exchange provides stock performance information on both of them. The tatamotors record has two years' worth of annual reports, dividends paid, management, insider trading information, where it is registered, and disclosures under Securities Exchange Board of India (SEBI) Regulations, 2011, of Substantial Acquisition of Shares and Takeovers" (SAST). The record also has a peer group section that identifies three other companies in the group, gives selected data for them, and provides a tool to choose other competitors. The information provided for comparison is for sales, equity, ratios, and ownership.

Interestingly, a search in Mergent Online revealed that this company trades on the New York Stock Exchange with the ticker symbol, TTM. Consequently, the researcher should be able to obtain the 20-F for the company. Furthermore, Reuters.com indicates that this company is trading on the National Stock Exchange of India (www.nse.india.com) with the ticker tamos.ns. A search at this site revealed that it was in the listing directory and trading with the ticker symbol tatamotors.

Earlier in this section a search strategy for finding stock exchanges was presented which involved using a search engine. Although using a search engine to find a specific exchange appears simple, it would not necessarily be the tool to use to find an exhaustive list of exchanges. Consequently one may have to use some standardized online and print sources. For example, there are stock exchange federations that "cover all the regulated stock exchanges in the world" and they may overlap.[11] One of these is the World Federation Exchange (WFE) (www.world-exchanges.org/). At the time of review, about seventy regulated exchanges that are members of this federation. This website also lists exchanges are identified as affiliates or correspondents of the WFE. Affiliates consist of newer, smaller, regulated exchanges and are not subject to peer review nor are they necessarily following the criteria for membership.[12] Correspondents are additional exchanges that have access to information and meetings of the WFE, and they are not subject to peer review or need to follow membership criteria.

Other sources for finding exchanges include:

- Asian and Oceanian Stock Exchanges Federation at www.aosef.org
- African Securities Exchanges Association (ASEA) www.africansea.org/ASEA
- Federation of European Securities Exchanges www.fese.be/en/
- Federation Iberoamericana de Bolsas (exchanges in Central and Latin America) www.fiabnet.org/en/index.asp
- NYSE Euronext at www.euronext.com/landing/indexMarket-18812-EN.html.[13]

There are also smaller exchanges to look at for countries in certain regions. For example, many North African public companies go to the Alternative Investment Market (AIM), which is the junior market of the London Stock Exchange. One can refer to the African Securities Exchanges as well for African companies.

Depositary receipts

Other sources of public company information are the financial institutions that manage depositary receipts. Depositary receipts (DR) are certificates representing company stock. These DRs can be American (ADRs), European (EDR), Global (GDR), and other country (ZDR—for Zambian DRs). The institutions that handle DRs include

- Bank of New York/Mellon (BNY Mellon; www.adrbnymellon.com)
- Citibank (www.citiadr.idmanagedsolutions.com/www/front_page.idms)
- Computershare (wwss.citissb.com/adr/common/linkpage.aspx?linkFormat=M&pageId=3&subpageid=19)
- Deutsche Bank (www.adr.db.com)
- J. P. Morgan Chase (www.adr.com).

More about DRs is covered in chapter 9, global investing.

Company and Regulatory Authority Websites

Companies that are trading worldwide will often provide their annual reports on their websites. For those companies that are trading in the United States, a website may include access to the 20-Fs that they filed with the US SEC. For example, Toyota Motors has 20-Fs from 2003 to the present that link to the SEC site where they are available via EDGAR.

They also provide annual reports to stockholders that they publish. Other companies that are trading internationally, but not on an American exchange, will often have annual reports on their website. In some cases they may provide an English version, but it may have a warning that says it is not the official document submitted to authorities.

Other sources for company information are websites for agencies that collect and administer the documents that companies in the country must submit to comply with regulations related to incorporation. In some cases, these interfaces will only have the companies that are listed in a county, but others will be more comprehensive. The latter will be discussed in the section for finding information about unlisted companies.

Canada's System for Electronic Document Analysis and Retrieval (SEDAR; www.sedar.com) is an online mechanism in which securities related information is submitted "to the Canadian securities regulatory authorities."[14] The researcher can find records for public companies and investment funds.

There are also websites that provide access to annual reports from different regions. Carol (www.carol.co.uk/) is an online service offering direct links to the financial pages of listed companies in Europe and the United States.

Some other sources for annual reports include Irasia (www.irasia.com) and infoline (www.infoline.es).[15] Irasia (Investor Relations Asian Pacific) provides annual reports for Asia Pacific companies. Infoline reports that it provides *memorias anales* (annual reports), as well as other documents for 90,000 companies covering 60 countries worldwide, whether they are trading or not. Some of the countries covered include Portugal, Finland, Hungary, Lithuania, and South Africa. There is also the *Financial Times'* Company Content Hub (markets.ft.com/markets/investorrelations.asp). This portal allows one to find company reports, and news releases, as well as videos for many European and US companies.

The official documents of a company are very important sources of information when conducting this type of research. This section identified several places to find these documents for listed companies. Sources of information for unlisted companies, including where to find this type of material, will be covered next.

Unlisted (Private) Companies

Although detailed financials or summaries are generally not available for US-based private/unlisted companies and subsidiaries, if a company is located in Europe or the United Kingdom the landscape changes. Thus, identifying a country's primary location will be useful for identifying sources.

For European companies, Bureau van Dijk (BvD) offers subscription databases that will have this type of data. Resources they provide with global company coverage include orbis and Mint Global. It also offers other databases that focus specifically on regions, such as the Amadeus database that covers European companies. Another source for unlisted companies is LexisNexis Academic Company Dossiers, although it is not as extensively as BvD. The ICC Financial Analysis Reports that are available come from ICC Information Limited, a major company forming Hoppenstedt Bonnier Information N.V. (HBI). It is widely acknowledged as a major publisher of corporate and industry analysis for the United Kingdom.[16]

Official Registries

For those who do not have access to subscription-based databases, a very important source of information are the portals provided by agencies that collect and administer the laws and regulations that companies must follow in order to be incorporated. As part of meeting these obligations, these portals have created interfaces where companies not only submit their documentation electronically, but that provide a way for researchers to find information about both listed and unlisted companies, and subsidiaries that have incorporated in a country worldwide.

In the United Kingdom, "all limited companies in England, Wales, Northern Ireland and Scotland are registered at Companies House, the authoritative agency who is sanctioned to administer registration matters by the Companies Act 2006."[17]

Companies House provides an online system in which all limited companies in the United Kingdom submit their required documents (referred to as WebFiling), as well as a search tool named WebCheck to find businesses that are incorporated in the UK, which is called WebCheck (www.companieshouse.gov.uk). Searching for companies in WebCheck is free.

As an example, a search in WebCheck on a company called Firesource Limited reveals that it is a private limited company classified as a holding company. Its UK SIC is 7415. As part of its official name it has Limited as its security identifier.[18] A private limited company may be defined in two ways, it is

1. A company with a small number of shareholders, whose shares are not traded on the Stock Exchange
2. A subsidiary company whose shares are not listed on the stock exchange, while those of its parent company are[19]

A holding company is "a company that owns or controls others. In the UK it implies that the company operates through its subsidiaries."[20]

One can then purchase a financial report for Firesource for as little as £1 (not accounting for exchange rates or transaction fees). A financial statement for the year ending December 31, 2010 reveals that the group's principal activity is that of "general retailers."[21] The report also mentions B&M Retail Limited. A financial report purchased for B&M Retail from WebCheck clearly says that Firesource Limited is the "ultimate parent undertaking."[22] This fits the definition of holding company provided previously. What this demonstration shows is that there are financials for unlisted companies outside the US; they can be used to verify information found elsewhere.

Many times a researcher finds that a major company, such as Walmart, has subsidiaries in other countries. There may be a belief that this information is completely unavailable, but this is not necessarily so. If a subsidiary is located in the UK, the researcher should use WebCheck to find out if it is incorporated. For example, one of Walmart's subsidiaries is a company called Asda Stores, which is located in the UK. A search in WebCheck informs the user that the formal name of this company is Asda Stores Limited, a private limited company, with UK SIC 47190, other retail sale in non-specialized stores, registration number 00464777.[23] A Report on Financial statements dated December 31, 2010, purchased in December 2010 had thirty-five pages of information to look through, two-year's worth of profit and loss accounts, a statement of total recognized gains and losses, a balance sheet, and the director's report that covered highlights, risks, and business activity for the year.

The financial documents retrieved for Firesource, B&M Retail Limited, and Asda Stores were not as robust as a US company's 10-K, but they are still important sources of information to verify or update any other information already found, to discover new information, and of course, to learn about the finances of a company.

In France, the Les Greffes Des Tribunaux de Commerce (Infogreffe) as well as the Institut National de la Propriété Industrielle (INPI) (www.inpi.fr/) serve as the central repository for official company documents according to the European Business Register (EBR). "There are about 4,500,000 companies entered on the French register, including historical data. These include Public Limited Companies, Private Limited Companies, General Partnerships, Cooperatives and Sole Traders."[24] Infogreffe (www.infogreffe.fr/infogreffe/index.do) provides an English interface in which to search for a company and/or its executive officer. One can then purchase documents, including those that are financial in nature.

For Germany, according to the EBR, "the bundesanzeiger is the official distributor of German company data registered at the Unternehmensregister" (business register per Google Translate). There are "about 3.4 million companies entered in the Unternehmensregister, of which 1.5 million are live companies."[25] The information provided via this source is in German, and its website is available at www.bundesanzeiger-datenservice.de/?main=prod. Another source for German company data is the Unternhmens-register (company register) https://www.unternehmensregister.de/ureg/, which has an English portal. It describes itself as "the central platform for the storage of company data." Consequently, if a company has operations in Germany, as is the case for the Canadian company Bombardier, either or both of these sources can be used to find more information. The individual will have to pay to obtain any documents from the first source. There are free documents through the second source, including accounting and financial documents listed at the site. They will be in German.

There is a system in Europe called the European Business Registry (EBR) (www.ebr.org) that has links to registries for several European countries. This registry was started in 1992 as a way to access official company information via a centralized system. To date there are twenty-six members in the system, twenty of which are members of the EU.[26] The EBR website has a list of members that contribute to the system, as well as links to their information distributors of company information. Some of the distributors and registries have an interface to search for companies and a way to purchase documents.

A centralized database in which company files are being distributed is Global Business Register, LTD (www.gbrdirect.eu), which also identifies and provides access to a member country's registry. GBRDirect (Global Business Register, Ltd., www.gbrdirect.eu/) is "an Irish HPSU (high potential start-up) company which has been backed and supported by Enterprise Ireland, the Irish government agency responsible for assisting the development of indigenous Irish industry. Operating under its flagship brand, GBRDirect, the company has built an electronic network that allows customers to access and retrieve information from the national registers that are members of the European Business Register and other unaffiliated national companies' registers."[27] To date, the system provides full availability for nineteen countries, including sixteen EU countries; it provides partial availability to one EU country, Italy. The other three non-EU countries covered in GBRDirect are the island of Jersey Latvia, and Norway. One can thus purchase documents for companies from these countries through GBRDirect. There are differences in price for documents from GBRDirect and a specific country's registry, such as Companies House. To obtain the official documents for the eleven EU countries that are not in the system, the individual business registries should be used.

To find the registries for other countries, there are several sites that list them. Companies House provides one on its website (www.companieshouse.gov.uk/links/introduction.shtml#reg). It links to sixty-six registries worldwide. Rhodes-Blakeman Associates (RBA) also provides a listing of company registration for several countries (www.rba.co.uk/sources/registers.htm). It has thirty-three for Europe, four for Asia, three for Oceania, eleven for the Americas, and one for Africa. Another source is Commercial Register (www.commercial-register.sg.ch/home/worldwide.html). It links to the European Business Register described earlier, with thirty-six registries from Europe, and twenty-three from Africa, America, Asia, and Australia. Wikipedia also has a list (en.wikipedia.org/wiki/List_of_company_registers).

Another source for regulatory agencies worldwide is the International Organization of Securities Commissions (IOSCO) (www.iosco.org/). This is an organization of member agencies dedicated to, among other matters, implementing "consistent standards of regulation and oversight . . . to protect investors"[28] worldwide. Membership consists of three categories. The first, ordinary, is made up of security commissions responsible for regulating securities in its jurisdiction. The second, associates, can be one of two types:

- a public regulatory body with jurisdiction in the subdivisions of a jurisdiction if the national regulatory body is already an ordinary member; and
- any other eligible body with an appropriate responsibility for securities regulation.[29]

The third category is affiliate, which is made up of a "self-regulatory body (SRO), or an international body with an appropriate interest in securities regulation."[30]

Chambers of Commerce

World chambers of commerce collectives are other sources to potentially find information about companies in a particular part of the world. These include the World Chamber of Commerce (www.worldchamberc.org), World Chambers Federation (www.iccwbo.org/wcf/), World's Chamber Network (chamberdirectory.worldchambers.com/), and American Chambers of Commerce Abroad (www.uschamber.com/international/directory). Each of these has a particular role. For instance, the American Chamber of Commerce Abroad is made up of voluntary American companies and individuals conducting business in a particular country, as well as firms and individuals of that country doing business in the United States. There are 115 chambers from 102 countries that are affiliated with the United States Chamber of Commerce. It is an advocacy group for the business community.

Online Product Directories

If the researcher cannot find a business in a company directory, he or she can try a search in other types of directories, such as a product or B-to-B directory. Although these types of directories may not provide tips or insights as to the legal structure of a company, it is possible to use them to identify where a company is located and the products and services it offers. Some sources include Kompass, Solusource, Europages Directory, WAND Directory, Alibaba, and MacRAE's Blue Book.

Kompass (www.kompass.com) is a business-to-business source that can be used for identifying the suppliers of products. The free portion of the website is its database, which consists of 3 million global companies in twenty-five languages, using different categories, including "Products and Services," "Company Name," and the different classification systems, including NACS, CPV, Harmonized system, NAICS, and one unique to Kompass. The researcher can also use categories or catalogues for searching, as well as selecting specific countries or states in the United States. A guided search is also available, allowing the user to start with one of sixteen product categories combined with a region, country, or US state. Using the product category allows an individual to drill down to a specific product level. For instance, under the Information Technology category, one can get down to seventeen subsets of desktop computers and personal computers (PC). This includes microcomputers, tablet PCs, electronic book readers, and media/Internet tablets. The information provided includes the address, telephone. and fax numbers. It may also provide the number of employees and registered capital. Registration is required in order to purchase any company reports from this service. A subscription allows the user to take advantage of the advanced search, which includes the ability to search by the Kompass classification system, retrieve the full records of a company (including legal structure, trade names, and countries to which it exports and from where it imports, catalogs), and the ability to download any data that is available.

A source of industrial product suppliers is Solusource (www.solusource.com). Solusource is a division of Thomas Publishing Company LLC, who also publishes the Thomas Register (www.thomasnet.com/), the latter being a source that librarians have relied on for information about private companies in the industrial sector. The database is searchable by "Global Product," category of supplier, and/or company name. Searching by Global Product or category of supplier retrieves a list of companies, which can be limited by country. The ability to search in eleven languages is also possible. The information provided includes the name of the company, address, telephone, and fax number, a website link, and a list of its products.

The Europages Directory (Euredit S.A.) (www.europages.com) is a B-to-B portal for locating products and their related producers. The site can be searched in one of twenty-six languages by company, product, or classifieds, as well as by twenty-six business sectors. Searching by product retrieves a list of products and the relevant companies. Information about a product and its wholesale prices are given. In addition to an address, telephone number, and website, there are company facts, such as the nature of the company's business, workforce numbers, and import and export zones. A map identifying the location of the head office is also shown.

With WAND directory (www.wand.com), one can search for suppliers using 11 different languages for over 170 countries. It is possible to start by selecting one out of eight possible regions: international, United States, Africa, Asia, Europe, North America, Oceania, and South America, and entering a product, service, or company name in the search box. The are thirty main categories from which to choose, such as consumer electronics, and then drill down to a more detailed level, which in this case could include tablet computers. An advanced feature allows the researcher to select a region, product/service, and a six-digit Harmonized Commodity Description and Coding System (HS) by which to search. In addition to identifying companies manufacturing a product or providing a service, this source also gives a description of the business and other products and/or services it offers. An address and phone number, contact name, and link to its website are included for a company.

Alibaba.com is a business-to-business portal which grew from an "online sourcing directory in China" in the latter part of the 1990s. It is made up of by products, suppliers, and buyers. It is possible to select a specific country or region in which to search, or search in over forty categories from which the researcher can then narrow into more specific groups. For instance, from the broader category of apparel one can narrow down to children's clothing. If a supplier is selected, a list of its products is given. The bulk of the suppliers are located in mainland China, but the list does include those from other world locations. The ability to "limit my country" is available from the list of products retrieved. Since this is a business-to-business portal, bulk prices are presented for the product, as well as the name of the supplier, and contact information. Information provided for a company includes its name, business type, products and services sold and bought, number of employees, main markets and customers, annual sales volume, and trade shows.

MacRAE's Blue Book Europe (www.maceuro.com) is one of several products from Owen Media Partners, Inc. It is an online directory consisting of more than 350,000 companies. One can search for industrial products and services from seven European countries: Austria, Belgium, France, Germany, Italy, Switzerland, and the Netherlands. A company record will have an address and a Google Map marking its location. There is also a Blue Book for the UK (www.macraesbluebook.co.uk), with 150,000 companies in eight manufacturing industries as well as wholesale trade and services. Yet another MacRAE directory is the Canadian Trade Index (www.ctidirectory.com/). It has manufacturers, exporters, distribution and service companies, and their products in over 100 categories. A US Blue Book also exists at www.macraesbluebook.com. With over

50,000 product headings for more than 2 million products, a user is able to identify companies for a given product or service. The free interface offers the ability to search by company or product/service using keyword, or to browse by using one of almost eighty headings. Results include the name of a company, the products it offers, its website address, and a link to a company profile. There is also a catalog of digital images of the products a business manufactures. Accessing the profile gives the address, the company's business activity, phone numbers, a link to email the company, and further description of the company.

Print Directories

The focus thus far has been on online sources, either commercially or publicly available. However, libraries still have print directories in their collections. This may be more prevalent in libraries that cannot afford the more expensive online databases. This section identifies some of these publications, although they also have online counterparts.

D&B Principal International Businesses is made up of more than 50,000 companies that come from D&B's extensive database of company information. Companies are arranged by geography, SIC (US), and alphabetically. These categories help identify major companies in a country, identify manufacturers or service providers worldwide for the specific industries covered in this source, and look up and verify the name of a company. An entry for a business includes its name, parent company if applicable, import/export indicator, business address, telephone and fax numbers, ownership date, annual sales data (in US dollars), total number of employees, relevant SIC codes, and the name of the chief executive.

Graham & Whiteside/Gale Cengage Learning (G&W) publishes print directories covering 92,000 companies, of which 70,000 are unlisted. These directories provide basic contact information such as address, phone, email, web address, company activities, two years of financial information, and parent company, if relevant. These publications are

- *Major Companies of the Arab World*
- *Major Companies of Europe*
- *Major Companies of Asia and Australasia*
- *Major Companies of Central and Eastern Europe and the Commonwealth of Independent States*
- *Major Companies of Latin America and Caribbean*
- *Major Companies of Sub-Saharan Africa*

Another set of directories identifies companies in different countries around the world by industry. They are

- *Major Chemical and Petrochemical Companies of the World*
- *Major Energy Companies of the World*

- *Major Telecommunications Companies of the World*
- *Major Pharmaceutical & Biotechnology Companies of the World*
- *Major Financial Institutions of the World*
- *Major Food and Drink Companies of the World,* and
- *Major Information Technology Companies of the World*

The industry collection identifies the companies in countries covered in seven regions, including Africa, the Arab World, Eastern Europe, and Latin America. Each entry provides address, website, principal activities, trade names, subsidiary companies if relevant, and legal structure.

Euromonitor is another publisher of print directories by industry, listed below:

- *World Cosmetics and Toiletries Marketing Directory*
- *World Drinks Marketing Directory*
- *World Food Marketing Directory*

Each one provides the major multinationals and their market share in a major industry (i.e., beer, soft drinks, sprits, and wine in the *World Drinks Directory*) for the World, and seven regions made up of Asia Pacific, Australasia, Eastern Europe, Latin America, the Middle East and Africa, North America, and Western Europe. For each country a directory covers, it also identifies the company operators in a country, along with their market share and rank, leading brands, and financial information when possible.

Uniworld publishes a unique set of print directories, *American Firms Operating in Foreign Countries* and *Foreign Firms Operating in the United States*. These sources help a user identify company worldwide operations. The firms included in this source consist of those that contribute significantly to the global economy by nature of their sales figures. Their scope is presented below:

- *Directory of American Firms Operating in Foreign Countries* presents information about US companies with overseas operations, specifically branches, subsidiaries, and affiliates. It consists of four parts. Part one is an alphabetical listing of companies that operate overseas. Information that is provided includes the company's website, directory, chief executive officer (CEO), international operations or international operations officer (IO), human resources director (HR), number of employees, revenue, an industry description as well as its NAICS codes, and the countries in which it has operations. Parts 2, 3, and 4 alphabetically list all the countries and includes the US companies operating in each one. Each country section has the name of the parent company, its US address, phone and fax number, website, and its industry description. It will then provide names of the US operations in the country, address, phone and fax numbers, and contact names.

- *Directory of Foreign Firms Operating in the United States* has two sections. The first one organizes the information alphabetically by country. Each country has the name of those companies that have US operations, arranged alphabetically. The entry includes the parent company's name, address, phone and fax number, website, CEO, business description, NAICS codes, revenue, and number of employees. It will then list the name of the US operations in the country with the associated address, CEO, telephone and fax number, and the description of the business at that location. Part 2 of this volume includes an alphabetical listing of the firms included in the volume.

Print directories can be a satisfactory alternative for libraries with tight budgets since they are less expensive than any online database. Furthermore, if a library cannot purchase an edition every year, the content is not lost as will happen when a subscription to an online database is canceled. However, more and more users want to access any source online, and publishers are meeting this need. For instance, in addition to publishing the print directories identified above, the three publishers of these sources also incorporate the content into online databases. Graham and Whiteside/Gale/Cengage directories are part of Business Insights: Essentials, as well as being available via Gale Directory Library; the Euromonitor publications are integrated in databases like PassportGMID and Uniworld offers Uniworld Online. Since the companies in these directories are described as either major or that have a global presence, they will not include the smaller ones that are a main part of the global business landscape. Furthermore, several directories that were once staples for business research are not available in print. This includes the PIERS Directory of US Exporters and PIERS Directory of US Importers. As the demand for more online content continues, no doubt there will be other print favorites that will cease to exist in this format.

Yellow Pages Directories

If one continues to be unsuccessful in finding a company, searching in a global online telephone directory like the International Yellow Pages (www.yellow.com/international.html), might at least verify that a company exists. This service has companies from Africa, the Americas, Asia, Europe, and Oceania. Another international phone directory is Infobel (www.infobel.com/world/default.aspx). This directory has over 130 million European telephone subscribers and is made available by a Belgian company called Kapitol. Regional online telephone directories are another possibility, but these appear to come and go.

IDENTIFYING COMPETITORS

Conducting company research also involves identifying competitors. If a company is public, there will be many ways to do this, from fee-based databases to free websites. Several of the databases identified at the beginning of this chapter will help a researcher to do this, including Hoovers Online, Mergent Online, Business Insights: Essentials, Corporate Affiliations, Mint Global, OneSource, and S&P NetAdvantage to name some of them. Uniworld Online, which is more comprehensive than the print version, allows the researcher to identify companies in a particular industry, in a city from a specific country.

As part of the process, one will probably want to do a competitive analysis. An advantage to using a company database such as Mergent Online is that the researcher is able to compile a list of competitors and their financials for those companies that populate it and compare them using different indicators, such as revenues, net income, price/earning ratios, and so forth. Doing a competitive analysis based on individual annual reports will be more time intensive.

Several of the freely available sources can help identify competitors. These include the stock exchanges, which would identify a few companies that are also trading in them and that are located in the country of the exchange. One can also identify competitors using those institutions that provide depositary receipt services. There are also websites like Reuters.com, Barron's (online.barrons.com), Bloomberg (www.bloomberg.com), Bloomberg Businessweek (www.businessweek.com), Financial Times (ft.com), MSN Money (money.msn.com), and Wall Street Journal's SmartMoney (smartmoney.com).

US companies can also contact a US commercial service representative for company profiles in a market they want to enter.

ARTICLES

Another step to take is to search for articles in trade journals, newspapers, and business magazines. Both listed and unlisted, major global companies tend to be covered in the press. Listed companies are covered daily because of their trading activity. This will include not just the stock information, but also negative and positive press coverage about any of the company's operations or plans that will affect its stock performance. Both listed and unlisted companies are covered if they are involved in a major project or activity. For example, if a company is involved in a merger or acquisition, or a lawsuit, chances are high that it will be covered by news sources that cover a nation or the world. The main sources of information for smaller types of unlisted companies are those that provide local and regional news.

Newspaper/news databases that have articles from local/regional newspapers, newsletters, and trade publications are a promising source of information if a company has been active in an area. If one does not know the local language, databases that translate the coverage into English, such as World News Connection, can be very useful for the researcher who only understands English.

There are many commercial databases that provide full-text content to these kinds of publications, and a wide array of public and academic libraries will have one or more of these. Some of the fee-based databases for news sources include ABI/Inform, Business Insights: Essentials, Business Source Premier/Complete, Factiva, and LexisNexis Academic. They provide articles from a wide range of global news sources, including regional newspapers and magazines, trade journals, newswires, television transcripts, and/or blogs. Access World News is a database to use for searching newspaper content. It contains full-text from over 600 US newspapers and more than 700 international sources. World News Connection (WNC), available through Dialog, is a source that provides translated as well as English-language information from local, regional, and country sources.

If a company is involved in something significant, using Internet search engines may find articles from reliable sources, such as Bloomberg BusinessWeek, or international news sources. In some cases if the results come in a language in which the user doesn't know, the search engine used to find the information may have a tool that will provide a rough translation. The translation can be used to get an idea of what is going on, but one should use a good translator if the research will be driving a company's strategy and/or affecting the bottom line.

Whatever the source used, the researcher will have to assess the news source for its reliability.

OTHER

There are also unconventional strategies and resources available. For example, one might look at free and fee-based sources that provide sanctions and/or enforcement lists. This type of material would be used to determine whether a company or person related to the company is on one or more of these lists. In an indirect way, they provide information about the company. For example, the Office of Foreign Asset Controls (OFAC) from the US Treasury provides a list of specially designation nationals (SDN) of entities and individuals considered to be laundering money for terrorist organizations (www.treasury.gov/resource-center/sanctions/SDN-List/Pages/default.aspx). A report dated June 29, 2012, consisted of 530 pages and hundreds of names.[31] The assets of persons and entities on the list are blocked and US persons are basically prohibited from dealing with them. Another source to try is the Denied Persons List (www.bis.doc.gov/dpl/default.shtm) from the US Department of Commerce, Bureau of Industry and Security (BIS). Persons on this list are prohibited from engaging in export transactions. Other links to check are provided at the BIS "Lists to Check" page located at www.bis.doc.gov/complianceandenforcement/liststocheck.htm.

As new social media tools are entering the scene, librarians and others are using sites like LinkedIn and Twitter to find pieces of information that will assist them in developing company profiles as well as market information. LinkedIn claims to have the over 161 million members from more than 200 countries and territories.[32] Sixty-one percent of its members come from outside of the United States, and information is available in seventeen languages.[33] Many business professionals are registering themselves in LinkedIn and at times may provide bits of information that can be used in research. Twitter is another tool that may yield results. Wikipedia is another source for company information. As is the case in any resource used in research, one should evaluate the information obtained from them because they could be very biased.

CONCLUSION

This chapter identified strategies and resources that could be used for finding information for both listed and unlisted companies (An appendix at the end of this chapter provides a list of articles with other strategies for finding international company information, written by Sylvia James for *Business Information Alert*). The various sources presented included those where one could find financial information for both of these types of companies as well as subsidiaries. How to identify competitors was also addressed. Alternative methods such as using government sites that provide sanctioned and enforcements lists was included, and use of social media tools like LinkedIn and Twitter was also introduced as part of a strategy.

As the Internet expands, there will no doubt be new ways of finding information, as well as new systems implemented by database providers that will help the person who is conducting company research. This should keep librarians and information professionals on their toes.

LIST OF SOURCES

Databases

This is an alphabetical list of the fee-based databases mentioned in this chapter.

ABI/Inform (Ann Arbor, MI: ProQuest, 1971–), www.proquest.com/products_pq/descriptions/abi_inform.shtml.

Access World News (Naples, FL: Newsbank 2004–), www.newsbank.com.

Associations Unlimited (Detroit, MI: Gale Research 1995-), www.gale.cengage.com/.

Business Insights: Essentials (Farmington Hills, MI: Gale Cengage Learning, 2012–), www.cengagesites.com/Literature/782/gale-business-insights-global-essentials/.

Business Source Complete (Ipswich, MA: EBSCO Pub., 2005–), www.ebscohost.com/public/business-source-complete.

Corporate Affiliations (New Providence, NJ: LexisNexis Group, 2002–), www.corporateaffiliations.com.

Country Commerce (New York: Economist Intelligence Unit, 2000–), www.eiu.com.

Factiva (New York: Dow Jones & Reuters, 2001–), www.dowjones.com/factiva/index.asp.

Hoovers Online (Austin, TX: Reference Press, 1996– www.hoovers.com (28 June 2012).

Mergent Online (New York: Mergent, 1997–), www.mergentonline.com (30 June 2012).

Plunkett Research Online (Houston, TX: Plunkett Research 2002–), www.plunkettresearch.com/ (28 June 2012).

Morningstar Investment Research Center (Chicago, IL: Morningstar, 2002–), library.morningstar.com.

Standard & Poor's NetAdvantage (New York: Standard & Poor's, 2001–), www.netadvantage.standardandpoors.com/.

World News Connection (Washington: NTIS: Dialog, 1995–), wnc.dialog.com.

Websites

This is an alphabetical list of association, government, and publisher websites mentioned in this chapter.

African Securities Exchanges Association, www.africansea.org/ASEA (28 June 2012).

American Chambers of Commerce Abroad, www.uschamber.com/international/directory (28 June 2012).

Asian and Oceanian Stock Exchanges Federation, www.aosef.org (28 June 2012).

BIS, "Lists to Check," www.bis.doc.gov/complianceandenforcement/liststocheck.htm (28 June 2012).

Bloomberg (www.bloomberg.com) (28 June 2012).

Bundesanzeiger, www.bundesanzeiger-datenservice.de/?main=prod (28 June 2012).

Bureau van Dijk, www.bvdinfo.com (28 June 2012).

Canada's System for Electronic Document Analysis and Retrieval (SEDAR), www.sedar.com (28 June 2012).

Canadian Trade Index, www.ctidirectory.com/ (28 June 2012).

Commercial Register, www.commercial-register.sg.ch/home/worldwide.html (28 June 2012).

Companies House, www.companieshouse.gov.uk (28 June 2012).

Country Commercial Guides, www.buyusainfo.net/adsearch.cfm? search_type=int& loadnav=no (28 June 2012).

Denied Persons List, www.bis.doc.gov/dpl/default.shtm (28 June 2012).

Dun & Bradstreet, www.dnb.com (28 June 2012).

Europages Directory (www.europages.com (28 June 2012).

European Business Registry, www.ebr.org (28 June 2012).

Federation Iberoamericana de Bolsas, www.fiabnet.org/en/index.asp (28 June 2012).

Federation of European Securities Exchanges, www.fese.be/en/ (28 June 2012).

Global Business Register, LTD, GBRDirect, www.gbrdirect.eu (28 June 2012).

Infobel, www.infobel.com/world/default.aspx (28 June 2012).

Infogreffe, www.infogreffe.fr/infogreffe/index.do (28 June 2012).

Institut National de la Propriété Industrielle, www.inpi.fr/ (28 June 2012).
International Organization of Securities Commissions, www.iosco.org/ (28 June 2012).
International Yellow Pages, www.yellow.com/international.html (28 June 2012).
Kompass, www.kompass.com (28 June 2012).
MacRAE's Blue Book Europe, www.maceuro.com (28 June 2012).
NYSE Euronext, www.euronext.com/landing/indexMarket-18812-EN.htm (28 June 2012).
Rhodes-Blakeman Associates, www.rba.co.uk/sources/registers.htm (28 June 2012).
Solusource, www.solusource.com (28 June 2012).
Thomas Register, www.thomasnet.com/ (28 June 2012).
Thomson Reuters, thomsonreuters.com (28 June 2012).
US *Blue Book*, www.macraesbluebook.com (28 June 2012).
Unternhmens-register, https://www.unternehmensregister.de/ureg/ (28 June 2012).
WAND directory, www.wand.com (28 June 2012).
Wikipedia, en.wikipedia.org/wiki/List_of_company_registers (28 June 2012).
World Chamber of Commerce, www.worldchamberc.org (28 June 2012).
World Chambers Federation, www.iccwbo.org/wcf/ (28 June 2012).
World Federation Exchange, www.world-exchanges.org/ (28 June 2012).

APPENDIX

James, Sylvia. "Pan-European Union Company Information." *Business Information Alert* 16, no. 3 (March/April 2004): 1, 3–15.

———. "The Challenges of Researching Pan-Asian Company Information: Pan-Asian company sources." *Business Information Alert* 16, no. 7 (July–Aug. 2004): 1, 6.

———. "Researching Central American company information." *Business Information Alert* 17, no. 2 (May 2005): 1, 5.

———. "Company Research and the Effect of New International Accounting Standards: International Financial Reporting Standards (IFRS) Part 1: The Background." *Business Information Alert* 18, no. 2 (Oct. 2006): 1, 3–5.

———. "Researching Company Information in Europe: General Principles (Report)." *Business Information Alert* 18, no. 9 (Oct. 2006): 1, 4.

———. "Official Company Information." *Business Information Alert* 19, no. 2 (Feb. 2007): 1, 4–5, 9.

———. "Pan-European Union Company Information: An Update (Report)." *Business Information Alert* 19, no. 3 (March 2007): 1, 5.

———. "Researching Company Information: France, Germany, and the UK," *Business Information Alert* 19, no. 5 (May 2007): 1, 4–6.

———. "Researching Western European company information outside the EU: Iceland, Norway, and Switzerland: Part 1: company research in Switzerland." *Business Information Alert* 19, no. 6 (June 2007): 1, 5.

———. "Researching Western European company information outside the EU: Iceland, Norway, and Switzerland: Part 2: Company Research in Iceland and Norway. (Company Overview)" *Business Information Alert* 19, no. 7 (July–Aug. 2007): 1, 4.

———. "Researching African Companies: Part 1 South Africa." *Business Information Alert* 20, no. 2 (May 2008): 1, 6.

———. "Researching African Companies: Part 2 North Africa." *Business Information Alert* 20, no. 3 (June 2008): 1, 5.

———. "Rich Lists and Business Research Part 1: Using Rich Lists." *Business Information Alert* 21, no. 4 (April 2009): 1, 5.

———. "Rich Lists and Business Research: Part 2: How Lists are Compiled and Source tables. (Bibliography)," *Business Information Alert* 21, no. 5 (May 2009): 1, 6.

———. "Mining Company Information from Stock Exchange Websites: Part 1: Basic Principles of Disclosure." *Business Information Alert* 21, no. 6 (June 2009): 4.

———. "Mining Company Information from Stock Exchange Websites: Part 2: Stock Exchange Sites and How to Use Them." *Business Information Alert* 21, no.7 (July–Aug. 2009): 1, 5.

———. " Mining Company Information from Stock Exchange Websites: Part 3: Listed Company Sources." *Business Information Alert* 21, no. 8 (Sept. 2009): 1, 5.

———. "Not Quite Listed Researching Large Unlisted Companies Part 1: Types of Companies." *Business Information Alert* 21, no. 9 (Oct. 2009): 1–6.

———. "Not Quite Listed Researching Large Unlisted Companies Part 2: Sources." Business Information Alert 21, no. 10 (Nov./Dec. 2009): 1, 4–6.

———. "Researching an IPO." Business Information Alert 22, no. 1 (Jan. 2010): 2.

———. "Researching annual reports, part 2: collections for companies outside North America." Business Information Alert 22, no. 7 (Jan. 2011): 1, 5.

NOTES

1. Ricky W. Griffin and Michael W. Pustay, *International Business*. 5th ed. (Upper Saddle River, NJ: Pearson Prentice Hall, 2007), 10.

2. Griffin and Pustay, *International Business*, 11.

3. UNCTAD, "Transnational Corporations," www.unctad.org/Templates/Page.asp?intItemID=3148&lang=1 (2011 Nov. 17).

4. European Commission, *The New SME Definition*, (Luxembourg, Office for Official Publications of the European Communities, 2005), 14 ec.europa.eu/enterprise/policies/sme/files/sme_definition/sme_user_guide_en.pdf (18 Nov. 2011).

5. EDGAR Dissemination Service Subscriber Information, www.sec.gov/info/edgar/dissemination/rel41.txt (6 June 2011).

6. Sylvia James, "Not Quite Listed Researching Large Unlisted Companies Part 1: Types of Companies," *Business Information Alert* 21, no. 9 (Oct. 2009): 1–6.

7. James, "Not Quite Listed . . . Part 1," 4.

8. This company now brands itself as S&P Capital IQ.

9. US Securities Exchange Commission, "Company Search," www.sec.gov/edgar/searchedgar/companysearch.html (13 Aug. 2011).

10. A search in BvD for Bombardier backed up this logic. The search revealed that the ticker symbol for this company is BBD.B, located in Montreal, Quebec, Canada. A search on the Toronto Stock Exchange provided stock information for the company.

11. Sylvia James, "Mining Company Information from Stock Exchange Websites: Part 2: Stock Exchange Sites and How to Use Them," *Business Information Alert* 21 no. 7 (July–Aug. 2009): 1 (5).

12. WFE World Federation of Exchanges, "Affiliates," www.world-exchanges.org/member-exchanges/affiliates (13 Aug. 2011).

13. James, "Mining Company Information from Stock Exchange Websites: Part 2," n/a.

14. SEDAR, www.sedar.com/homepage_en.htm (19 Feb. 2012).

15. Sylvia James, "Researching Annual Reports, Part 2: Collections for Companies Outside North America," 22 no. 7 (Jan. 2011): 1(5).

16. LexisNexis Academic. Source Information, "ICC Financial Analysis Reports," w3.nexis.com/sources/scripts/info.pl?154113 (20 Jan. 2012).

17. Companies House, "About Us," www.companieshouse.gov.uk/about/functionsHistory.shtml (14 Aug. 2011).

18. For a description of various security identifiers and company extensions go to www.corporateinformation.com/Company-Extensions-Security-Identifiers.aspx.

19. Dictionary of Business, s.v. "private limited company," www. credoreference.com/entry/acbbusiness/private_limited_company (30 June 2012).

20. Ruth A. Pagell and Michael Halperin, *International Business Information: How to Find It, How to Use It*, 2nd ed. (Phoenix, AZ: Oryx Press, 1998), 74.

21. Grant Thornton, "Financial Statements Firesource Limited," 31 Dec. 2010, www.companieshouse.uk (8 Nov. 2011).

22. Grant Thornton, "Financial Statements B&M Retail Limited," 31 Dec. 2010, www.companieshouse.uk (8 Nov. 2011).

23. UK companies may provide their Companies House registration number on their websites. It can then be used to search WebCheck.

24. European Business Register, "France," ebr.org/section/24/index.html (29 June 2012; 2011 Nov. 30).

25. European Business Register, "Germany," www.ebr.org/section/26/index.html (30 June 2012).

26. European Business Register, "EBR History," www.ebr.org/section/68/index.html (30 June 2012).

27. GBR Direct, "GBR Direct Profile," www.gbrdirect.eu/GBRDirectProfile.aspx (30 Nov. 2011).

28. OICU/IOSCO, "About IOSCO," www.iosco.org/about/ (19 Feb. 2012).

29. OICU/IOSCO, "Membership Categories and Criteria," www.iosco.org/about/index.cfm?section=membership (19 Feb. 2012).

30. OICU/IOSCO, "Membership Categories and Criteria."

31. Office of Foreign Assets Control, "Specially Designated Nationals and Blocked Persons," www.treasury.gov/resource-center/sanctions/SDN-List/Pages/default.aspx (29 June 2012).

32. LinkedIn, "About," press.linkedin.com/about (28 June 2012).

33. LinkedIn, "About."

SIX

Classification Systems for Industry

The United Nations (UN), through its Statistical Division and units, as well as other international organizations like the Organization for Economic Co-operation and Development (OECD), compile and disseminate a wide range of statistics that they obtain from national statistics offices. There are also regional communities such as the European Union and governments that gather statistics on a wide range of categories. In order to collect and deliver these statistics in a way that is comparable among countries, there are numerous classifications by which national statistics offices must submit to international organizations like the UN or OECD. These classification systems are based on the nature of the data and how they are to be used. For example, national statistics agencies must submit their industrial production data using the International Standard Industrial Classification (ISIC) code to the responsible agency, such as the United Nations Statistics Division. The latter will then be responsible for ensuring that the data is comparable and then disseminating the data through print sources and/or databases.

There are several types of statistics that one can utilize to evaluate an industry worldwide. This includes import/export data, production data, number of establishments in an industry, size of establishments, and sales figures. There are several sources available that can provide these, and depending on that source, the taxonomy used to retrieve or present the data may be different. Being aware of such classification systems enables the researcher to understand the information that retrieved from numerous sources. For example, the United Nations Industrial Development Organization uses ISIC rev. 3 to provide manufacturing statistics in the undata.org database, and its print source *International Yearbook of Industrial Statistics*. This code reflects the activity that yields an output. Consequently, when one is reviewing data that is categorized with a specific ISIC, it reflects the establishments whose primary economic activity is the same, and not the output. Often, these sources will have an introduction that explains the system that is being used to present the data. In other cases, the code is needed to retrieve the data. For instance, the Interactive Tariff and Trade DataWeb portal from the US International Trade Commission provides an option to search by several international codes, including ISIC. To find export and import data from US government sources, a researcher will have use the Schedule B code for export data and the Harmonized Tariff Schedule code for import data.

Nine systems will be covered in this section. They have been selected because they are used extensively in a wide range of sources that provide statistics that can be used in industry research. These are listed below.

- Harmonized Commodity Description and Coding System (HS)
- Schedule B: Statistical Classification of Domestic and Foreign Commodities Exported from the United States
- Harmonized Tariff Schedule of the United States
- United Nations Standard International Trade Classification (SITC)
- International Standard Industrial Classification (ISIC)
- Central Product Classification (CPC)
- North American Industry Classification System (NAICS)
- United Kingdom's Standard Industrial Classification of Economic Activities (UK SIC)
- Extended Balance of Payments Services Classification (EBOPS)

There are publications consisting of hundreds of pages that describe most of these systems. The descriptions provided here will be just the basics. If one wants to look at each in detail, URLs are provided.

The Harmonized Commodity Description and Coding System, most commonly referred to as the Harmonized System (HS) was developed and is administered by the World Customs Organization (WCO). This system helps harmonize trade and customs procedures worldwide. It is used by over 200 countries to set their customs tariffs and collection of international trade statistics.[1] The HS is a six-digit system that is used to classify over 5,000 products. There are 5,300 article/product descriptions that appear as headings and subheadings, arranged in 99 chapters, grouped in 21 sections. One can get an idea as to the nature of the system by looking at some of the section headings. For example, Section I covers live animals and animal products. Items in Section VI are products of the chemical or allied industries. Section XI is textile and textile articles. The focus of this system is on the actual output, which differs from later codes that will be presented that focus on similarity of process. Using the HS code for snow-skis, 950611, these six digits are broken down as follows:

- The code falls under Section XX, "Miscellaneous manufactured articles."

- The first two digits, HS-95, indicate the chapter in which a good is classified, which in this case is "Toys, games and sports requisites; parts and accessories thereof."
- The third and fourth digits, HS-06, refer to the grouping within the chapter and is described as "Articles and equipment for general physical exercise, gymnastics, athletics, other sports (including table-tennis) or outdoor games, not specified or included elsewhere in this chapter; swimming pools and paddling pools."
- The fifth and sixth digits, 11, identify the specific item, with the fifth digit being—"Snow-skis and other snow-ski equipment" and the full code, 9506.11 referring to skis.[2]

HS codes are available at www.wcoomd.org/home_hsoverviewboxes_tools_and_instruments_hsnomenclaturetable2007.htm.

The two classification codes that the United States uses for trade are based on the international Harmonized System. One covers exports from the United States and the other deals with imports into the country. The system that is used for exports is *Schedule B: Statistical Classification of Domestic and Foreign Commodities Exported from the United States*, and is referred to as Schedule B. Using the Harmonized System's four- to six-digit headings and subheadings as its foundation, it is made up of ten digits and classifies over 8,000 commodities. US export statistics are compiled and reported using this method.[3] Schedule B is available for browsing or searching using keywords at the US Census Foreign Trade page at www.census.gov/foreign-trade/schedules/b/.

Commodities coming into the US (imports) are classified using the *Harmonized Tariff Schedule of the United States (HTS)*. "The 4- and 6-digit HS product categories are subdivided into 8-digit unique US rate lines and 10-digit non-legal statistical reporting categories."[4] The US Bureau of Customs and Border Protection uses HTS to assign tariffs on goods coming into the country as well as for gathering, compiling, and disseminating statistics.[5] The United States International Trade Commission maintains and publishes this schedule. One can search for codes and rates for imported products at the HTS Online Reference Tool located at hts.usitc.gov/.

Comparing each of the classification codes covered so far for snow skis, it is possible to see the similarity among HS, Schedule B and HTS, as well as where they each veer off at the seventh digit (Table 6.1). Consequently, if a code for an item is found, one can conclude that the other codes will be virtually the same. These codes can be used to obtain trade data from US sources like TradeStats Express and USATrade Online.

There are also several important international codes. These are the Standard Industrial Trade Classification (SITC), the International Standard Industrial Classification (ISIC), Central Product Classification

Table 6.1. Codes for Skis from Three Classifications Systems

Classification Systems	Description	Code
Harmonized Schedule (HS)	Skis	9506.11
Schedule B	Skis	9506.11.5000
Harmonized Tariff Schedule (HTS)	Country Skis Other Skis	9506.11.2000 9506.11.40

(CPC), General Industrial Classification of Economic Activities with the European Communities (NACE), and Extended Balance of Payments Services Classification (EBOPS).

The original version of the SITC code was drawn up in 1950 by the UN secretariat with the help of experts and the cooperation of governments.[6] SITC has been revised several times due to increases in volume, changes to geographical patterns, and the need by countries, intergovernmental agencies, and international organizations for comparability of trade statistics. This code is presently at revision 4, and all basic headings (except for 911.0 and 931.0) are defined in terms of HS07 (Harmonized System 2007) subheadings.[7] It takes into consideration the following elements:

a. The nature of the merchandise and the materials used in its production
b. The processing stage
c. Market practices and the uses of the product
d. The importance of the commodity in terms of world trade
e. Technological changes[8]

It is a hierarchical system made up of ten major sections, 67 divisions, 262 groups, 1,023 subgroups, and 2,970 basic headings.[9] Taking the example for skis, whose SITC Rev. 4 code is 894.73, the breakdown is as follows:

- The section is 8, "Miscellaneous manufactured articles."
- Its division is 89, "Miscellaneous manufactured articles, n.e.s."
- The group is 894, "Baby carriages, toys, games and sporting goods."
- It's in subgroup 894.7—"Sports goods."
- The basic heading is 894.73—"Snow-skis and other snow-ski equipment."

Unlike classification systems that will be presented later, this code does represent a product of commodity. Although at revision 4, some countries still use revision 3 to submit their national trade statistics. Sources will often have an explanation of the revision that is being used to report the data. To find a code for a product using SITC Rev. 3, go to the United Nations page for the "Detailed structure and explanatory notes" at the following URL: unstats.un.org/unsd/cr/registry/regcst.asp?Cl=14. For revision 4, use unstats.un.org/unsd/cr/registry/regcst.asp?Cl=28.

Several sources use the SITC to provide data. This includes the following United Nations publications: *UN Monthly Bulletin of Statistics*; *International Trade Statistics Yearbook* (*ITSY*), available in print and electronically; the *United Nations Commodity Trade Statistics* database (most commonly known as *UN Comtrade* and located at comtrade.un.org/db); and OECD's *International Trade by Commodity Statistics*. One can also use SITC to retrieve import and export data from TradeStats Express.

The International Standard Industrial Classification of all Economic Activities system (ISIC) was adopted in 1948 and has been revised four times. ISIC allows economic and social data such as production, value added, and employment to be compared internationally. For the purposes of identifying ISIC, "an industry is defined as the set of all production units engaged primarily in the same or similar kinds of productive activity."[10] The United Nations Statistics Division sends out a questionnaire designed to gather industrial production data to national statistics offices, and then publishes indices in monthly, quarterly, and yearly publications.[11] ISIC data is structured as follows:

- Section—There are twenty-one sections made up of letters that represent the main type of activity. For example, Section A represents "Agriculture, forestry and fishing" and has three divisions.[12]
- Division—This is represented by the first two numerical digits of the code. There are a total of 99 divisions spread out across the sections. For example, in ISIC Rev. 4, digits 10–33 belong with Section C, Manufacturing, while 41–43 are under Section F, which is construction, etc.
- Group—Incorporates the first three digits.
- Class—Is made up of four digits.

To see this illustrated, consider 3230, the ISIC rev. 4 code for snow-skis.

- The section under which this code falls is C, Manufacturing.
- The first two digits, 32, reflect the Division, which is "Other Manufacturing."
- The third digit is the Group, 323, "Manufacture of Sports Goods."
- The fourth digit, 0, is the Class, "manufacture of articles and equipment for sports, outdoor and indoor games, of any material would include other types of sporting goods."[13] One can see that this relates to the process of producing this item and not the product itself, in that 3230 includes various types of sports equipment, including skis, bindings, and poles; hard and soft balls; sailboards and surfboards; and bows and crossbows.

An ISIC code can be found for an item at unstats.un.org/unsd/cr/registry/regcst.asp?Cl=27.

Sources that disseminate industry data using ISIC include the following United Nations publications: the *Monthly Bulletin of Statistics*, the *United Nations Statistical Yearbook*, and the *World Statistics Pocket Book*.[14] Industry statistics in OECD iLibrary are also presented using ISIC.

The Central Product Classification (CPC) "presents categories for all products that can be the object of domestic or international transactions or that can be entered into stocks. It includes products that are an output of economic activity, including transportable goods, non-transportable goods and services."[15] It is a hierarchical system made up as follows:

- Sections—identified by the first digit, ranging from 0 to 9
- Divisions—identified by the first and second digits
- Groups—Identified by the first three digits
- Classes—Identified by the first four digits
- Subclasses—Identified by all five digits[16]

Consequently, the CPC Ver. 2 code for skis would be 38410, where

- 3 is the section known as "Other transportable goods, except metal products, machinery and equipment."
- 38 is the division described as "Furniture; other transportable goods n.e.c."
- 384 is the group known as "Sports Goods."
- 3841 is the class, while 38410 is the subclass. In this case, both 3841 and 38410 have the same description, "Snow-skis and other snow-ski equipment; ice skates and roller skates."[17] A "0" is used in CPC when the classification isn't further subdivided, as is the case here.[18]

The United Nations' *Industrial Commodity Statistics Yearbook* organizes the data using CPC. CPC ver. 2 codes can be found at unstats.un.org/unsd/cr/registry/cpc-2.asp.

The final international system to be covered in this chapter is the Extended Balance of Payments Services Classification (EBOPS), a method used to categorize service statistics. EBOPS is an extension of the four modes of service that were identified in the General Agreement on Trade in Services (GATS). "GATS constitutes the first set of legally enforceable disciplines and rules at the multilateral level established to cover international trade in services."[19] EBOPS service components consist of the following:

1. Manufacturing services on physical inputs owned by others
2. Maintenance and repair services n.i.e.
3. Transport
4. Travel
5. Construction
6. Insurance and pension services

7. Financial services
8. Charges for the use of intellectual property n.i.e.
9. Telecommunications, computer, and information services
10. Other business services
11. Personal, cultural, and recreational services
12. Government goods and services n.i.e. [20]

The United Nations and the OECD both produce resources that provide statistics using this system. For instance, the print and digital publications of *OECD Statistics on International Trade in Services* present data by this system. The UN Service Trade database does as well (unstats.un.org/unsd/servicetrade/). EBOPS codes can be found at unstats.un.org/unsd/tradeserv/TFSITS/msits2010/ebops2cpc.htm.

In addition to these standard international classification systems, there are also codes that have been developed to compile statistics for a region. One of these is NACE, which describes the European Community Classification of Economic Activities, and the other is the North American Industry Classification System (NAICS) code.

NACE is the statistical classification of economic activities of the European Union and has been used since 1970. It is derived from ISIC with additional levels that "reflect European activities that were inadequately represented in ISIC."[21] It is a hierarchical system consisting of four levels: sections, divisions, groups, and classes. The first level consists of twenty-one sections and is represented by the alphabet A–U, where A is "Agriculture, forestry, and fishing" and U is "Activities of Extraterritorial Organizations and Bodies." The second level, divisions, is made up of the first two digits of a code. The third level, groups, consists of the first three digits. The fourth level, classes, is represented by four digits.[22] Using the example of skis, its NACE code would be 32.30. This code falls under C, the manufacturing section. The division, 32, is described as "Other manufacturing." The number 32.3 represents groups, "Manufacture of Sports Goods." The class, 32.30 is referred to again as "Manufacture of Sports Goods," and includes the manufacture of sports goods from "hard, soft and inflatable balls," "skis, bindings and poles," and "bows and crossbows."[23]

NACE is mandatory within the European Statistical System (ESS), and the statistics derived from this method allow comparability on the European level and in general on the world level.[24] The ESS, "is a partnership between Eurostat and national statistical institutes or other national authorities in each European Union (EU) Member State responsible for developing, producing and disseminating European statistics."[25] One can search for data using NACE at the Eurostat statistics page, epp.eurostat.ec.europa.eu/portal/page/portal/statistics/search_database. Codes can be found at ec.europa.eu/eurostat/ramon/nomenclatures/in-

dex.cfm?TargetUrl=LST_NOM&StrGroupCode=CLASSIFIC&StrLangua-
geCode=EN.

It is important to recognize these international standards when looking at data produced by different organizations because a different standard is used depending on what is being reported (i.e., export/import
data will be presented by SITC while ISIC is used for production). In
addition, the United Nations provides lists and access to the various
versions of classification systems at its "UN Classifications Registry"
page, along with a link to correspondence tables for the various systems
and versions that exist (i.e., ISIC Rev. 3 – ISIC Rev. 4; HS 2007 – SITC Rev.
4.; ISIC Rev. 3.1 – NACE Rev. 1.1). The classification registry is at un-
stats.un.org/unsd/class/.

Another regional classification scheme is the North American Industry Classification System (NAICS) code. NAICS

> was developed as the standard for use by Federal statistical agencies in
> classifying business establishments for the collection, analysis, and
> publication of statistical data related to the business economy of the
> U.S. NAICS was developed under the auspices of the Office of Manage-
> ment and Budget (OMB), and adopted in 1997 to replace the old Stan-
> dard Industrial Classification (SIC) system.[26]

The role of the NAICS to produce common industry definitions for Canada, Mexico, and the United States. "NAICS is based on the economic
concept that establishments using the same production processes to produce a good or service should be grouped together."[27] It is important to
note that the NAICS code is based on establishments and not commodities. An establishment is defined as "generally a single physical location
where business is conducted or where services or industrial operations
are performed."[28] Every five years NAICS is reviewed to make sure of
relevance, accuracy, and timeliness of the data, and determine whether
there should be any revisions.[29] The first version was NAICS 1997, and
2012 is the most current. The code is a hierarchical system representing
twenty economic sectors, made up of two to six digits, with each level
becoming more specific. For example, consider 339920, the NAICS code
for ski equipment manufacturing.

- The first two digits, 33, represent an economic sector named Manufacturing.
- The third digit, 339, corresponds to a subsector called "Miscellaneous Manufacturing."
- The fourth digit, 3399, characterizes an industry group, which in
  this case is described as "Other Miscellaneous Manufacturing."
- The fifth, 33992, represents the NAICS industry called "Sporting
  and Athletic Goods Manufacturing."
- The six-digit code, 339920, designates the national industry, which
  is the same as 33992, "Sporting and Athletic Goods Manufactur-

ing."[30] The sixth digit allows Canada, Mexico, and the United States to "have a country-specific detail."[31]

Statistics for the United States, Canada, and Mexico can be compared beginning at the fifth level for most NAICS codes. The US government, through its designated bureaus and units, gathers and classifies economic activity using this system, and statistics are reported through these categories. Such reports include the *Economic Census, Monthly Retail Trade and Food Services*, and *Monthly Wholesale Trade: Sales and Inventories*. Data for these items can be retrieved at the US Census website for "Business and Industry" at www.census.gov/econ/currentdata/.

NAICS can also be used to search in fee-based databases. For instance, in company databases like Mergent Online, Hoovers Online, Bureau van Dijk databases, Corporate Affiliations, and Thomson ONE, an individual can use the NAICS field search to identify companies in industry. In databases like Business Source Complete, ABI/Inform Complete, and Business Insights: Essentials, it is possible to use the NAICS search field to retrieve articles from trade journals or regional newspapers and other content such as industry overviews or profiles. For example, one can use the NAICS code search field in Business Source Complete (BSC) to pull up various reports that cover an industry either globally or by a specific country. BSC has reports from several key providers, including Business Monitor International, MarketLine (Datamonitor), Economist Intelligence Unit (EIU), and Icon Group International. NAICS codes can be found at www.census.gov/eos/www/naics/.

There are also individual codes that countries use to gather their statistics. For example, the United Kingdom uses the UK Standard Industrial Classification 2007 (UK SIC 2007), not to be confused with the SIC system that the United States used up until 1997, when NAICS replaced it. As a member of the European Union, the UK SIC must match NACE rev. 2 down to and including the fourth level. A fifth digit is included to form subclasses. The UK SIC reflects a classification system that takes into account the type of economic activity which involves "an input of resources, a production process and an output of products (goods or services)."[32] Data from the UK is released through the Office for National Statistics. Current industry codes can be found at www.ons.gov.uk/ons/guide-method/classifications/current-standard-classifications/standard-industrial-classification/index.html. The UK SIC 2007 code for skis is 32.30, described as the "Manufacture of Sports Goods," which is the same as the NACE code explained earlier.

Before NAICS was launched in 1997, the system that the United States used was also called SIC, which stood for Standard Industrial Classification. This was a four-digit system that was used to categorize US economic statistics through 1996. It is a hierarchical system made up of ten divisions representing US economic activity. This is made up of the letters A–J, where A represents agriculture, forestry, and fishing, and Division J represents public administration. These are divided into major groups, which are represented by two digits ranging from 01–99. Each of these categories has industry groups made up of three digits, which are broken down to four digits that represent the code for an industry. SICs are available at the website located at www.osha.gov/pls/imis/sic-search.html. Using the query tool, one finds that the SIC code for skis is 3949, Sporting and Athletic Goods, Not Elsewhere Classified. The breakdown for this code is as follows:

- The first two digits, 39, correspond to "Miscellaneous Manufacturing Industries," which is one of twenty major groups that fall under Division D, Manufacturing.
- The next three digits, 394, is an industry group referred to as "Dolls, Toys, Games, and Sporting and Athletic."
- 3949 is the ultimate SIC and is described as "Establishments primarily engaged in manufacturing sporting and athletic goods, not elsewhere classified, such as fishing tackle; golf and tennis goods; baseball, football, basketball, and boxing equipment; roller skates and ice skates; gymnasium and playground equipment; billiard and pool tables; and bowling alleys and equipment."[33]

Although the US SIC code isn't used to group official US government statistics anymore, there are still some fee-based databases that allow searching by this code. Some of these include company databases like Mergent Online and industry databases like First Research.

Table 6.2 presents the codes for skis using ten different classifications previously described (EBOPS is excluded since it is a system for categorizing services). One can see that the methods dealing with trade, HS HTS, Schedule B, and SITC have codes that are specific to the product. It makes sense to have codes at such a level of specificity to have an efficient system of processing goods in and out of countries and keeping track of them. The CPC comes close, reflecting its underpinnings as a system designed to represent products. The rest of the codes, ISIC, NACE, US SIC, NAICS, and UK SIC include skis in a broader category; that is, the manufacturing of sporting goods that includes an array of products, from billiards to surfboards. They reflect the similarity of process that it takes to produce the output.

Other countries have their own classification systems as well. The United Nations provides a list of national classifications at the following URL: unstats.un.org/unsd/cr/ctryreg/ctrylist2.asp?rg=7. One will be able to identify a country's classification for activities, products, "expenditure according to purpose," "other classifications in the System of National Accounts," and previous versions used.[34] The Ramon database from Eurostat provides a list of almost 200 "Metadata Classification" systems at ec.europa.eu/eurostat/ramon/nomenclatures/in-

Table 6.2. Codes for Skis from Ten Classification Systems

Classification Systems	Description	Code
Harmonized Schedule (HS)	Snow-skis	9506.11
Schedule B	Skis	9506.11.5000
Harmonized Tariff Schedule (HTS)	Cross-Country Skis Other Skis	9506.11.2000 9506.11.40
SITC Rev. 3	Snow-skis and other snow-ski equipment	894.73
SITC Rev. 4	Snow-skis and other snow-ski equipment	894.73
ISIC Rev. 3.1	Section D – Manufacturing … Manufacture of Sports Goods	3693
ISIC Rev. 4	Section C–Manufacturing … Manufacture of Sports Goods	3230
CPC Rev. 2	Snow-skis and other snow-ski equipment; ice-skates and roller-skates	38410
NACE Rev. 2	Manufacture of Sports Goods	32.30
NAICS (1997, 2002, 2007, 2012)	Sporting and Athletic Goods Manufacturing	339920
SIC (U.S.)	Sporting and Athletic Goods, Not Elsewhere Classified	3949
UK SIC 2007	Manufacture of Sports Goods	32.30

dex.cfm?TargetUrl=LST_NOM&StrGroupCode=CLASSIFIC&StrLanguageCode=EN.

There are a range of other classification systems that an individual may run into when doing international business research. For instance, there is Standard & Poor's Global Industry Classification Standard (GICS®). Developed by Standard & Poor's and MSCI, GICS® consists of 10 sectors, 24 industry groups, 68 industries and 154 sub-industries."[35] It forms the basis for investment research, portfolio management, and asset allocation. One can use this code in S&P's *Compustat* database.

Another classification system is Dun and Bradstreet's (D&B) Data Universal Numbering System, or as it is most commonly known, the D-U-N-S number. This is a unique number that is owned and assigned by D&B to a company based on location[36]; it is an industry standard used to keep track of world businesses[37] and can also be used to search D&B databases and other vendor resources.

CONCLUSION

The classification systems discussed in this chapter are used with the list of sources provided later in chapter 7, which deals with industry research. These systems and others not included here have documentation from the sponsored agencies consisting of hundreds of pages that describe the reasons for developing a classification scheme, on what they are based, as well as the codes for the different economic activities or product. Scrutinizing such publications will help the user understand the data he or she is looking at.

Whenever one uses a print resource, the introduction will usually inform the user of the system that is being used to report the data. If the information is retrieved from an online source, there will often be a link to get a description of that system. These codes are periodically revised as new industries and changes in the world economy occur and the need for data presents itself. Concordances or correspondence tables that relate the codes from an earlier version to a new one, or to other coding systems that enable statistics to be compared, are common features of websites that identify classification systems, including Ramon and the UN classification registry.

As the researcher finds other sources, he or she will see that other methods are used. Some examples include the Classification by Broad Economic Categories (BEC), Classification of Individual Consumption According to Purpose (COICOP), International Classification of Activities for Time-Use Statistics (ICATUS), National System of Accounts, and Balance of Payments and International Investment Position Manual (BPM6). There are also alphabetical and numerical country codes that have been developed.

LIST OF SOURCES

Websites

This is an alphabetical list of publicly available websites for classification systems referred to in this chapter.

CPC Ver. 2 Detailed Structure and Correspondences of CPC Ver. 2 Subclasses to ISIC Rev. 4 and HS 2007, unstats.un.org/unsd/cr/registry/docs/CPCv2_structure.pdf (27 June 2012).

European Commission. eurostat, "Metadata Classification," ec.europa.eu/eurostat/ramon/nomenclatures/index.cfm?TargetUrl=LST_NOM&StrGroup-Code=CLASSIFIC&StrLanguageCode=EN (27 June 2012).

European Commission, eurostat, *NACE Rev. 2. Statistical Classification of Economic Activities in the European Community*, epp.eurostat.ec.europa.eu/portal/page/portal/nace_rev2/introduction (16 Oct. 2012).

Office for National Statistics, *UK Standard Industrial Classification of Economic Activities 2007 (SIC 2007)*, www.ons.gov.uk/ons/guide-method/classifications/current-standard-classifications/standard-industrial-classification/index.html (27 June 2012).

United Nations, Department of Economic and Social Affairs, *International Standard Industrial Classification of All Economic Activities*, unstats.un.org/unsd/publication/seriesM/seriesm_4rev4e.pdf (27 June 2012).

United Nations, Department of Economics and Social Affairs, Statistics Division, *Manual on Statistics of International Trade in Services 2010 (MSITS 2010)*, unstats.un.org/unsd/tradeserv/TFSITS/msits2010/M86%20rev1-white%20cover.pdf (27 June 2012).

United Nations Statistics Division, "Detailed Structure and Explanatory Notes,ISIC Rev. 4," unstats.un.org/unsd/cr/registry/regcst.asp?Cl=27 (27 June 2012).

United Nations Statistics Division, "Detailed Structure and Explanatory Notes, SITC Rev. 3," unstats.un.org/unsd/cr/registry/regcst.asp?Cl=14 (27 June 2012).

United Nations Statistics Division, "Detailed Structure and Explanatory Notes, SITC Rev. 4," unstats.un.org/unsd/cr/registry/regcst.asp?Cl=28 (27 June 2012).

United Nations Statistics Division, "Industry Statistics," unstats.un.org/unsd/industry/ (27 June 2012).

United Nations Statistics Division, *Manual on Statistics of International Trade in Services 2010*, "Correspondence Between the EBOPS 2010 and the Central Product Classification (CPC, version 2), EBOPS 2010 Services Components," unstats.un.org/unsd/tradeserv/TFSITS/msits2010/ebops2cpc.htm (27 June 2012).

United Nations Statistics Division, "National Classifications," unstats.un.org/unsd/cr/ctryreg/ctrylist2.asp?rg=7 (27 June 2012).

United Nations Statistics Division, "UN Classifications Registry," unstats.un.org/unsd/class/ (27 June 2012).

United States Department of Labor, Occupational Safety and Health Administration, www.osha.gov/pls/imis/sicsearch.html (27 June 2012).

United States International Trade Commission, "HTS Online Reference Tool," hts.usitc.gov/ (27 June 2012).

United States Census Bureau, "North American Industry Classification System," www.census.gov/eos/www/naics/ (27 June 2012).

United States Census Bureau, "Schedule B Export Codes," www.census.gov/foreign-trade/schedules/b/ (27 June 2012).

World Customs Organization, "HS Nomenclature 2007 Edition," www.wcoomd.org/home_hsoverviewboxes_tools_and_instruments_ hsnomenclaturetable2007.htm (27 June 2012).

NOTES

1. World Trade Organization, "Nomenclature—Overview—What is the Harmonized System (HS)?" www.wcoomd.org/home_hsoverviewboxes_hsharmonizedsystem.htm (28 June 2012).

2. World Customs Organization, HS Nomenclature 2007 Edition, "Chapter 95, Toys, games and sports requisites; parts and accessories thereof," www.wcoomd.org/home_hsoverviewboxes_tools_and_instruments_hsnomenclaturetable2007.htm (4 Oct. 2011).

3. United States Census Bureau. Foreign Trade, "Schedule B," www.census.gov/foreign-trade/schedules/b/ (28 Sept. 2011).

4. "Schedule B."

5. United States International Trade Commission, "About Harmonized Tariff Schedule," www.usitc.gov/tariff_affairs/about_hts.htm (28 Sept. 2011).

6. Department of Economic and Social Affairs, Statistics Division, Statistical Papers, *Standard International Trade Classification. Revision 4*, unstats.un.org/unsd/publication/SeriesM/SeriesM_34rev4E.pdf, v (28 Sept. 2011).

7. *Standard International Trade Classification, Revision 4*, viii.

8. *Standard International Trade Classification, Revision 4*, vii.

9. *Standard International Trade Classification, Revision 4*, vii

10. United Nations, Economic and Social Affairs, *International Standard Industrial Classification of All Economic Activities, Rev. 4*, unstats.un.org/unsd/publication/seriesM/seriesm_4rev4e.pdf, 9 (29 Sept. 2011).

11. United Nations Statistics Division, "Industry Statistics," unstats.un.org/unsd/industry/ (29 Sept. 2011).

12. United Nations, Economic and Social Affairs, *International Standard Industrial Classification of All Economic Activities*, 43.

13. United Nations, Economic and Social Affairs, *International Standard Industrial Classification of all Economic Activities, Rev. 4*, 158.

14. United Nations Statistics Division. Industrial Statistics, "Industry Statistics," unstats.un.org/unsd/industry/ (29 Sept. 2011).

15. United Nations Statistics Division, Department of Economic and Social Affairs, *Central Product Classification (CPC), Version 1.1* (Statistical Papers. Series M, No. 77, Ver.1.1), (New York: United Nations: 2004), 7, unstats.un.org/unsd/publication/SeriesM/SeriesM_77ver1_1E.pdf (29 Sept. 2011).

16. *Central Product Classification, (CPC), Version 1.1*, 9.

17. "CPC Ver. 2 Detailed Structure and Correspondences of CPC Ver. 2 Subclasses to ISIC Rev. 4 and HS 2007," unstats.un.org/unsd/cr/registry/docs/CPCv2 _structure.pdf (27 June 2012).

18. *Central Product Classification, (CPC), Version 1.1*, 9.

19. United Nations, Department of Economics and Social Affairs, Statistics Division, *Manual on Statistics of International Trade in Services 2010* (*MSITS 2010*), 12, unstats.un.org/unsd/tradeserv/TFSITS/msits2010/M86%20rev1-white%20cover.pdf   (3 Nov. 2011).

20. United Nations Statistics Division, *Manual on Statistics of International Trade in Services 2010*, "Correspondence Between the EBOPS 2010 and the Central Product Classification (CPC, version 2), EBOPS 2010 Services Components," unstats.un.org/unsd/tradeserv/TFSITS/msits2010/ebops2cpc.htm (3 Nov. 2011).

21. European Commission, eurostat, "NACE Backgrounds," epp.eurostat.ec .europa.eu/statistics_explained/index.php/NACE_backgrounds (9 Sept. 2011).

22. "NACE backgrounds."

23. European Commission, eurostat, *NACE Rev. 2. Statistical Classification of Economic Activities in the European Community*, epp.eurostat.ec.europa.eu/cache/ITY_OFFPUB/KS-RA-07-015/EN/KS-RA-07-015-EN.PDF (3 Nov. 2011).

24. European Commission, eurostat, *NACE Rev. 2. Statistical Classification of Economic Activities in the European Community*.

25. European Commission, eurostat, "Glossary. European Statistical System," epp.eurostat.ec.europa.eu/statistics_explained/index.php/Glossary:European_statistical_system (ESS) (30 Sept. 2011).

26. United States Census Bureau, North American Industry Classification System. Frequently Asked Questions (FAQs), "What Is NAICS and How Is It Used?" www.census.gov/eos/www/naics/faqs/faqs.html), (16 Sept. 2011).

27. Carole A. Ambler, US Census Bureau, "Developing a Product Classification System for the United States," June 1998, www.census.gov/eos/www/napcs/papers/related3.pdf (16 Sept. 2011).

28. United States Census Bureau, (FAQs), "What Is an Establishment?"

29. United States Census Bureau, "NAICS Update Process Fact Sheet," www.census.gov/eos/www/naics/reference_files_tools/NAICS_Update_Process_Fact_Sheet.pdf (6 Dec. 2011).

30. United States Census Bureau, "North American Industry Classification System," www.census.gov/cgi-bin/sssd/naics/naicsrch?code=339920&search=2012   (21 June 2012).

31. "What Is the NAICS Structure and How Many Digits Are in a NAICS Code?" (16 Oct. 2012).

32. Office of National Statistics, *UK Standard Industrial Classification of Economic Activities 2007 (SIC 2007)*, www.ons.gov.uk/ons/guide-method/classifications/current-standard-classifications/standard-industrial-classification/sic2007-explanatory-notes.pdf 9 (3 Oct. 2011).

33. United States Department of Labor. Occupational Safety and Health Administration, "Division D: Manufacturing," www.osha.gov/pls/imis/sic_manual.display?id=880&tab=description (6 Dec. 2011).

34. United Nations Statistics Division, "National Classifications," unstats.un.org/unsd/cr/ctryreg/ctrylist2.asp?rg=7 (1 Nov. 2011).

35. MSCI, "GICS®," www.msci.com/products/indices/sector/gics/ (16 Oct. 2012).

36. D&B, "About the D-U-N-S Number," fedgov.dnb.com/webform/pages/dunsnumber.jsp (9 Oct. 2012).

37. Dun & Bradstreet, Credibility Group, "D-U-N-S Center," smallbusiness.dnb.com/establish/12137020-1.html (6 Dec. 2011).

SEVEN

International Industry Research

Anyone who wants to enter a certain market, whether domestic or international, needs to conduct an industry analysis for the country of interest. The *Dictionary of Business* defines industry as "a group of companies making the same type of product or offering the same type of service"[1] (2006). The *Collins Dictionary of Economics* defines it as "a group of related economic activities classified according to the type of good or service supplied"[2] (2006).

The industry analysis will include a structural as well as a competitive analysis. Michael Porter describes five competitive forces that affect industry structure. These are threat of new entrants (which is influenced by barriers to entry), the bargaining power of suppliers, the bargaining power of buyers, the threat of substitute products or services, and rivalry among existing competitors.[3] A place to begin is using sources that have already been published (secondary research). The strategies and resources covered in this chapter focus on this type of study. In addition to finding information that already exists, the results from this activity should help the researcher identify any gaps that will require primary research. Michael Porter recommends the following internal sources for getting field data that will help one to do the analysis: the company's market research staff, sales force, former employees of competitors, engineering staff, purchasing department, and R&D department.[4] Depending on the type of researcher (i.e., a student, a corporate librarian, independent information professional), he or she might not have access to these types of resources. Fortunately, there publicly available sources that have information about industry.

Some of the questions that need answers are

- What is currently happening in this industry globally or in the country I want to enter?

- What is the forecast for the industry?
- Are any environmental forces impacting the industry (political/legal, economic, socio/cultural, and/or technological)?
- Who are the competitors in the industry? How many? What are their sizes? What is the market share? What type of competition exists (monopolistic, oligopolistic, pure competition, monopolistic competition)? How do they differentiate their product?

Industry research is often part of market research and/or competitive analysis. Consequently, some of the sources used for market and company research can be used in the industry analysis and vice versa. For instance, Euromonitor's Passport GMID, a resource presented in this chapter, is also included in chapter 7, which deals with market research. Another example is a company's annual report (10-Ks, 20-Fs), which contains information about the industry that may be impacting the business positively and/or negatively. In addition, industry profiles produced by vendors often deal with trends, threats, opportunities, and other factors that may help in developing the opportunities and threats portion of a company SWOT[5] analysis.

Many times a student or other type of researcher will begin the research process with a search engine. Although these are valuable tools to use, they may not be effective in finding the information that is needed for an industry analysis. Even if leads are discovered, they might be market research reports that cost thousands of dollars. If the individual is going to be conducting international business research, he or she should be aware that the US government provides significant assistance to a US business that is interested in entering global markets, and that there are international organizations that provide a wide range of data at no cost. Like the US, governments of other countries also have support for businesses that want to enter global markets. Consequently, this would be a good place to begin. Furthermore, academic libraries often subscribe to several industry and market research databases, as well as to those that index and provide full-text articles to trade journals and newspapers; some public libraries in metro areas do as well. Keeping this in mind, one could use the following strategy for industry research:

- Utilize government resources provided to support businesses that want to enter the international market. The focus in this chapter will be from the US.
- Use sources on how to do business in a country.
- Search in fee-based resources that provide industry profiles and market research reports.
- Assess export data to find out if there are industry trends globally and/or from the United States to a country of interest.
- Gather industrial statistics from international organizations such as the United Nations (UN) and Organisation for Economic Co-opera-

tion and Development (OECD), US and other official regional national statistical agencies, and fee-based sources for analysis.

- Search for articles published in trade journals, magazines, and regional/local newspapers.
- Identify trade and industry associations and/or organizations and search their websites for relevant data and information; attend trade show events, if possible.
- Identify contacts and reach out to them for further assistance.
- Leverage the sources cited in a specific document and investigate it for further information.
- Review company reports as well as market research reports and extract any information that might be written about the industry, which could include economic factors that are affecting it and/or new trends that must be addressed.

These strategies, along with selected resources, are covered in the rest of this chapter. Reference to various classifications will be named for certain sources. These schemes are described in more detail in the chapter on "Classifications for Industry."

US GOVERNMENT SOURCES

One of the most important sources with which to begin doing international business research was the GLOBUS/National Trade Data Bank (NTDB) from the US Department of Commerce. This database ceased on September 30, 2010.[6] However, some of the information that was available through it is now dispersed through various US government websites, including Export.gov and the Market Research Library (MRL) via the US Commercial Service (www.buyusainfo.net). The University of Central Florida has created a research guide that organizes the information that was on GLOBUS/NTDB along the lines of this terminated database. It is located at guides.ucf.edu/content.php?pid=141826&sid=1209051.

The International Trade Administration (ITA), a bureau under the US Department of Commerce, supports companies, large, medium, and small in their efforts to conduct business beyond US borders, either by helping them start or by promoting their efforts. One way they do this is through Export.gov, which they manage in collaboration with ten government agencies, including the US Department of Commerce, the US Department of State, and Overseas Private Investment Corporation (OPIC). This website has trade data; Doing Business Guides—which are the *Country Commercial Guides* discussed later in this chapter; tips on shipping a product, links to Schedule B and the Harmonized Tariff Schedule—discussed in more detail in the "Classifications for Industry" chapter; training opportunities, and contacts for export assistance. Another unit ITA administers in promoting overseas trade is its US Commercial Services.

ITA also manages the Market Research Library (MRL), which is currently accessed through the US Commercial Services at the following URL: www.buyusainfo.net. To access any of the reports available one must be from a US company or be a student/researcher and register at Export.gov. There are three sources of information in the MRL. These are the *Country Commercial Guides*, Market Research Reports, and Best Market Reports.

The *Country Commercial Guides* category currently has over 12,686 reports, 253 of which are current. These guides provide information on how to do business in a particular country. Each is organized as follows:

- Chapter 1: Doing Business In [specific country]
- Chapter 2: Political and Economic Environment
- Chapter 3: Selling US Products and Services
- Chapter 4: Leading Sectors for US Export and Investment
- Chapter 5: Trade Regulations, Customs and Standards
- Chapter 6: Investment Climate
- Chapter 7: Trade and Project Financing
- Chapter 8: Business Travel
- Chapter 9: Contacts, Market Research and Trade Events
- Chapter 10: Guide to Our Services

These guides have certain pieces of information that would be useful to know about industry in a particular country. Specifically, the guide describes the leading sectors for US export and investment, reveals trade barriers that might impact specific industries, points out licensing requirements for specific goods, identifies trade agreements, and trade publications, and lists the names of industry trade associations, events, leads, and contacts.

The Market Research Report section has over 53,156 reports, 1,500 of which are current. These reports are generally two to ten pages in length, and cover a wide range of industries in countries and regions. Because of the diversity of these reports, it is worth searching this database for a specific product or service because there might be more information about it. Even if they are not very long, these reports provide information that would potentially be useful for the industry analysis. For example, the report retrieved from MRL called "Motorcycles in the Czech Republic" dated 6/6/2011, identifies the number of motorbike manufacturers in the country, provides import data for the first quarter in 2011 for new bikes from the top six firms, and gives the number of new motorbike registrations for the top ten companies in 2010. It also identifies sources for the data provided, trade events, and associations to investigate for more information. The same report would be useful for market research as well.

The Best Market Report section at this time is made up of over 186 documents, 57 of which are current. This section also consists of a wide range of topics similar to the Market Research Reports section and that can be used in an industry analysis. For example, the report dated June 2011 on *The Broadcast Industry: Thailand* includes the key subsectors of this industry, broadcasting rules and regulations, its infrastructure, suppliers of broadcast communication equipment, information about tariffs and duties, trade events, and contacts.

The ITA website (trade.gov) also provides links to industry information (see figure 7.1). The Data & Analysis button links to a page that lists the following industries listed:

- Aerospace
- Automotive
- Building Products
- Construction
- Consumer Goods
- E-Commerce
- Energy
- Environmental Industries
- Financial Services
- Health
- Information and Telecom
- Machinery

Figure 7.1.

- Textiles and Apparel
- Service Industries
- Travel and Tourism

Each of these industries links to the webpage of a relevant US government division for the industry. For example, the Aerospace, Automotive, and Machinery sectors are linked to the Transportation and Machinery Office page; Consumer Goods links to the Office of Consumer Goods, a division of the Office of Health and Consumer Goods; Electronic Commerce and Information and Telecommunications links to the Office of Technology and Electronic Commerce website; and Travel and Tourism takes one to the Office of Travel and Tourism Industries page. Each of these sites has a different interface, and each of them will include not only information for the US market, but also information useful for international business engagement.

SOURCES ON HOW TO DO BUSINESS IN A COUNTRY

The resources that are identified in this section could easily fit in the chapter on market research. They are placed here because these types of reports provide information about regulations and laws that a company must deal with to conduct business in a country. These set of laws can create barriers to foreign business if they are very strict. By reviewing these documents, a business can be aware of what it has to deal with in this area, and take steps to deal with it, or not. In addition, they also provide other information that can be useful in the industry analysis. One of the fundamental sources to use when planning to do business abroad is the World Bank's Doing Business series (www.doingbusiness.org/). This is a project that began in 2004 and in which the World Bank is engaged to provide measurements of regulations applicable to conducting business in over "183 economies and selected cities at the subnational level."[7] The series includes annual updates about the state of doing business worldwide, and thematic reports such as *Paying Taxes* or *Getting Electricity*.

Except for those published in 2008 and 2009, the "Doing Business" annual reports have had a theme. For example, the theme in 2004 was *Understanding Regulations* and in 2012 the theme is *Doing Business: Doing Business in a Transparent World*. These reports look at small and medium sized companies and the regulatory environment (the ease of doing business) in a defined area compared to other similar countries. The regulations measured and compared relate to the following stages of a company's life cycle (for 2012):

- Starting a business
- Dealing with construction permits

- Getting electricity
- Registering property
- Getting credit
- Protecting investors
- Paying taxes
- Trading across borders
- Enforcing contracts
- Resolving insolvency
- Employing workers[8]

A report for a country will provide indicators that allow the researcher to compare the ease of taking each of these steps in the targeted country as compared to other countries. For example, in the *2012 Doing Business* report for Brazil ranks it 126 out of 183 economics in the category of "Ease of Doing Business." It ranks 120 in "Starting a Business" and 150 for "Paying Taxes." Within each of the stages more information is provided. For instance, in the "Ease of Doing Business" category, the report states that it requires 13 procedures, takes 119 days, and costs 5.4 percent of income per capita to start a business in Brazil.[9] Within each of these categories, the procedures to set up a business are identified and the time and cost of each one is provided. For instance, in Brazil, the first step in setting up a business is to "Check company name with State Registry Office," which takes one day at no cost. Similar information is provided for fourteen other procedures.

Another source on how to do business in a country is EIU's *Country Commerce* series. Depending on the country, these publications can include information about the regulatory environment; the position of the country in the global economy; the political and market conditions; the conditions for foreign direct investment and the steps required to invest in a country; labor conditions and structure (i.e., union, non-union); national incentives that can be general, industry specific, or regional; competition policies; the control system for handling exchange rates; and relevant conditions for human resources, including laws.

A source that has already been mentioned is the *Country Commercial Guides* from the US Commercial Services. Chapter 5: Trade Regulations, Customs and Standards is the relevant section to use here.

Another strategy the researcher can use is to search Amazon.com or a library catalog using keywords like "doing business in" or "how to do business in [name of country]" to find publications from other publishers. If using a library catalog in an academic library, that catalog is probably using the Library of Congress classification system. If so, the official Library of Congress subject headings for this type of document are:

- Name of Country—Commerce—Handbooks, manuals, etc.
- Name of Country—Description and travel.

Although these reports don't specifically focus on an industry, they are helpful in terms of judging the regulatory barriers that have to be dealt with in a specific country.

FEE-BASED SOURCES FOR INDUSTRY PROFILES—US COVERAGE

A number of fee-based databases will help the researcher when conducting industry research. These researchers will often provide information about the state of the industry, how the economy might be affecting it, technological trends that are having an impact, main competitors, and social and demographic trends. There are several sources for industry profiles that primarily focus on the United States. These are described below.

First Research

This industry database comes from Hoover's LEARN Division (Library Education Academic Research Network Affiliates).[10] Information is provided for more than 900 industry segments. A profile will include an industry overview, recent developments, business challenges, trends and opportunities, executive insight, call prep questions, financial information, industry forecast and rating, and suggested web links and acronyms. Although the reports primarily cover the United States, First Research does have twenty-five brief reports focusing on the manufacturing sector in Canada.

Freedonia Focus Market Research Portal

The Freedonia Focus Market Research Portal is a source for the academic community. It has 600 reports covering 18 industries, such as "Automotive and Other Transportation Equipment" and "Security, Electronics, and Communication" for the United States, China, and the world. The publications are about twenty pages in length and give highlights of what is happening in the industry in the United States, an industry overview that includes market share and regulatory considerations, industry trends and forecasts that deal with the market environment and product forecasts, and the structure of the industry that describes the composition of the industry and its leaders. These reports also have a one-page description of what may be happening globally in the industry. There are also reports that cover industry and markets in selected countries.

IBISWorld

The industry reports provided by this publisher cover 700 market segments and include market analysis, industry growth and statistics, market size, industry trends, and market share. Although primarily focused on the US market, the reports will include information about international markets and the effect of globalization on an industry. IBISWorld also provides global reports for industries in major categories that consist of Business Activities; Community, Social, and Personal Services; Financial Intermediation; Hotels & Restaurants; Manufacturing; Mining; Telecommunications; Tourism; Transport; and Wholesale and Retail Trade.

Plunkett Research

Plunkett Research (www.plunkettresearch.com/) is available in print and online. Its series of publications cover thirty broad industry categories, including traditional industries like *Automobiles & Trucks*, and newer ones like *Alternative & Renewal Energy, Games, Apps & Social Media*, and *Green Technology*. One can purchase these reports, or subscribe to them or the database, *Plunkett Research Online* or the print material, or purchase the reports individually. A report will include market research and trends, statistics from sources that include the US Census and the US International Trade Association (if relevant), as well as trade associations. Depending on the industry, import and export data is included as well. Other components of a publication include companies and executives, industry associations, and a glossary. There are also links to videos that introduce the user to the industry. Plunkett also creates custom reports when requested.

Standard & Poor's (S&P) Capital IQ Industry Profiles

S&P's *Industry Profiles* provides detailed information for more than fifty industries. They are included in S&P's *NetAdvantage* database (www.netadvantage.standardandpoors.com) and continue to be available in print. The reports are written by S&P industry analysts and include an overview of the current environment, an industry profile, trends, a discussion on how the industry operates, some key industry ratios and statistics, how to analyze a company, a glossary of terms, industry references, and a presentation of revenues, net income, profit ratios, balance sheet ratios, equity ratios, and per-share data for the major companies in an industry.

FEE-BASED SOURCES FOR INDUSTRY PROFILES—GLOBAL COVERAGE

In addition to the sources that cover the United States, there are several that provide industry reports not only on a broad, global scale, but profiles for specific countries. This section identifies some of the companies and the products they offer. In addition to covering global industries, the companies in this section also provide other tools that will be useful in other international business research; some will provide country risk, while others may cover companies. The focus of the information presented here is on industry.

Business Monitor International (BMI)

BMI's analysts contribute to industry profiles for twenty-two sectors in seventy markets across the world. Included in the reports are five- to ten-year forecasts based on BMI's proprietary method. They include an industry SWOT (strengths, weaknesses, opportunities, and threats), information about the business environment (legal framework, foreign investment policy, tax regime, and security risk), industry forecasts, infrastructure, and competitive landscape. One can buy individual reports through the online store, subscribe to the database Business Monitor Online, or use the consulting service for customized deliverables. There are also industry profiles from this publisher via EBSCOHost's Business Source Complete. BMI also offers company intelligence and country business forecasts.

Datamonitor Group

Through various platforms, this company provides reports for automotive, consumer packaged goods, energy and sustainability, financial services, logistics and express, pharmaceutical and healthcare, and retail industries around the world. Industry reports, company and country profiles and data models are available for purchase through its Research Store. A business can also subscribe to their Knowledge Center.

This publisher used to provide the Datamonitor 360 database to academic libraries. This resource is now called MarketLine Advantage. It has more than 3,500 industry profiles, covering aerospace and defense, to government and non-profit organizations, to transport and logistics; they incorporate Porter's five forces of competitive analysis. Business Source Complete provides past Datamonitor industry reports, as well as those from MarketLine.

Several databases that include Datamonitor industry reports, although they generally do not include everything that is offered by the publisher. Databases that provide them include Business Source Complete, Business Insights: Essentials, BvD's Mint Global, and infogroup's OneSource.

Consulting services are also provided by this company.

Euromonitor International

Euromonitor covers almost thirty industry categories in consumer goods, services, and industrial markets on an international and country level. Reports include "data and analysis of market size, distribution channel analysis, market trends, competitive landscape, legislation, local company profiles, company and brand shares and five year forecasts."[11] Online databases are available for three target groups:

- Passport (for corporations)
- Passport GMID (Global Market Information Database) for government and export departments, business schools and university libraries, information centers in banks, consultancies, and advertising agencies
- Research Monitor for libraries

Passport GMID is a rich source of information for many elements of international research, and is especially strong with industry. Not only does it provide reports on different types of industry areas (such as pet care in Brazil, vitamins and dietary supplements in the Netherlands), but it also provides a wide range of socioeconomic data, such as annual disposable income, consumer expenditures, and a country's gross domestic product (GDP). A strong feature of the statistical portion of the database is the ability to change the time series to include historical and/or future data. Euromonitor continues to offer its print reference books for sale for various industries and markets. Many Euromonitor reports can be used for market and company analysis as well. It also offers consulting services.

IHS

IHS provides solutions for fifteen global industries. One of these is the Global Insight database. This resource provides industry intelligence for the world's major sectors, which includes agriculture, construction, consumer goods, commerce and transport, energy, healthcare and pharmaceutical, telecommunication, finance and investments, and steel.[12] IHS also provides consulting and advisory services.

EMIS, Emerging Markets Information Service

EMIS provides industry information for 100 countries in Asia-Pacific, the Caucasus and Central Asia, Central and Southeast Europe, Latin

America and the Caribbean, and the Middle East. It also provides industry reports from Business Monitor and Euromonitor. This source can also
be used for finding company information in these emerging markets.

The success one has with any of the databases identified in this section, or that one finds elsewhere will depend on the industry one is
researching and/or the level of granularity one wants. For example, if one
is researching scuba diving instruction in the United States, an *IBISWorld*
report on scuba diving instruction should be perfect. However, if researching this industry in a Central American country other strategies
will have to be undertaken, such as identifying associations and contacting them for information.

There are many academic libraries that have access to industry databases, including the ones just identified and others they have selected to
meet their users' needs. A current student or faculty member should
always contact his or her educational institution's library to determine
whether it might have any databases that can be used for researching an
industry. There are also public libraries or library districts that may subscribe to them. A community member should be aware of this type of
resource. Depending on the licensing agreements between a library and
publisher, a nonaffiliated member of a library may be able to access databases to which it subscribes and use the information found.

STATISTICS

Statistics are very important in the industry analysis. Some of the information that would be useful includes import/export (trade) data, sales
figures, number of companies in the industry, market share, and production levels. Depending on the product, service or industry, these and
other types of data may or may not be available on a significant scale. For
instance, if one is researching the automobile industry, which contributes
a significant amount to the US economy, one should be able to find a
considerable amount of data. This would not be the case for sunscreens.
This section identifies some resources for import and export data as well
as nontrade statistics.

Trade Statistics

Cullen and Parboteeah point out that "a high volume of trade in an
industry is a strong indicator of a globalized industry and suggests that
success is related to cross borders. That is, it shows an already existing
high level of international competition and acceptance of products from
different countries."[13] Consequently, one can look at import/export data
to determine if they reveal any industry trends. In addition, one may be
able to identify those countries to which the United States is exporting a

product, or countries exporting that same product to other countries. One could call this a competitive analysis of the countries trading the same product.

A publicly available source for US import and export data is TradeStats Express located at tse.export.gov/TSE/TSEhome.aspx. This service is provided by the US Department of Commerce's International Trade Administration. Presently the database provides access to two separate components, National Trade Data (figure 7.2), which includes US merchandise exports, imports, and trade balances, and State Export Data, which consists of state and regional exports of merchandise.

The interface provides access to annual and quarterly trade data. If one begins with National Trade Data, one then has a choice of selecting either the "Global Patterns of US Merchandise Trade" or "Product Profiles of US Merchandise Trade with a Selected Market" (figure 7.3).

The first component, Global Patterns of US Merchandise Trade allows one to find the US trade balances with the world and its trading partners for the last twenty years, as well as total exports and imports. One can also find figures for total merchandise being exported or imported to and from the US to the world and with its trading partners. One can also identify the top import and export trading partners for specific merchandise. The search interface allows use of either NAICS, Harmonized System, or SITC to identify the commodity desired.

The other section of the Global Patterns of Merchandise Trade offers "Product Profiles of US Merchandise Trade with a Selected Market" (figure 7.3). Trade Partners can be a specific country, geographic regions

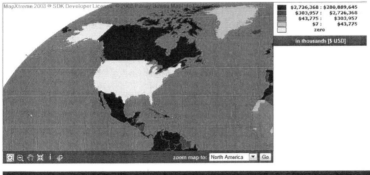

Exports of NAICS Total All Merchandise			
Partner	2005	2006	2007
World	901,081,812,545	1,025,967,497,363	1,148,198,722,191
Canada	211,898,689,378	230,656,013,599	248,888,144,575
Mexico	120,247,580,142	133,721,712,754	135,918,138,711
China	41,192,010,123	53,673,008,343	62,936,891,576
Japan	54,680,579,847	58,458,978,071	61,159,582,766
United Kingdom	38,568,083,046	45,410,106,533	49,981,491,297
Germany	34,183,656,274	41,159,115,809	49,419,703,142

Figure 7.2. National Trade Data

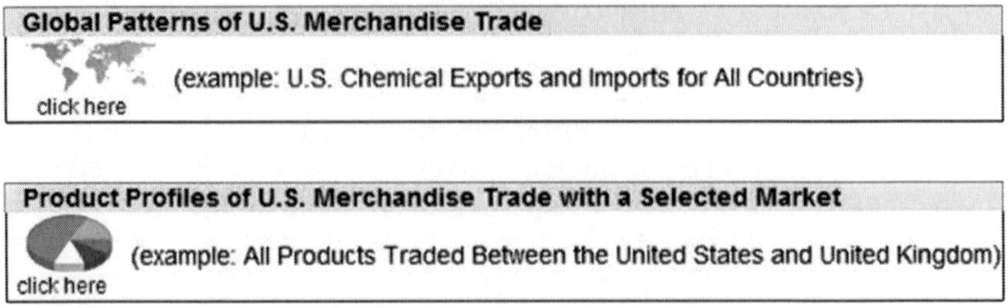

Global Patterns of U.S. Merchandise Trade

(example: U.S. Chemical Exports and Imports for All Countries)

click here

Product Profiles of U.S. Merchandise Trade with a Selected Market

(example: All Products Traded Between the United States and United Kingdom)

click here

Figure 7.3.

(such as the World, Africa, Middle East, etc.), and trading and economic regions such as EU27, Free Trade Agreement of the Americas, Gulf Cooperation Council, South African Customs Union, and so forth. This side allows the researcher to find the value of selected product exports or imports of US merchandise worldwide, by regions, or individual countries. To select a product, one would use NAICS, Harmonized System, or SITC.

The other section of TradeStats Express is State Export Data section (figure 7.4). It offers the ability to find three types of product data based on three-level NAICS code, going back twenty years as well as quarterly year-to-date data. One should be aware that NAICS codes can go to the sixth level. Since one can only go to the third level with TradeStats Express, this means that the data obtained probably won't be as specific as desired. For example, the NAICS code for ski manufacturing is 339920, Sporting and Athletic Manufacturing. The data that TradeStats Express provides is at the third level, 339, described as Miscellaneous Manufactured Commodities.

The first type of information that is available in the State Export Data section is categorized as "Global Patterns of a State's Exports." One would be able to find exports from an individual state in the US, a global region, the world, and to individual countries, including the United States. An example would be Miscellaneous Manufactured Commodities exported from Washington to the world as well as to each country. The second type available in the State Export Data category is referred to as "State-by-State Exports to a Selected Market." Data for exports to a country, geographic region, or trading and economic region from every state would be accessible here. An example of this would be the exports of Miscellaneous Manufactured Commodities from each state to the EU 27. The third type of information is the "Export Product Profile to a Selected Market." One can get an export product profile from a state to a country, geographic regions, or trading and economic region. An example of this would be all merchandise exports from California to Belgium, which would be returned in three-digit NAICS codes.

Global Patterns of a State's Exports
(example: Exports from Texas to each country) click here

State-by-State Exports to a Selected Market
(example: Exports to Ireland from each state) click here

Export Product Profile to a Selected Market
(example: Products from Texas to Iceland) click here

Figure 7.4.

Another source for US trade data is USA Trade Online (https://www.usatradeonline.gov/), from the Foreign Trade Division of the US Census Bureau. This division is the official source for collecting data for goods and services exported and imported from the United States.[14] The statistics available here are more current than TradeStats Express and provides more up-to-date detailed import and export data for district, port and state. One can find information for over 18,000 export commodities and 24,000 import commodities using either the Harmonized System (HS) or North American Industrial Classification System (NAICS) codes. Data is provided up to the ten digits for HS and six digits for NAICS and is reported forty-five calendar days after the month reported.[15]

Repository libraries can access the information freely from this source, so a user should contact his or her local library if he or she is interested in using it.

One can also obtain US international trade data at the US Census Bureau Foreign Trade Division website, www.census.gov/foreign-trade/about/index.html. The Foreign Trade Division also has the NAICS Related–Party portal (http://sasweb.ssd.census.gov/relatedparty/), which provides import and export trade data between parties based on the NAICS code. An example of what one might find is the total import value of trade (for the United States) for storage batteries (NAICS 335991) from Antigua, Andora. United Arab Emirates for each of the years from 2007–2011.

Another source of trade statistics is the US International Trade Commission's

Interactive Tariff and Trade Dataweb (dataweb.usitc.gov/). Although this source is publicly available one does have to register. The following information is provided through this portal:

- US imports for consumption
- US domestic exports
- US general imports
- US total exports
- Trade balance

One can search for this data using HTS, US SIC, SITC, or NAICS codes.

A source of trade data for cross country comparison is Wisertrade (www.wisertrade.org). Not only does it give US trade data, it also provides import/export data for 27 European Union countries, the Canadian Provinces, the Chinese Provinces, Taiwan, and Japan; and imports for 184 UN countries.[16] This is a subscription-based database.

There are several sources that provide global trade statistics. One of this is the United Nations' *International Trade Statistics Yearbook*, which is available both in print and through the UN comtrade portal (comtrade.un.org). Data for the print resource is obtained from comtrade. Figures for the comtrade database are obtained by the United Nations Statistics Division (UNSD) from over 170 reporter countries. This data is then standardized.[17] The portal provides detailed annual trade data for commodities and their partner countries. Information for a commodity is retrievable using SITC and HS. This resource has import/export trade value of a product, its net weight in kilograms, and quantities traded from one country to another. For instance, one would be able to identify the import/export trade value of "beauty or make-up preparations and preparations for the care of the skin . . . including sunscreen or suntan" (HS 3304) in US dollars, from Brazil to any country for several years. As of 8 October 2012, the most recent annual statistics available are for 2011. Although this can't be done with the two-volume print set, it is possible to identify the top ten export and import commodities (based on three-digit SITC) for a country and the top ten exporting and importing countries for a specific commodity (based on four-digit HS). The online database is publicly available; however, one has to agree to its usage terms in order to access the data. In addition, there are restrictions for dissemination of large data sets, set out in a 190-page document available at unstats.un.org/unsd/tradekb/Attachment55.aspx.

The United Nations Statistics Division provides the United Nations International Trade Services Database, which is branded as UN Service-Trade (unstats.un.org/unsd/servicetrade/), for trade data on services. This is a publicly available system for storing and disseminating international trade in services statistics. Data is presented using the Extended Balance of Payments System (EBOPS) and the partner country. The data that populates this database comes primarily from central banks, national statistical offices, and the statistical office of the European Communities.[18] A researcher would be able to find the trade value of a service exported or imported from one country (referred to as Reporter) to another country (called Partner). For example one could find the trade value of business and management consulting and public relations services (EBOPS 9.3.1.3) from each partner country in the system to the world. Registration is required before using this database.

Yet another source of trade data is the World Trade Organization (WTO). The WTO provides trade and tariff data through its print publication *International Trade Statistics*. Current and editions going back to 2000 are available on the WTO "International trade and tariff data" page (www.wto.org/english/res_e/statis_e/statis_e.htm). On this page is a link to an online statistics database. This database offers trade, tariff, and services profiles, as well as an interactive database that allows one to obtain time series of trade data. Trade profiles cover over 180 economies and include basic economic indicators; data related to trade policies, such as WTO accession, tariffs, and duty free imports; and contribution to the WTO budget. The tariff profile section includes a summary for tariffs and imports as well as duty ranges, tariffs on imported product groups, and exports to a country's main trading partners and the duties it faced. The services profiles cover transportation telecommunications, finance and insurance, showing "100 indicators relating to investment, market performance, production, employment, trade, as well as performance rankings," for more than ninety economies. The tariff profiles are also distributed through WTO's print publication, *World Tariff Profiles*.

Not to be ignored as a source of trade data is the United Nations Conference on Trade and Development (UNCTAD). Its UNCTADStats (unctadstat.unctad.org/) database is a freely accessible database that provides a number of statistical reports related to merchandise imports and exports. This includes trade trends, trade by partner and category/product, trade indicators, and market access. There is also the potential to get data from 1948 through 2011 in certain categories, such as the values and shares of merchandise exports and imports data for merchandise. This database also has other types of statistics that are valuable when doing business research, including information on economic trends, foreign direct investment, external financial resources (such as development assistance, external debt, and international reserves), population and labor force, commodities, the information economy, and maritime transport.

Other sources of trade data include IMF's *Direction of Trade Statistics (DOTS)*, the Organisation for Economic Co-operation and Development's (OECD) *International Trade by Commodities Statistics, Monthly Statistics of International Trade*, OECD Statistics on *International Trade in Services* and its online database OECD iLibrary. These resources were covered in chapter 2, which deals with the international monetary system and financial system.

In addition to these sources, other country governments also gather trade data for their own needs. One can go to the sites of a country's official statistical department and look for such data if desired. The US Census Bureau provides a list of worldwide statistical agencies at www.census.gov/aboutus/stat_int.html.

Nontrade Statistics—International Organizations

In addition to trade data, there are other types of statistics published by international organizations such as the United Nations and OECD, commercial vendors, trade associations, and the US government that one can utilize for industry research. The information provided will vary by source. For instance, some will include population counts for countries or large cities that would be useful to know. Others might provide industry sales data; still others may reveal the market size of a particular product or service. The sources identified next will help with environmental scanning, which involves identifying political/legal, economic, socio/cultural, technological factors that affect the industry. These sources may also be used for market research.

The United Nations Statistics Division collects, processes, and disseminates data through several publications, including the *Statistical Yearbook* and the *Industrial Commodity Statistics Yearbook*. The *Statistical Yearbook* is published annually and presents social and economic conditions for the world, as well as all the countries and regions for which there is data available. The volume consists of four parts made up of nineteen tables. Part one includes world statistics for population, production, external trade and finance, including selected data for regions of the world, such as population figures; indices for agricultural, food and industrial production; commercial energy (production, trade and consumption data); and import and export indices. Part two covers population and social statistics. Part three deals with economic activity, providing gross domestic product (GDP) and GDP per capita, and related GDP figures (i.e., GDP by type of expenditure at current prices). Part three of the volume focuses on industrial production in the major sections of an economy, which consists of agriculture, hunting, forestry; mining and quarrying; manufacturing; electricity, gas and water supply; construction; wholesale, retail trade; restaurants and hotels; transport storage and communication; and other activities. Part four covers international economic relations, including international merchandise trade, international tourism and transport, balance of payments, international finance, and development assistance. According to the publisher, the staff of the *Statistical Yearbook* work hard to ensure that the statistics received from numerous national sources and then published are comparable. A downside to these data is that often it is not as timely as someone doing an industry analysis wants. For instance, the most current data in a *Yearbook* published in 2009 is for 2006, which was based on the information that was provided by statistical offices worldwide as of June 30, 2008.[19] One of the reasons for this is that only a small number of countries may have provided most of the current data and, for a print publication such as this one, the publisher tries to balance the presentation of current information with suitable country coverage.[20]

The *Industrial Commodity Statistics Yearbook* is a two-volume set providing both the physical number and the monetary value on approximately 600 industrial commodities for about 200 countries and areas. This is not an all inclusive presentation of all the commodities worldwide; instead, the ones that are in this source have been selected because of their overall importance in the world, as well as that of the outputs of certain ISIC industries.[21] Volume I presents information based on Physical Quantity Data, while volume II expresses it in monetary value. Each page is made up of a table populated with ten years' worth of data for each commodity and country covered in this source. The products are a selection representing industrial production from the list of ISIC rev. 3.1 of mining (Section C), manufacturing (Section D), and electricity and gas (Section E) of ISIC. It is presented by Central Product Classification (CPC). The UN Statistics Division is responsible for gathering and distributing these industrial commodity production statistics.

Another source of industry data is the United Nations Industrial Development Organization's (UNIDO) *International Yearbook of Industrial Statistics*. The purpose of this source is to provide a way to make worldwide comparisons of the manufacturing sector by providing statistical indicators.[22] Data for this publication is obtained from international sources such as the "World Bank, OECD, the United Nations Statistics Division, the International Monetary Fund, . . . regional development banks, . . . industrial censuses, statistics supplied by national and international organizations, unpublished data collected in the field by UNIDO as well as estimates made by the UNIDO secretariat."[23] It is made up of two parts.

Part I consists of summary tables for the global manufacturing sector. It provides major growth and distribution trends, leading producers in selected manufacturing divisions (based on ISIC Rev. 3), characteristics of branches (i.e., value added per employee, costs of labor, etc.) in certain industries for a country, and other statistical indicators. Part II is made up of country tables. Each country table includes the following information for each industry covered based on ISIC Rev. 3: output and value added in producers' prices, number of enterprises and employees, and wages and salaries. The most current data provided in the 2011 edition is for 2008.

Table 7.1 presents the main highlights of these two publications. Data from each of these are available through the Undata database, as indicated in the fourth column.

Data from other sources as well non-industry publications are also publicly available via the United Nations Undata portal at data.un.org (figure 7.5). One can use the search interface to look for a commodity or select specific databases, such as the Industrial Commodity Statistics Database and UNIDO's INDSTAT resource.

Other industry specific content that is included in Undata includes:

- Energy Statistics Database
- World Telecommunication/ICT Indicators Data from the International Telecommunications Union (ITU)
- World Tourism Data from the World Tourism Organization

This portal also provides access to the UN's *Monthly Bulletin of Statistics* which continues to be available in print. There is also an interactive interface for this source at unstats.un.org/unsd/mbs. This resource provides economic and social data for more than 200 countries, as well as industry figures. For example, it has industrial production indices; energy produc-

Table 7.1. Highlights from two sources that provide worldwide industry statistics

Title	Publisher	Description	URL
Industrial Commodity Statistics Yearbook	United Nations Statistics Division (UNSD)	Commodities (about 600) by country (200) and geography; ISIC Rev. 4, but 3.1 for some countries. Commodities (about 600) by country and region (around 200); ISIC Rev. 4, but 3.1 for some countries. Not exhaustive. Commodities included because of their overall importance to the world economy, as well as that of the outputs of certain ISIC industries. Data presented by Central Product Code. unstats.un.org/unsd/industry/icsy_intro.asp	data.un.org
International Yearbook of Industrial Statistics	United Nations Industrial Development Organization (UNIDO)	Statistics on level, growth, and structure of manufacturing at world, regional, and country levels. In the second part, data for major indicators of industrial statistics are presented at 3- and 4-digit level of ISIC by country. It is designed to facilitate international comparisons relating to manufacturing activities and industrial development and performance. www.unido.org/index.php?id=1001196	data.un.org (referred to as INDSTAT [UNIDO])

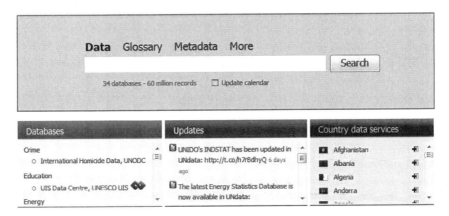

Figure 7.5.

tion figures; fuel imports; production figures for mining, manufacturing, and construction; international merchandise trade data; and retail trade indices. Data is available from 2000 to 2012 for certain series, such as gross domestic product (GDP).

OECD disseminates trade and other statistics gathered from its member countries and selected non-nonmember economics via its print publications, and online through the subscription database OECD iLibrary. In addition to providing the full-text content in electronic format for many of its print publications, the researcher is able to generate data on numerous topics at www.oecd-ilibrary.org/statistics. There is also a free version called OECD.Stat Extracts (stats.oecd.org) that has selected data. It provides statistics for thirty-four member countries as well as for Brazil, China, India, Indonesia, the Russian Federation, and South Africa on the "themes" in table 7.2.

More than one of the topics in table 7.2 could be relevant, depending on the industry being researched. The most obvious category with which to begin is "Industry and Services." This section has data for production and sales, figures from structural analysis (STAN) databases, structural and demographic business statistics, and timely indicators of entrepreneurship. Data offered via the STAN databases include the following variables:

- Number of persons engaged (total employment)
- Production (gross output), current prices

Table 7.2. Themes for OECD.Stat Extracts

General statistics	Agriculture and fisheries
Demography and population	Development
Economic projections	Education and training
Environment	Finance
Globalization	Health
Industry and services	International trade and balance of payments
Labor	Monthly economic indicators
National accounts	Prices and purchasing parities
Productivity	Public sector, taxation, and market regulation
Regional statistics	Science, technology, and patents
Social and welfare statistics	Transport
Transport	Other international organizations data
Others	

- Production (gross output), volumes
- Intermediate inputs, volumes
- Value added, volumes
- Labor costs, compensation of employees
- Wages and salaries

STAN data is provided for thirty-two OECD countries and can be used to analyze "industrial performance at a detailed level of activity across countries."[24] It is based on ISIC rev. 3, covering all activities including services. New data is incorporated in STAN as soon as it is obtainable. However, information is still dated by two years.

Nontrade Statistics — United States Government Sources

Other US government sources would potentially be useful for international industry research. If an industry is related to agriculture, the US Department of Agriculture (USDA) has important resources, one of which is the Economic Research Services (ERS) (www.ers.usda.gov/). Under the Data portion of the ERS website is the subject "Trade and International Markets" that could provide relevant information. For those working on a project related to transportation, the RITA Bureau of Transportation Statistics should not be ignored (www.bts.gov). Selected international data is also available in the *Statistical Abstract of the US* (www.census.gov/compendia/statab/). Categories for international-related statistics include agricultural production and trade, climate, environment, economy, finance expenditures, foreign commerce and aid, military, natural resources and energy, and prices. Another way to use this source is as an index. The tables that are in it identify the source of the data, as well as the website URL. The researcher can follow up on this and go directly to that site for more information. The 131st, 2012 edition is the last one to be published by the United States Census Bureau. However, access to this edition and others from 1878 to 2011 is available at the site for *Statistical Abstract*. In addition, Bernan Press, a ProQuest company, will continue to produce it with the 2013 edition.

As mentioned earlier, other countries have national statistical agencies that are responsible for the gathering and disseminating of their country's data. For example, the United Kingdom has its national statistics site at www.statistics.gov.uk/hub/index.html. Here, an individual can browse by theme and find international trade statistics in the "Business Energy" section.

There are online directories that provide links to these official national statistical websites. For example, the US Bureau of Labor Statistics provides a list linking to its "Statistical Sites" on the World Wide Web at www.bls.gov/bls/other.htm. The United Nations Economic Commission for Europe (UNECE) has one on its site at www.unece.org/stats/links.html.

COMMERCIAL PUBLICATIONS

In addition to the statistics available through international organizations and statistical offices of other governments, there are also commercial publications of international data.

Barnes Reports (www.barnesreports.com) is one example of a commercial product that provides industry statistics. In addition to publishing data for US industries organized by NAICS codes, Barnes has a series called World Industry & Market Outlook. Published annually, this series covers over 120 worldwide industries and more than 500 minor industries. Over 250 pages in length, a report will include the number of establishments, employment and sales totals for each industry, five-year trends in establishments and sales totals, industry financial ratios, and industry figures for the previous year. Barnes also has a Worldwide Industry series covering 120 industries for 45 of the largest countries in the world. For each of the countries covered, the latter will include industry descriptions, number of establishments in the industry, sales and employment trends, selected industry ratios, country comparisons, estimates of the number of firms by size (based on the number of employees), sales and employment estimated figures by size, estimated number of establishments, employment, and sales figures for subindustries. One can purchase these reports in print or in PDF format. The Worldwide Industry series is currently available through Business Source Complete.

Another commercial source of data comes from Icon Group International (www.icongrouponline.com), which, along with other statistics, annually produces industry/product reports "across 200 countries for over 2000 industry and product categories."[25] Selected series are:

- Global Industry Outlooks—Projected worldwide latent demand across countries.
- Global Trade Reports—Detailed import/export forecasts for 550+ categories: worldwide, by region, and for 180 countries.
- Regional Industry Outlooks—Latent demand, pro-forma financials, and more, for 2000 products across six regions.
- Industry Financial and Labor Productivity Benchmarks—Compares an industry's financial performance and gaps to global benchmarks.
- World City Segmentation Reports—Forecasts latent demand for each major city of the world.[26]

The data in these series are forward looking, and derived from or based on different information sources and/or econometric models; consequently there is always the possibility that actual data may be different from what was projected.[27] Reports are also available for purchase through market research aggregators like MarketResearch.com. An embargoed version of "World Market Forecasts," which is part of the Global Trade Reports series, is also available via Business Source Complete.

ProQuest Statistical Insight (formerly from LexisNexis) includes global data that comes from the Index to International Statistics (IIS). Sources include international organizations like the UN and its regional commissions and affiliated agencies, OECD, and the European Union. Types of data include "information on the population, business and financial activities, foreign trade, education, health, and other economic, demographic, and political characteristics of nations and world regions."[28] A subscription to this part of ProQuest Statistical Insight will provide access to the full-text reports. If not, there is a chance of obtaining a report through interlibrary loan as several universities will have the microfiche collection, which has 97 percent of the full text of the abstracts in IIS.

A strategy to use when in Statistical Insight is to note the citation for a desired item and check to see if a library has the source. For example, a search in this database found the following citation: Annual World Bank Conference on Development Economics, 2000. A search in the University of Denver's online catalog revealed that it was available electronically via the eLibrary database. One can also search for citations in search engines like Google and sometimes find an online version at no cost for certain reports. If a citation in this ProQuest database points to a periodical or journal, search in databases that index and provide full-text coverage of a specific publication to obtain the full-text from that database. An individual should contact his or her library's reference or information desk and ask for assistance if unfamiliar with navigating a library's online website and databases.

Another source for both international and US data is Responsive Data Services' (RDS) TableBase, available through Gale/Cengage. This source provides statistics originally published in other sources, such as trade publications, in tabular form. A search in this database has the potential to retrieve a relevant table because each table is indexed with appropriate subject headings. The full-text of the pertinent article in many cases is also available in TableBase. Each record for an item provides the citation to the source from where the tables were extracted, providing the researcher with a lead to more information, similar to the steps taken in the previous example.

ASSOCIATIONS AND ORGANIZATIONS

Many associations are set up to support a wide range of industries. These trade associations provide information and assistance to those who are affiliated with them, and often conduct research that is shared with their members either at a reduced price or as part of the membership. Most, if not all, of these associations have websites and where they might provide information about governmental policies that affect them, market research that they have undertaken, contact names, and conferences and events they are sponsoring. Although the majority of the content might be limited to its members, to get the most out of such a site, there are cases when some information is publicly available. If not, there might be an option enabling an individual to purchase a report, although at a nonmember rate. Associations may have the granular data in the timely manner that a researcher wants, but this type of data does not come freely.

One may be able to find a specific association for an industry, but may have to go broader. For instance, the product is sunscreen, it might be necessary to settle for an association for the cosmetics industry. On the other hand, an industry like scuba diving might have several relevant associations, although it may be outside the area of interest. For example, the National Association of Underwater Instructors (NAUI) and PADI: Professional Association of Diving Instructors are associations for scuba diving training, but they may have statistics useful for conducting an industry, as well as for market analysis.

Depending on the industry, international organizations and nongovernmental organizations (NGOs) can also be sources of industry information. NGOs are voluntary organizations that are usually focused on international relief development efforts. Examples are Amnesty International and the International Statistical Institute. This chapter has already identified sources for industry data provided by international organizations, including the United Nations, OECD, and the International Monetary Fund.

To identify worldwide associations or organizations, as well as nongovernmental organizations, print and electronic directories like Gale/Cengage's *Encyclopedia of Associations* (which focuses on the United States) and its companion, *Encyclopedia of Associations, International Organizations* are useful. There is also the database, Associations Unlimited, which includes both US and international content.

Another source is the *Yearbook of International Organizations*, edited by the Union of International Associations since 1948, and published by Brill as of 2011.[29] This source offers more that 65,000 "civil society organizations in 300 countries and territories."[30] Content includes international nongovernmental organizations (INGOs) and intergovernmental organizations (IGOs), but excludes those that are for-profit. It is offered in print, online, and by data streaming. Customized directories can be designed for a user and delivered either in print or PDF format.

There are also free online sources that provide listings of international organizations and/or associations. For example, the United Nations provides a directory of organizations that have an official relation with it at ngo-db.unesco.org/s/or/en. Michigan State University's GlobalEDGE provides a list of international organizations at globaledge.msu.edu/Global-Resources/organizations. The Federation of International Trade Associations (www.fita.org/) is yet another source. FITA has "450 association members and 450,000 linked company members dedicated to the promotion of international trade, import-export, international logistics management, international finance and more."[31] The associations included in the directory are primarily from the United States, with a few coming from Canada, Mexico, and one from Bermuda.

Many associations and organizations are already on the web, so one can also use a search engine like Google or Yahoo! and have a chance of locating relevant groups.

Associations and organizations may also sponsor conferences or trade shows. Since these types of events may have presentations on certain industry trends, as well as vendor exhibits, a researcher may learn about what is happening in the industry by attending one.

ARTICLES

Whether researching a niche industry or a traditional one, the strategy should also include searching for articles from trade publications, newspapers, regional/local publications, and newswires. Because these publications are often published daily, weekly, or monthly, the articles in these sources enable the researcher to update and supplement the information obtained from industry overviews, statistical sources, and other secondary resources. Some newspapers and wire services, such as the *Wall Street Journal* or *Financial Times* provide some free content on the web, although relevant articles will probably have to be purchased. In addition, sometimes a news item reports the release of a recent market report or provides current statistical information about an industry. Trade publications may have information about competitors, and economic, regulatory, social, technological issues that are affecting an industry. Regional or local newspapers and magazines may have information about an industry on a regional/local level. Databases rich in trade journals, national/regional/local newspapers/publications, and/or newswires include ABI/Inform, Business Insights: Essentials, Business Source Complete, Business Source Premier, Factiva, LexisNexis Academic, RDS Business & Industry, and Access World News. Another source, World News Connection, available from Dialog, is a database that provides English translations of articles that were originally published in the language of the source country.

There are also websites that identify to international newspapers. For instance, NewsLink (newslink.org/) identifies newspapers in a country, and provides links with access to them. GlobalEDGE has a listing of global regional sources at globaledge.msu.edu/Global-Resources/regional-news/.

LEVERAGING OTHER SOURCES

During the research process, be sure to take note of the sources cited in the information discovered and follow up on any leads. Other sources that could potentially provide important information about the industry are the annual reports from companies in an industry. For instance, such a publication might discuss the impact the state of the economy is having on a company as well as the industry. It often addresses competitive factors and might refer to social trends that the company may be dealing with.

Although market research databases focus primarily on the market for products or services, they also provide information about the industry. Researchers should try to determine whether a library has such sources and seek to access them. There are numerous market research databases available, including those from Frost & Sullivan, Gartner, IBC, Jupiter Research, Marketresearch.com, and Mintel. However, no single market research database covers all the types of industries researchers can come up with. One should be aware that some market research database publishers will prohibit their use in academic libraries if the information is for a field study or if it is be provided in any way to an actual company.

SOCIAL MEDIA

Other approaches that are becoming prevalent as a result of the rapid advancement of technology and the Internet include utilizing social media tools like LinkedIn, RSS feeds, and blogs. For instance, there are business executives who have signed up for LinkedIn, and they might provide some information about their companies that might be useful for industry research. A recent *Financial Times* article reported on the entry of Rupert Murdoch, a media tycoon, on Twitter.[32] Blogs are another source of information, especially given the trend for major newspapers, business publications, and government organizations to utilize this social media tool to provide information. For example, the *Financial Times* has several blogs at www.ft.com/intl/comment/blogs. The US Census Bureau and International Trade Administration have blogs at blogs.census.gov/ and blog.trade.gov respectively. Twitter feeds can also provide some information.

CONCLUSION

This chapter presented some of the strategies and sources that are available for researching industries. However, there are numerous situations when other approaches are needed in order to discover a unique resource that is only relevant to a given industry. In addition, as the researcher begins to require more detailed information or is researching niche industries, he or she will probably have to contact experts from sources around the world, including embassies, chambers of commerce, and those available through national governments, such as the export contacts provided by the United Kingdom at www.ukti.gov.uk/export/contactus.html or the United States at Export.gov.

LIST OF SOURCES

Databases

This is an alphabetical list of the fee-based databases mentioned in this chapter.

ABI/Inform (Ann Arbor, MI: ProQuest, 1971–), www.proquest.com/products_pq/descriptions/abi_inform.shtml.
Access World News (Naples, FL: Newsbank, 2004–), www.newsbank.com.
Associations Unlimited (Detroit, MI: Gale Research, 1995–), www.gale.cengage.com/.

Business Insights: Essentials (Farmington Hills, MI: Gale Cengage Learning, 2012–), www.cengagesites.com/Literature/782/gale-business-insights-global-essentials/.

Business Source Complete (Ipswich, MA: EBSCO Pub., 2005–), www.ebscohost.com/public/business-source-complete.

Country Commerce (New York: Economist Intelligence Unit, 2000–) www.eiu.com.

Emerging Markets Information Service (EMIS) (New York: Internet Securities, 2009–), www.securities.com/.

Factiva (New York: Dow Jones & Reuters, 2001–), www.dowjones.com/factiva/index.asp.

First Research (Austin, TX : First Research Inc., 2007–), www.firstresearch.com.

Freedonia Focus Market Research Portal (Cleveland, OH: Freedonia Group, 2001–), www.freedoniagroup.com.

Global Insight (Englewood, Co: IHS/Global, 2000–) www.ihs.com/products/global-insight/index.aspx.

Industry Profiles (New York: Standard & Poor's, 1998–), www.standardandpoors.com.

LexisNexis Academic (Dayton: OH: LexisNexis, Division of Reed Elsevier, 2002–), academic.lexisnexis.com/online-services/academic/academic-overview.aspx.

OECD iLibrary (Washington, D.C.: OECD, 2000–), www.oecd-ilibrary.org/statistics.

Passport Global Research System (for corporations) (London: UK; Chicago, IL: Euromonitor International, 1990s–), www.euromonitor.com/solutions.

Passport GMID (London: UK; Chicago, Il: Euromonitor International, 1990s–), www.euromonitor.com/passport-gmid.

Plunkett Research Online (Houston, TX: Plunkett Research, 2002–), www.plunkettresearch.com/ (28 June 2012).

ProQuest Statistical Insight (Ann Arbor, MI: ProQuest, 2010–), cisupa.proquest.com.

RDS Business and Industry (Farmington Hills, MI: Gale Group, 1994–), www.gale.cengage.com.

RDS Tablebase (Farmington, MI: Gale, 1996–), www.gale.cengage.com.

Yearbook of International Organizations Online (Leiden, the Netherlands: Brill, 2000–), www.uia.be/yearbook.

World News Connection (Washington: NTIS : Dialog, 1995–), wnc.dialog.com.

Websites

This is an alphabetical list of association, government, and publisher websites mentioned in this chapter.

Barnes Reports, www.barnesreports.com (28 June 2012).

Business Monitor, www.businessmonitor.com (28 June 2012).

Bureau van Dijk, www.bvdinfo.com/Home.aspx?lang=en-GB (28 June 2012).

Datamonitor, www.datamonitor.com (10 October 2012).

Export.gov (28 June 2012).

Federation of International Trade Associations, www.fita.org/ (28 June 2012).

Financial Times, www.ft.com/ (28 June 2012).

Financial Times Blogs, www.ft.com/intl/comment/blogs (28 June 2012).

GlobalEDGE, "Organizations," globaledge.msu.edu/Global-Resources/organizations (28 June 2012).

GlobalEDGE, "Regional News," globaledge.msu.edu/Global-Resources/regional-news/ (28 June 2012).

Icon Group International, www.icongrouponline.com (28 June 2012).

Infogroup, www.infogroup.com (28 June 2012).

International Trade Administration, www.trade.gov (28 June 2012).

International Trade Administration blog, blog.trade.gov (28 June 2012).

NewsLink, newslink.org/ (28 June 2012).

OECD.StatExtracts database, stats.oecd.org (28 June 2012).

Research and Innovative Technology Administration (RITA), Bureau of Transportation Statistics, www.bts.gov (28 June 2012).

UK National Statistics, www.statistics.gov.uk/hub/index.html (28 June 2012).

UN comtrade portal, comtrade.un.org (28 June 2012).

UN Monthly Bulletin of Statistics, unstats.un.org/unsd/mbs (28 June 2012).

UN Service Trade, unstats.un.org/unsd/servicetrade/ (28 June 2012).

UNCTADStats database, unctadstat.unctad.org/ (28 June 2012).

United Nations Economic Commission for Europe, "Links to Official Statistical Organizations," www.unece.org/stats/links.html (28 June 2012).

United Nations Educational, Scientific, and Cultural Organization (UNESCO), "Organizations Maintaining Official Relations with UNESCO," ngo-db.unesco.org/s/or/en (28 June 2012).

United Nations Statistics Division, *Industrial Commodity Statistics Yearbook*, unstats.un.org/unsd/industry/icsy_intro.asp (28 June 2012).

United States Census Bureau blog, blogs.census.gov/ (28 June 2012).

United States Census Bureau, Foreign Trade, www.census.gov/foreign-trade/about/index.html (28 June 2012).

United States Census Bureau, Foreign Trade, NAICS Related—Party portal, sasweb.ssd.census.gov/relatedparty/ (28 June 2012).

United States Census Bureau, Foreign Trade Division, *USA Trade Online*, https://www.usatradeonline.gov/ (28 June 2012).

United States Census Bureau, International Statistical Agencies, List of Official Statistical Sites, www.census.gov/aboutus/stat_int.html (28 June 2012).

United States Census Bureau, *Statistical Abstract of the United States*, www.census.gov/compendia/statab/ (28 June 2012).

United States Department of Agriculture (USDA), Economic Research Services (ERS), www.ers.usda.gov/ (28 June 2012).

United States Department of Labor, Bureau of Labor Statistics, "Statistical Sites on the World Wide Web," www.bls.gov/bls/other.htm (28 June 2012).

University of Central Florida Libraries, STAT-USA—links to sources, "GLOBUS & NTDB," guides.ucf.edu/content.php?pid=141826&sid=1209051 (28 June 2012).

US Commercial Service, Market Research Library (MRL), www.buyusainfo.net (28 June 2012).

US Department of Commerce, International Trade Administration, TradeStats Express, tse.export.gov/TSE/TSEhome.aspx (28 June 2012).

United States International Trade Commission, "HTS Online Reference Tool," hts.usitc.gov/ (28 June 2012).

United States International Trade Commission, Interactive Tariff and Trade DataWeb, dataweb.usitc.gov/ (28 June 2012).

Wall Street Journal, online.wsj.com (27 June 2012).

Wisertrade, www.wisertrade.org (28 June 2012).

World Bank, Doing Business series, www.doingbusiness.org/ (28 June 2012).

WTO International Trade and Tariff Data website, www.wto.org/english/res_e/statis_e/statis_e.htm (28 June 2012).

NOTES

1. *Dictionary of Business*, s.v. "industry," www.credoreference.com/acbbusiness/industry (15 Sept. 2011).

2. *Collins Dictionary of Economics*. (London: Collins, 2006). s.v. "industry," www.credoreference.com/entry/collinsecon/industry (15 Sept. 15, 2011).

3. Michael Porter, "Five Competitive Forces that Shape Strategy," *Harvard Business Review* 86, no. 1 (Jan. 2008).

4. Michael Porter, *Competitive Strategy: Techniques for Analyzing Industries and Competitors* (New York: The Free Press, 1980), 378.

5. SWOT means "strengths, weaknesses, opportunities, and strengths." The first two characteristics refer to internal variables over which a company has control, while the last two are external factors over which the company has no control.

6. Internet Archive Wayback Machine, "STAT/USA® Internet™," web.archive.org/web/20110711142100/http://www.stat-usa.gov/ (19 Sept. 2011).

7. World Bank. "About Doing Business," www.doingbusiness.org/about-us (27 Sept. 2011).

8. World Bank, *Doing Business 2012, Doing Business in a More Transparent World,* (Washington D.C.: The International Bank for Reconstruction and Development/The World Bank, 2012), www.doingbusiness.org/reports/global-reports/doing-business-2012 (5 March 2012).

9. IFC, International Finance Corporation, The World Bank, *Doing Business, Ease of Doing Business in Brazil, 2012,* www.doingbusiness.org/data/exploreeconomies/brazil/ (5 March 2012).

10. At the time of this writing, *First Research* was being managed and distributed by Mergent.

11. Euromonitor International, Industries, "Industry reports," www.euromonitor.com/industries (7 Oct. 2011).

12. IHS Global Insight, www.ihs.com/products/global-insight/ (13 Oct. 2011).

13. John Cullen and Parboteeah K. Praveen, *International Business: Strategy and the Multinational Company* (New York: Routledge, 2010), 51.

14. US Census Bureau, "Foreign Trade," www.census.gov/foreign-trade/ (20 Oct. 2011).

15. USA Trade Online, https://www.usatradeonline.gov/ (20 Oct. 2011).

16. WISER, "WISERTrade," www.wisertrade.org/home/about/wisertrade_info.pdf (20 Oct. 2011).

17. United Nations International Trade Statistics Knowledgebase, "What is UN Comtrade," unstats.un.org/unsd/tradekb/Knowledgebase/What-is-UN-Comtrade (20 Oct. 2011).

18. United Nations. Department of Economic and Social Affairs, "Read Me First," http://unstats.un.org/unsd/servicetrade/docs/read%20me%20first%20-%20UN%20Service%20Trade.pdf (29 Oct. 2011).

19. United Nations. Department of Economic and Social Affairs. Statistics Division, *Statistical Yearbook* (New York: United Nations, 2008), iii.

20. *Statistical Yearbook* (New York: United Nations, 2008), 5.

21. United Nations. Industrial Commodity Statistics Yearbook (New York: United Nations, 2009), vii.

22. United Nations Industrial Development Organization, *International Yearbook of Industrial Statistics* (MA: Edward Elgar Publishing, Inc., 2010), 7.

23. *International Yearbook of Industrial Statistics*, 7.

24. STAN database for Structural Analysis, "Metadata," stats.oecd.org/Index.aspx (29 Oct. 2011).

25. Icon Group International, "About Us," www.icongrouponline.com/about.asp?sid=342481099 (29 Oct. 2011).

26. Icon Group International, "About Us."

27. Icon Group International, "Disclaimers, Warrantees, and User Agreement Provisions," www.icongrouponline.com/disclaimers.asp?sid=342481099 (29 Oct. 2011).

28. *ProQuest Statistical Insight.* "LexisNexis Statistical User Guide," cisupa.proquest.com/ksc_assets/subscriber_resources/LexisNexis_Statistical_User_Guide.pdf (29 Oct. 2011).

29. *Yearbook of International Organizations*, www.uia.be/ybvolall (28 June 2012).

30. Union of International Associations, *Yearbook of International Organizations*, www.uia.be/yearbook (31 Oct. 2011).

31. FITA, The Federation of International Trade Associations, "Welcome to the FITA.org Global Trade Portal," www.fita.org (31 Oct. 2011).

32. Tim Bradshaw and Richard Waters, "Twitter Turns Up Heat on Ambitions," *Financial Times*, 6 Jan. 2012, www.ft.com/intl/cms/s/0/e3182574-3886-11e1-9ae1-00144feabdc0.html#axzz1ii4AzOsC (6 Jan. 2012).

EIGHT

International Market Research

Market research is undertaken when a company wants to sell a product or service to a consumer. The American Marketing Association defines market research as "the systematic gathering, recording, and analyzing of data with respect to a particular market, where market refers to a specific customer group in a specific geographic area."[1] Market research is used to develop a marketing plan, "a document composed of an analysis of the current marketing situation, opportunities and threats analysis, marketing objectives, marketing strategy, action programs, and projected or proforma income (and other financial) statements."[2] Market research provides the facts that allow a company to choose the market (consumer, customer) for its product or service based on the potential, accessibility, and similarity of buyers or users.[3] International marketing extends these activities beyond national borders.[4]

The research process includes identifying those external, uncontrollable factors that will affect the performance of a product or service in a market. This involves conducting a PESTLE analysis, which consists of finding out what political, economic, socioeconomic–cultural–religious, technological, legal, and environmental factors exist that will have a positive or negative impact on efforts to enter a market. The research will also include finding information about the target market, whether it has money to spend, and determining where it is spending its money. Thus, market research should include the following:

1. Identify the market—Who are they (country, demographics, culture, idiosyncrasies, income, buying behavior, lifestyles)?
2. Screen the political situation—What politics are applicable that will affect the situation for marketing this product globally? Is the political situation stable? What are government attitudes on foreign investment?[5]

3. Determine economic trends—What is the country's economic growth rate? Unemployment? Foreign direct investment? Exchange rates?[6] What effect is the global financial crisis having? What other economic indicators will have an impact?
4. Screen for sociocultural factors—Consider language and communication, religion, dietary if relevant, cultural orientation (cognition styles), attitudes, beliefs and value systems, trends, income distribution, and any other elements that will affect the market.
5. Identify technological developments—Are there any innovations that must be dealt with or that can be harnessed in order to be successful? What is the state of Internet availability?
6. Screen the legal setting—What laws or regulations in a country will affect the efforts of marketing the product or service.
7. Determine if environmental movements exist—Are there environmental regulations that must be followed?[7] Green issues, recycling?
8. Match product to country—It wouldn't make sense to introduce wool ponchos in a country or region that is consistently warm.

The marketing plan is made up of the marketing mix, referred to as the four P's; these are product, price, promotion, and place. A business has control over these items. Product is made up of its features, brand name, packaging, service, and warranty.[8] Part of dealing with this "P" is ensuring that it is appropriate for the target. This may involve modifying it to meet any factors that would affect the success of a product in a specific market, such as those dealing with culture, religion, and/or regulations. Depending on the product, price will deal with what the item sells for before any reductions in price, discounts offered, allowances, credit terms, and/or payment period. Promotion is done to entice the consumer to purchase the product, which could be made up of any of the following methods: advertising, personal selling, sales promotion, and/or direct marketing. Place deals with distribution channel, which would be any of the following: outlets, channels, coverage, transportation, stock level.[9]

Market research is crucial to making the most effective decisions when developing the marketing plan. It will require one to do secondary research and primary research. "Secondary research is the most widely used method of collecting data and involves summarizing or synthesizing existing research from sources such as books, magazine articles, white papers, websites, etc."[10] Other sources of secondary information are worldwide government entities like the US Department of Commerce and the US Census, UK Trade and Investment, trade associations, and commercial publishers like Business Monitor International, Datamonitor, Economist Intelligence Unit (EIU), and Euromonitor. The process usually begins with information from secondary sources to find out what has already been published, potentially decreasing the cost of the overall research process.

The individual will probably have to engage in the next step, primary research, because the information that is found may not be as granular as needed to make a decision to enter a market. This will be especially true if the product or service is in a niche market. Primary research involves collecting new or primary data by "(1) observing people and (2) asking them questions."[11]

The next part of this chapter identifies secondary sources that are available for market research. The researcher should be able to extract from them the answers to those questions posed earlier as well as reveal others that need to be dealt with. In addition, while reviewing sources, the individual should also be able to extract information related to the 4Ps. These resources are grouped under the following categories:

- Sources for country background
- Resources for culture
- Market research reports and aggregators
- Statistical sources
- Resources for advertising and channels of distribution

SOURCES FOR COUNTRY BACKGROUND

Some of the answers to the questions posed earlier will be found in the resources that provide overviews of countries, and are covered in chapter 3, Resources with World Coverage. For example, using the *CIA World Factbook* will provide some general answers to a country's political situation and economic trends, as well as information about the culture and regulations related to international trade. The researcher will be able to identify some of the environmental factors (socioeconomic indicators, political environment, and culture) that are relevant.

The *CIA World Factbook* comes from the US government's Central Intelligence Agency. This source will enable the researcher to become familiar to the country being studied. Each report has nine sections, any of which would provide important background information. For instance the economy section includes gross domestic product (GDP), labor force, and unemployment-rate data. The section referred to as people and society provides the population, and identifies ethnic groups, religions, languages, and age structure.

EIU (www.eiu.com) produces several sources for country information. These include the Country Report series focusing on the political and economic outlook for 190 countries; Country Forecast, dealing with the business environment in 92 countries; and Country Risk, providing insight on the credit risks a business might face when doing business in more than 120 countries.

Country Watch is another producer of several series of country information. One of these is Country Reviews, which includes demographic,
political, economic, business, cultural, and environmental information. It
also has indexes for political risk, political stability, economic performance, foreign investment, and human development.

An important component for a researcher to consider is the political
risk associated with a specific country. Knowing the perils informs the
researcher whether or not to enter a market, or educate him or her of
elements that have to be addressed. *Political Risk Yearbook* is a source that
can assist in such an evaluation. Updated annually, the resource is produced by the Political Risk Services (PRS) Group. A monthly newsletter
that summarizes PRS' latest forecasts for economic and political changes
is available by subscription.

Numerous other sources that provide country information have not
been covered here. These include free websites that focus on a region or
country, such as those created for economic trade blocs like MERCOSUR
or ASEAN. Some of these types of resources are identified in chapter 4,
which covers regional sources. There are also other sources from international organizations like the United Nations, World Bank, International
Monetary Fund, OECD, United Nations Conference on Trade and Development (UNCTAD), and the World Trade Organization (WTO). These
particular international organizations provide databases or specific reports from which one can obtain a wide range of statistics that can be
used for market research. Sources from these organizations were covered
in chapter 7, which deals with industry research.

RESOURCES FOR CULTURE

It is important to find out about a country's culture when planning to
enter a market. Failure to do this has resulted in a few embarrassments
for companies around the world. There are various sources that focus on
this, including *CultureGrams, Executive Planet,* and *Kiss, Bow, or Shake
Hands.*

CultureGrams was developed by the David Kennedy Center for International Studies at Brigham Young University. It provides a synopsis of
the daily customs, lifestyle, politics, and economics for 200 countries,
each US state, and all 13 Canadian provinces and territories. It is available
in print and offered online through ProQuest, A researcher can also purchase individual units in PDF format for download.

Kiss, Bow, or Shake Hands provides background on a country, tips on
doing business, cultural orientation (which includes cognitive styles, values, decision making), protocol for addressing people, dress, dining, gift
giving, business practices, and cultural notes. The most recent edition is
dated 2006. There is a subscription available for the online version of this

resource. *Kiss, Bow, or Shake Hands* is also available for Asia, Europe, and Latin America. These are *Kiss, Bow, or Shake Hands Asia: How to Do Business in 12 Asian Countries*; *Kiss, Bow, or Shake Hands Europe: How to Do Business in 25 European Countries*, and *Kiss, Bow, or Shake Hands Latin America: How to Do Business in 18 Latin American Countries*.

The researcher can also identify other sources by searching Amazon.com, other bookseller websites, or using a search engine like Google. For example, when searching for the book *Kiss, Bow, or Shake Hands* at Amazon.com, the results will identify other sources on the topic. Included are *Multicultural Manners: Essential Rules of Etiquette* (2005) by Norine Dresser; *Cultural Intelligence: A Guide to Working with People from Other Cultures*, (2004) by Brooks Peterson; and *Do's and Taboos Around the World* (1993) by Roger E. Axtell. Amazon.com sells print and some electronic versions of this type of book for a nominal amount; the latter can be downloaded to a Kindle. For those who don't want to purchase anything, a nearby library, either academic or public, will most likely have some sources that deal with culture around the world. Search a library's online catalog using a keyword search strategy like "international business and culture." If one is not familiar with how to search in a library catalog, contact a local library's reference desk or information desk for assistance in identifying books on this topic.

In addition to sources that specifically focus on culture, one can also look in sources that provide information on how to do business in a country, such as the US Commercial Services' *Commercial Guides* that will be presented later in this chapter. This series provides business etiquette for a country in the chapter, "Business Travel." This section also covers language, local time, business hours, and holidays.

MARKET RESEARCH REPORTS

A researcher often seeks that ideal market research report that deals with the specific product or service one wants to sell as well as the specific country/market. These reports often have answers to many of the questions posed earlier, such as who is buying the product, what is the income for those who purchase it, on what does the target market spend its money, and whether there are any consumer trends of which to be aware. They might also cover other elements of market research, such as promotion and advertising. Depending on the product and/or service, it may or may not exist. There are a wide range of sources, from the Internet to market research aggregators, to a specific market research firm that may have such a document. Such a report usually costs several thousands of dollars. In addition, as the need for information becomes more granular, the researcher will undoubtedly have to conduct some primary research. For example, a researcher might need information about the market for snowboards in a city in France, including the psychographics of the population in that area. Although there might be general demographics for the location, data for the number of snowboards owned by the population of that location, or the psychographics in the area might not exist. Even so, it never hurts to look for the information because one can be surprised by what is available.

A source that freely provides research reports is the US Commercial Services Market Research Library (MRL) (this was also covered in the industry section). The US Commercial Service "is the trade promotion arm of the US Department of Commerce's International Trade Administration. US Commercial Service trade professionals in over 100 US cities and in more than 75 countries help US companies get started in exporting or increase sales to new global markets."[12] The MRL interface provides access to *Country Commercial Guides*, *Market Research Reports*, and *Best Market Reports* (figure 8.1). These reports were discussed in the industry chapter, but will be covered in this chapter as it relates to market research. To access any of the reports available, one must be a US company or student/researcher and register at Export.gov.

Country Commercial Guides is a series that provides information about how to do business in over 100 countries. These guides are a good beginning for anyone who wants to introduce a product or service into a spe-

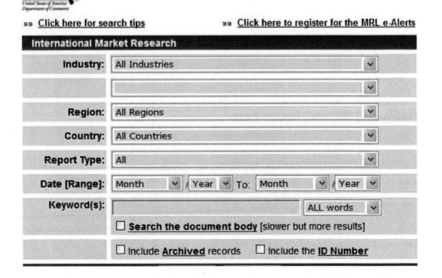

Figure 8.1.

cific country. These publications are written by experts located in US embassies worldwide. The *Doing Business in Russia: 2011 Country Commercial Guide for US Companies* includes the following chapters (all guides in the series have the same structure):

- Chapter 1: Doing Business in Russia
- Chapter 2: Political and Economic Environment
- Chapter 3: Selling US Products and Services
- Chapter 4: Leading Sectors for US Export and Investment
- Chapter 5: Trade Regulations, Customs, and Standards
- Chapter 6: Investment Climate
- Chapter 7: Trade and Project Financing
- Chapter 8: Business Travel
- Chapter 9: Contacts, Market Research, and Trade Events
- Chapter 10: Guide to Our Services

Chapter 3, "Selling US Products and Services," includes information about market challenges; strategies for entering a market; and how to sell products in the country, including distribution channels, trade promotion and advertising, pricing, and information about ten main sectors and the opportunities available. For example, the Cosmetics/Toiletries section in chapter 4 provides the following information that can be related to channels of distribution and consumer attitudes:

> The assortment of products in retail chains has changed too with middle-market and mass-market brands complementing exclusive products. The share of mass-market products in retail chains has grown to 20%. An additional channel for mass-market and middle-market brands, as well as curative cosmetics, is pharmacies, especially pharmacy chains. Russian consumers perceive [sic] cosmetics sold through pharmacies to be safer and more effective.[13]

MRL also provides *Market Research Reports* and *Best Market Reports*. These can be retrieved by using one of the nineteen categories listed in table 8.1.

It is also possible to select from over 230 countries or regions, ranging from ADB (Asian Development Bank) to Newly Independent States to World Bank, or search across "All Regions."

Both the Market Research and Best Market Reports identify and explain the opportunities that are available to US exporters for specific industries in specific countries and/or regions. Depending on the individual report, it may include relevant market data, demand, prospects, and issues; regulations, tariffs, and taxes; and resources and contacts. The contacts will be useful if one needs to conduct primary research.

The Market Research Report section has more than 52,700 reports, and around 1,500 that are current. These reports are generally two to ten pages in length, and cover a wide range of industries in countries and regions. It is possible get an idea of what is covered by looking at some of

Table 8.1. Industry categories in MRL

All Industries	
Aerospace and defense	Agribusiness
Apparel and textiles	Automotive and ground transportation
Chemicals, petrochemicals, and composites	Construction, building, and heavy equipment
Consumer goods and home furnishings	Energy and mining
Environmental technologies	Food processing and packaging
Health technologies	Industrial equipment and supplies
Information and communication	Marine industries
Paper, printing, and graphic arts	Security and safety
Services	Used and reconditioned equipment

the titles listed below. Although these reports are not long, they provide resources and contacts which to use for further research.

- Canada: Medical Tourism to Florida (8/16/2011)
- Franchising in Portugal (9/22/2011)
- Germany: The Plastics Market: Situation and Trends (July 2011)
- Italy: Overview of Toiletries and Cosmetics (10/03/2011)
- Japan: Cloud Computing Market (9/27/2011)
- The Leisure Boats Market in Turkey (9/23/2011)
- Mexico: Overview of the Artwork Industry (6/19/2012)
- Motorcycles in the Czech Republic (6/6/2011)
- Plastics Raw Material in Turkey (6/1/2012)

The Best Market Report section consists of over 180 documents, 60 of which are current. This section also covers a wide range of topics. For example, another one is Austria: Dental Industry Market Brief 2011. This nine-page report provides information about market demand for dental products, best product prospects to consider introducing into the market, tips for entering the market and marketing the product, and contacts.

Publications included in both the Market Research Reports and Best Market Reports section are written by commercial specialists at US embassies around the world; they provide an analysis of selected industries and markets.

It is reasonable to conclude that if the US government has agencies that provide support and information to the US business that wants to take its products and services abroad, that other country governments do as well. Consequently, one strategy is to identify the government agency that supports trade in a country of interest and then, once found, explore the site for information. To find these agencies for different nations, one can use the International Trade Centre's "Directory of Trade Promotion

Organizations and Other Trade Support Institutions" webpage (www.intracen.org/exporters/trade-support-institutions-by-country/). This source identifies both private and official government organizations that support trade in a country. For example, it identifies the Australian Trade Commission as one of the support groups for Australia. Information provided for it includes the URL for the website, location address, contacts emails, and phone numbers. This website has a section called "Invest in Australia," which includes a link for "Opportunities in Australia." By clicking on the link, the researcher will be able to learn about the available options for investing in Australia in nine sectors: financial services, clean energy, advanced manufacturing, biotechnology, infrastructure, agribusiness, food and beverage, ICT, and resources.

As the research process advances and information needs become more specific and granular, and conducting primary research, it might be useful to identify market research reports or publishers who produce material in specific areas. With more than 720 publishers and consulting firms from around the world using MarketResearch.com as a way to deliver their publications, this is a good place to look for material. This site is freely searchable, but the reports will have to be purchased. Some of the publishers in this portal also have websites where one can search for their specific reports. Several of them are listed next. The reports from these companies can also be scrutinized for industry information.

BCC Research

This firm covers and conducts detailed analysis for industries in nineten major sectors. The reports are technical in nature. For example, the food and beverage industry covers food testing, supplements, sweeteners, and packaging technology. Reports in this category include *Nutraceuticals: Global Markets* and *Processing Technologies, World Markets for Fermentation Ingredients*. The price of individual reports is several thousands of dollars.

Euromonitor International

Euromonitor researches industry, country, company, and consumer lifestyle. It covers 200 market and company categories across 80 countries, and their demographic, lifestyle, and socioeconomic data covers 206 countries. Reports include "data and analysis of market size, distribution channel analysis, market trends."[14] Online databases are available for three target groups: Passport for the commercial market; Passport GMID (Global Market Information Database) for government and export departments, business schools and university libraries, information centers in banks, consultancies, and advertising agencies; and Research Monitor for libraries. To get an idea of what Euromonitor publishes, consider the

following report: "Emerging Spending Habits of Pet Owners for 2010."
Learn about the trend in pet cosmetics if interested. Consumer lifestyle
and demographic print series include *Consumer Lifestyles in . . . [name of
country] in 2030: The Future Demographic.* Their global print reports include *World Consumer Income and Expenditure Patterns, World Consumer
Lifestyles Databook,* and *Future Demographic—Global Population Forecasts to
2020.*

Forrester

This company provides insight into technology-related industries
worldwide. Geographical coverage includes Africa, Asia Pacific, Latin
America, the Middle East, and North America. The reports fall under ten
industry categories which includes consumer electronics and technology,
energy and utilities, financial services, healthcare and life sciences, manufacturing, media and entertainment, public sector, retail, transportation
and logistics, and travel. Reports include analysis of new markets, consumer behavior, and new technology trends.

Frost and Sullivan

Frost and Sullivan's analysts provide detailed coverage of the following industries: aerospace and defense, automotive and transportation,
chemicals, materials and food, electronics and security, energy and power supplies, environment and building technologies, healthcare, industrial automation and process control, information and communication technologies, and measurement and instrumentation. They also do custom
research.

Gartner

This firm's research and analysis focuses on information technology
worldwide. Industries covered are banking and investment services, education, energy and utilities, government, healthcare providers, insurance,
manufacturing, media, and retail. Their reports provide scenarios, key
management issues, and strategic planning assumptions for the industry
covered. Intelligence on the impact of employing initiatives such as Ap-
plication Overhaul, Cloud Computing, and Virtualization, as well as insights on how to implement them is available. They also do customized
research.

International Data Corporation

IDC is a company that conducts worldwide market intelligence on
information technology, telecommunications, and consumer technology.

They have over 1,000 analysts providing "global, regional, and local expertise on technology and industry opportunities and trends in over 110 countries worldwide."[15] Reports can be purchased as needed, or one can set up a subscription to their various services, such as their tracking services for certain IT products in specific markets (i.e., *Middle East Quarterly PC Tracker Expanded Country Set: Segment by Channel* or *Africa Quarterly PC Tracker Expanded Country Set: Notebook by Screen Size* and a range of other offerings).

Mintel

Mintel provides market intelligence for consumer products and services. Reports include consumer attitudes and spending, market segmentation, and trends that will affect the market and its customers. Its Global Market Navigator provides an interactive portal where the researcher can get market snapshots for products in nineteen industries for forty-seven countries. These fact sheets include market size and forecast for a product, socioeconomic data for the country, and market share by company.

e-Marketer

This company provides analysis and insights into digital marketing, media, and commerce as well as Internet trends. Its process filters information conducted by thousands of worldwide sources and presents that information within the context of a specific topic. One can also subscribe to its daily newsletter and receive it for free.

Instead of searching the individual sites of the market research firms previously described, another strategy would be to search a market research report aggregator website. An individual can also purchase reports directly from them. Several are covered in the next section.

Global Information, Inc.

This company covers hundreds of market research publishers worldwide. In addition to providing market research reports, it serves as a facilitator to identify research analysts for clients requiring customized research.

MarketResearch.com

This company, mentioned earlier, has a pool of over 300,000 market research reports from more than 700 main global publishers. Areas covered are consumer goods, food and beverage, heavy industry, life sciences, marketing and market research, public sector, service industries, technology, and media. Users can freely search the site and, if a report is identified, it can be purchased from MarketResearch.com or directly from the publisher. This company offers an academic package for university and college libraries referred to as MarketResearch.com Academic. It includes reports published by Packaged Facts, Kalorama Information, MarketLooks, and Specialists in Business Intelligence; it is a subset of everything the company covers.

ReportLinker

This is a search engine designed to find information from publicly available resources, such as embassies and governments, and premium content provided by publishers such as BCC Research, Business Monitor, Datamonitor, Euromonitor, Freedonia, and IBISWorld. Areas covered are agribusiness, consumer goods, heavy industry, high tech and media, life sciences, and services. The database is freely searchable, but to access either the publicly available content or the premium content, one has to pay for it.

Research and Markets

With this company's pool of 1,517,100 documents, it is possible to identify reports or monographs published by well-known firms like Business Monitor International, Frost & Sullivan, IBISWorld, and John Wiley & Sons. The following categories can be searched: telecommunications and computing, business and finance,manufacturing and construction, pharmaceutical and healthcare, consumer and retail, government and public sector, and energy and transport. There is also a way to search for reports for a country or company reports at the website for this aggregator.

There are many academic libraries and major public libraries that subscribe to some of the commercial services that have already been mentioned. Consequently, anybody who is a student or faculty at an academic institution should contact its library and find out if it might subscribe to any market research databases. If the researcher is not affiliated with a college or university, but lives in a metro area, use the area's public library and determine whether it might have subscriptions to market research databases. Depending on the terms of a license between the publisher and the library, a user not associated with the library may be able to access a report.

STATISTICAL SOURCES

Demographic (sex, age, ethnicity) statistics and socioeconomic data (income, level of education, etc.) are some of the categories of data needed in the market research process. Success in finding relevant information will depend on the type of product and the country being considered. For instance, obtaining general demographic and socioeconomic data will be easier to gather as opposed to finding the demographics and psychographics of snowboarders in a specific town in France. This portion of the chapter will identify some of the standard sources for statistics. One would then have to incorporate other research methods to find data linked closer to a product.

Several international organizations provide demographic and socioeconomic data. These include the United Nations (UN), Organization for Economic and Co-operative Development (OECD), and World Bank. The US Census Bureau's International Program also participates in gathering and disseminating selected worldwide data. The first three sources publish print and electronic versions of titles that would potentially be useful. For instance, the United Nations publishes *Demographic Yearbook*, OECD has the *Economic Surveys*, and World Bank puts out *Gender Statistics*. They also provide interactive databases that allow one to retrieve information for different types of data sets, such as demographic (age, sex), economic (GDP), and social (education and employment) statistics.

The United Nations provides a wide range of data that can be used by market researchers. An obvious source is the *Demographic Yearbook*. Data in this source is derived from surveys received by the UN Statistics Division that had been sent to 230 national offices. The *Yearbook* provides demographic and vital statistics, including population by age, sex, and urban and rural residence; live births by age of mother and sex of child; and mortality and nuptiality data. It also issues special editions covering topics such as "economic activity, educational attainment, household characteristics, housing, ethnicity and language, among others."[16] This yearbook is available electronically at unstats.un.org/unsd/demographic/products/dyb/dybsets/2008%20DYB.pdf. Individual sets of data from this yearbook are available at: unstats.un.org/unsd/demographic/products/dyb/dyb2008.htm.

Currently the UN also provides data from this source, as well as other key UN databases and international sources such as the OECD, the International Telecommunication Union, and World Bank, through the Undata portal (data.un.org). Covering over 200 countries, users are able to access a large number of data sets in various areas. Some specific ones for market research include gender information, indicators on women and men, and demographic statistics.

If the researcher wants to know the population for various cities in a country for a range of years, Undata is a good option. The downside to the database is that, although it does have recent data, some of it may be older than desired.

OECD is another international organization that gathers and disseminates through a wide range of print and digital publications and through interactive databases. Currently OECD provides a free searchable database called OECD StatExtracts (stats.oecd.org/Index.aspx) that contains selected data. This database allows browsing and searching on twenty-two OECD-defined themes, including demography and population, economic projections, monthly economic indicators, pricing and purchasing power parities, and social and welfare statistics. Country-specific statistical profiles are provided as well. Although there is some free data provided at this site, a subscription to OECDIlibrary is needed to get fuller access to the data.

OECDIlibrary offers online access to OECD's books, papers, and statistics, as well as a gateway to its data and analysis. The researcher can select specific data sets relevant to the PESTLE analysis described earlier in the chapter. For instance, the database has economic indicators, education statistics, employment and labor market statistics, and social expenditure statistics. Key tables are available for the same topics; that is, economics, education, employment, labor markets, and social issues.

OECDIlibrary also provides access to flagship monographs like OECD Economic Factbook and OECD Outlook. Another publication available is *Society at a Glance*, which has general context indicators (i.e., household income), self-sufficiency indicators (i.e., employment, education spending), equity indicators (poverty, income difficulties), health indicators (life expectancy, water and air quality), and social cohesion indicators (trust, confidence in social institutions).

The World Bank is an organization that provides financial and technical support to developing countries across the world. Its publications cover twenty-nine subjects, including culture and development, education, gender, health, nutrition, and population. Data can be obtained from data.worldbank.org/. This is an open initiative project whereby one uses a single interface to pull data from such World Bank publications as World Development Indicators, Africa Development Indicators, and Gender Statistics.

US Census also gathers and analyzes demographic, economic, and geographic statistics around the world. Its "International Programs" website (www.census.gov/population/international/) provides the International Data Base (IDB). The website also provides links to other international statistical agencies, survey and census activities, and some of the older publications (such as *An Aging World*: 2008).

IDB consists of demographic indicators for countries and areas of the world with a population of 5,000 or more. These indicators include population, growth rate, fertility rate, births, life expectancy at birth, infant mortality rate, deaths, and net number of immigrants. This data is available for a country or region from 1950 to 2050. The database also provides tables and graphs for world population by age and sex, trends, growth rates, and population change from 1950 to 2050. It even has historical world population estimates going back to 10,000 BC.

Euromonitor's Passport GMID has already been mentioned in this chapter, but it has a rich set of data from which one can extract relevant market information. For example, an individual would be able to find the market size of pet care in Australia or find the size of the pet population for over fifty countries.

A major source for market statistics are industry and trade associations, as well as other international organizations not identified before. Strategies and sources for identifying these entities were discussed in chapter 7, which deals with industry research. One of the sources identified there was Gale/Cengage's Associations Unlimited.

This section identified some of the general sources that provide data. However, the market research reports available from companies identified earlier in this chapter will also provide statistics that a researcher could use for a market analysis. In addition, several of the sources identified in the statistics section of chapter 7, such as the UNCTADSTAT database and RDS TableBase, can also be used to find potential market research data.

ADVERTISING AND CHANNELS OF DISTRIBUTION SOURCES

Some of the resources mentioned earlier in this chapter should provide some insight for the 4Ps of a marketing plan. For example, market research reports should have covered person and product, and they may discuss price. Chapter 3 of the Country Commercial Guide, "Selling US Products and Services," provides information about distribution channels, pricing, trade promotion, and advertising in a specific country. Advertising and channels of distribution are examples of two of the 4Ps of a marketing plan, with the former being an example of promotion and the latter of place. This section will identify some sources that focus specifically on advertising and channels of distribution.

Advertising Sources

Advertising is one of the elements of promotion. It is a way of sending a message to the target market using suitable modes of communication, including magazines, newspapers, television, the World Wide Web, and social media tools like blogs, emails, Facebook, Twitter, and YouTube in order to convince them to buy a product or use a service. This section will identify some of the sources that can be used to find data and media relevant to this type of promotion.

Warc, originally known as World Advertising Research Center, provides information that is valuable for all aspects of marketing strategy. It provides market analysis from its own researchers and links to relevant Euromonitor reports. It is included in this section because of the databases that provide advertising expenditures and forecasts for eighty global markets and for seven media types. It also partners with TGI to provide time use data for TV, radio, Internet, newspapers, magazines, and cinema across more than fifty global markets,[17] with a one-year embargo.

Advertising Redbook has been around for almost 100 years. It is a directory that can be used to identify US and international advertisers and the agencies they use, total advertising expenditures and media outlets used, as well as identify agencies worldwide. Reports about advertisers provide name of the company, address, phone and fax number, relevant email addresses, business description, and industry group, as well as NAICS and SIC codes, affiliated advertisers, revenue, advertising expenditures by media, and personnel, competitors, agencies utilized, and brands. Agency reports provide name of the company, address, phone and fax number, relevant email addresses, agency type, NAICS and SIC codes, markets served (i.e., above-the line, e-commerce, business-to-business, etc.), billings, billings breakdowns, personnel, competitors, clients, and company hierarchy.

SRDS (Standard Rate and Data Service), now a business unit of Kantar Media, has been publishing resources for over ninety years. Its products can be used to identify advertising opportunities as well as the related costs. For example, the *SRDS International Media Guides* series can be used to identify specific publications and their advertising rates worldwide. These are categorized as follows:

- Business publications include those from Asia-Pacific/Middle East/Africa (over 2,400 trade publications), Europe (covers 7,900 trade publications), and the Americas (2,200 trade publications from North and South America as well as the Caribbean)

- Newspapers worldwide—has over 2,100 global newspapers.
- Consumer magazines worldwide—covers more than 4,400 consumer magazines.

Content for each of the sources in the *International Media Guides* series includes the following:

- Publication title
- Address, phone, fax, email, and URL
- Advertising, editorial, and production contacts
- Publisher's representatives/sales office
- Rates (in US dollars and local currencies)
- Closing dates
- Circulation
- Trim sizes (inches and millimeters)
- Readership/editorial description
- Geographic distribution
- Frequency[18]

This international content is available online and as an add-on module via SRDS Media Solutions.

A researcher can also look for advertising association websites that provide names of agencies. One of these is the Transworld Advertising Agency Network (www.taan.org).

Members of this association (TAAN) are selected to represent independently operated marketing communications agencies from Asia/Pacific, Europe, South America, and the United States. It included the names of agencies for Africa, Asia, Europe, North America, and South America. Information provided includes the address, phone number, and a web address. It also has an interface for sending a message to an agency.

Channels of Distribution Sources

Place, another element in the 4Ps, requires a business to determine channels of distribution to get the product to the customer. This section will identify some ways to find export assistance that national governments may provide, sites that have resources for logistics, and sources where one can find shippers.

Getting the product to the global market is a complex process requiring numerous steps and documents. This includes determining the mode of transportation to be used, identifying and getting quotes from companies selected for review, setting delivery times, and filling out invoice forms, to name a very few.

The US government has an extensive support system for those involved in exporting. For example, the Export.gov website provides an international logistics page where one can get guidance on what needs to be done to engage globally. It includes links to information on tariffs and import fees, a video on how to calculate duties and taxes for foreign countries, links to the most common types of documentation needed, and free trade agreements for the United States. There are also export assistance centers in 109 US cities and International US commercial offices in over 70 countries where a business can get assistance (export.gov/locations/index.asp).

The US Department of Homeland Security, Customs and Border Protection (CBP) is also a source for both export and import information (www.cbp.gov). There are links at its "Basic Importing and Exporting" webpage that provide access to export documents, licenses and requirements, legal decisions, import and export requirements established by the US Toxic Substances Control Act (TSCA), and automated tools for searching CBP rulings and submitting required documents online.

For a business to export items, duties and tax must be calculated. In the US, it is necessary to find the export code using Schedule B (www.census.gov/foreign-trade/schedules/b/), the classification system that is used to export goods. Products and other type of merchandise (including skis and live animals) are referred to as commodities in this system. Once this is found, export.gov advises one to go to CUSTOMS Info "Global Tariffs" page (export.customsinfo.com/Default.aspx) to find the duties and rates to use. The researcher will need to register in order to find out what they are.

Those that are importing into the United States would use the US International Trade Commission's Harmonized Tariff Schedule (HTS) online reference tool to find tariffs (hts.usitc.gov/).

Other governments provide similar support to businesses exporting from their countries. The International Trade Centre's "Directory of Trade Promotion Organizations and Other Trade Support Institutions" webpage (www.intracen.org/exporters/trade-support-institutions-by-country/) referred to earlier identifies such websites. The downside is that these agencies may only use their language to provide information or data, which could reduce their value significantly.

Another step to take is to identify a company or companies that have the knowledge and expertise to transport the commodities being sold. A fee-based source for doing this is *Piers Directory of United States Exporters* (directories.piers.com/default.aspx). Now available online, with US importers (www.piers.com/directories/), the interface allows searching by keyword, company name, location, SIC code, HS code, or commodity keyword. It provides information for 50,000 company exporters and 150,000 importers.

To identify importers or exporters, a possible strategy would be to search company databases like Hoovers Online, OneSource, Mergent Online, and ReferenceUSA using the relevant NAICS code. For example, one could use NAICS 4488510, which represents freight transportation arrangement, and includes shipping agents, freight forwarding, and customs brokers, in these databases. The online sources have facets for limiting the search to those businesses that are in a particular city.

There are also free websites that have information like shippers and ports. GlobalEDGE has a page on "Logistics" to find leads to relevant sources (globaledge.msu.edu/Global-Resources/logistics). For example, it has links to the Hong Kong Shipping Directory, Seaports Info Page, World Shipping Directory, and Worldwide Seaports.

One cannot dismiss the potential for finding sources using Internet search engines. But be aware that there is a chance that illegal companies might pass themselves off as legitimate.

ARTICLES

Always search for articles when doing market research. There are many domestic and international trade magazines that are published, and they will often deal with topics related to the consumer, products, market trends, or economic issues that will affect the market. One can choose to focus on one or more trade magazines to read regularly, or use databases that provide content to a wide range of sources, not only trade magazines, but also industry and market research reports. As mentioned in other chapters, these sources include ABI/Inform, Business Insights: Essentials, Business Source Complete, Business Source Premier, Factiva, LexisNexis Academic, RDS Business and Industry, and Access World News. Another source, World News Connection, which is available through Dialog, is a database that provides English translations of articles that were originally published in the language of the source country.

CONCLUSION

In this chapter market research was defined and potential questions to be answered were identified in order to develop a marketing plan. The 4Ps (product, place, promotion, and price) were also introduced as part of the plan. Throughout the chapter, sources were provided that a researcher could use to find the answers to these and other questions he or she might have. These sources fell under the following categories: country backgrounds, resources for culture, market research reports and aggregators, statistical sources, resources for advertising and distribution channels, and articles. This was not an exhaustive list of strategies and resources to use for market research. Part of the reason for this can be found in the advancement of technology and the effect it has on globalization. For instance, the ability for shoppers to access online storefronts and buy products easily across country boundaries offers a range of new opportunities for an entrepreneur to reach markets worldwide. Although some of the mainstream sources can still be helpful in these cases, including those that provide country information, other strategies will have to be employed. In addition, the growth of the Internet makes it possible that the ideal source is out there for someone to find. It may also be necessary to do primary research.

Refer to the sources in other chapters of this book, such as chapters 3 and 4, which provide alternative sources around the world and by regions, as well as chapter 7, which deals with industry.

LIST OF SOURCES

Databases

This is an alphabetical list of the fee-based databases mentioned in this chapter.

ABI/Inform (Ann Arbor, MI: ProQuest, 1971–), www.proquest.com/products_pq/de-scriptions/abi_inform.shtml.

Advertising Redbook (New Providence, NJ: LexisNexis Group), www.redbooks.com.

Associations Unlimited (Detroit, MI: Gale Research 1995–), www.gale.cengage.com/.

Business Insights: Essentials (Farmington Hills, MI: Gale Cengage Learning, 2012–), www.cengagesites.com/Literature/782/gale-business-insights-global-essentials/.

Business Source Complete (Ipswich, MA: EBSCO Pub., 2005–), www.ebscohost.com/public/business-source-complete.

Factiva (New York: Dow Jones and Reuters, 2001–), www.dowjones.com/factiva/index.asp.

LexisNexis Academic (Dayton: OH: LexisNexis, Division of Reed Elsevier, 2002–), academic.lexisnexis.com/online-services/academic/academic-overview.aspx.

OECDIlibrary (Washington, D.C.: OECD, 2000–), www.oecd-ilibrary.org/statistics.

Passport GMID (London: UK; Chicago, IL: Euromonitor International, 1990s–), www.euromonitor.com/passport-gmid.

RDS Business and Industry (Farmington Hills, MI: Gale Group, 1994–), www.gale.cengage.com.

RDS Tablebase (Farmington, MI: Gale 1996–), www.gale.cengage.com.

World News Connection (Washington: NTIS: Dialog, 1995–), wnc.dialog.com.

Websites

This is an alphabetical list of association, government, and publisher websites mentioned in this chapter.

Australian Trade Commission, www.austrade.gov.au/ (29 June 2012).

BCC Research, www.bccresearch.com (29 June 2012).

CIA World Factbook, https://www.cia.gov/library/publications/the-world-factbook/index.html (29 June 2012).

Country Watch, Country Reviews, Country Wire, Country Data, Country Maps, and Forecasts, www.countrywatch.com (29 June 2012).

CultureGrams, www.culturegrams.com/ (29 June 2012).

Economist Intelligence Unit (EIU), Country Reports, Country Forecast, Country Risk, www.eiu.com (29 June 2012).

eMarketer, www.emarketer.com (29 June 2012).

Export.gov, "Locations," export.gov/locations/index.asp (29 June 2012).

Forrester, www.forrester.com (29 June 2012).

Frost & Sullivan, www.frost.com (29 June 2012).

Gartner, www.gartner.com (29 June 2012).

Global Information Inc., www.giiresearch.com (29 June 2012).

Global Tariffs, CUSTOMS Info, export.customsinfo.com/Default.aspx (25 June 2012).

IDC, www.idc.com (29 June 2012).

GlobalEDGE, "Logistics," globaledge.msu.edu/Global-Resources/logistics (29 June 2012).

Google Translate, translate.google.com (29 June 2012).

IMF World Economic Outlook databases, www.imf.org/external/ns/cs.aspx?id=28 (11 June 2012).

International Trade Administration, www.trade.gov (29 June 2012).

International Trade Administration blog, blog.trade.gov (29 June 2012).

International Trade Centre, "Directory of Trade Promotion Organizations and Other Trade Support Institutions," www.intracen.org/exporters/trade-support-institutions-by country/ (25 June 2012).

MarketResearch.com (24 June 2012).

Mintel, www.mintel.com (29 June 2012).

NewsLink, newslink.org/ (29 June 2012).

Norid, "Domain Name Registries Around the World," www.norid.no/domenenavn-baser/domreg.html (11 June 2012).

OECD.Stat Extracts database, stats.oecd.org (11 June 2012).

Piers Directories of U.S Importers and Exporters, directories.piers.com/default.aspx (25 June 2012).

ReportLinker, www.reportlinker.com (29 June 2012).

Research and Markets, www.researchandmarkets.com/ (24 June 2012).

Reuters, www.reuters.com (29 June 2012).

SRDS International Media Guides, www.srds.com/frontMatter/ips/img/index.html (29 June 2012).

Transworld Advertising Agency Network, www.taan.org/ (29 June 2012).

Undata portal, data.un.org (11 June 2012).

UNCTADStat database, unctadstat.unctad.org/ReportFolders/reportFolders.aspx (11 June 2012).

United Nations, www.un.org (29 June 2012).

United Nations, Demographic Yearbook, unstats.un.org/unsd/demographic/products/dyb/dybsets/2008%20DYB.pdf (29 June 2012).

United Nations, Demographic Yearbook, unstats.un.org/unsd/demographic/products/dyb/dyb2008.htm (28 June 2012).

United Nations Economic Commission for Europe, "Links to Official Statistical Organizations," www.unece.org/stats/links.html (29 June 2012).

United Nations Educational, Scientific, and Cultural Organization (UNESCO), "Organizations Maintaining Official Relations with UNESCO," ngo-db.unesco.org/s/or/en (17 Oct. 2012).

United States Census Bureau blog, blogs.census.gov/ (29 June 2012).

United States Census Bureau, International Programs, www.census.gov/population/international/ (24 June 2012).

United States Census Bureau, International Statistical Agencies, "List of Official Statistical Sites," www.census.gov/aboutus/stat_int.html (11 June 2012).

United States Census Bureau, "Schedule B Export Codes," www.census.gov/foreign-trade/schedules/b/ (29 June 2012).

United States International Trade Commission, "HTS Online Reference Tool," hts.usitc.gov/ (29 June 2012).

University of Central Florida Libraries, STAT-USA—links to sources, "GLOBUS and NTDB," guides.ucf.edu/content.php?pid=141826andsid=1209051 (29 June 2012).

US Census. International Programs, www.census.gov/population/international/ (29 June 2012).

US Commercial Service, Market Research Library (MRL), www.buyusainfo.net (29 June 2012).

US Department of Commerce. Bureau of Economic Analysis, www.bea.gov (11 June 2012).

US Department of Homeland Security, Customs and Border Protection (CBP), www.cbp.gov (25 June 2012).

Warc, www.warc.com/AboutUs.info (25 June 2012).

Wall Street Journal, online.wsj.com (29 June 2012).

Wall Street Journal's Market Data Center, online.wsj.com/mdc (11 June 2012).

Wayback Machine, web.archive.org (29 June 2012).

World Bank, Data, data.worldbank.org/ (24 June 2012).

NOTES

1. American Marketing Association, "Definition of Marketing Research," www.marketingpower.com/AboutAMA/Pages/DefinitionofMarketing.aspx (15 Sept. 2011).

2. American Marketing Association, "Definition of Marketing Plan," www.marketingpower.com/_layouts/Dictionary.aspx?dLetter=M (22 Oct. 2011).

3. *The Handbook of International Trade: A Guide to the Principles and Practice of Export,* Consultant eds. Jim Sherlock and Jonathan Reuvid (Sterling, VA: Kogan Page), 49–51.

4. American Marketing Association. Resource Library. Dictionary "M," www.marketingpower.com/_layouts/Dictionary.aspx?dLetter=M 20 Sept. 2011.

5. Andrew Harrison, *Business Environment in a Global Context"* (New York: Oxford University Press, 2010), 15.

6. Harrison, *Business Environment in a Global Context,* 15.

7. Harrison, *Business Environment in a Global Context,* 15.

8. Roger A. Kerin, Steven W. Hartley, Eric N. Berkowitz, and William Rudelius, *Marketing* (New York: McGraw-Hill Irwin, 2006), 46.

9. Kerin et al., *Marketing,* 46.

10. US Small Business Administration. "Conducting Market Research," www.sba.gov/content/conducting-market-research (22 Sept. 2011).

11. Kerin et al., *Marketing,* 213.

12. International Trade Administration, "U. S. Commercial Service," trade.gov/cs/ (23 Sept. 2011).

13. US Commercial Service, *Doing Business in Russia: 2011 Country Commercial Guide for US Companies,* www.buyusainfo.net/docs/x_2871072.pdf (17 Oct. 2012).

14. Euromonitor International. Industries, "Industry reports," www.euromonitor.com/industries (7 Oct. 2011).

15. IDC, "About IDC," www.id c.com/about/about.jsp?t=1318531883170 (13 Oct. 2011).

16. United Nations, *Demographic Yearbook,* unstats.un.org/unsd/demographic/products/dyb/default.htm (14 Oct. 2011).

17. Warc, "About Warc," www.warc.com/AboutUs.info (25 June 2012).

18. *SRDS International Media Guides,* www.srds.com/frontMatter/ips/img/index.html (25 June 2012).

NINE

Global Investing

Global investing occurs when buyers and sellers trade assets, such as equities, bonds, and currencies around the world. Capital markets like the stock and bond markets, as well as the foreign exchange market, provide the mechanisms by which this can be done. Buyers (investors) and sellers include institutions such as banks and investment companies, businesses who need capital for expansion, governments, pension funds, and individuals. With the evolution of globalization and the World Wide Web, more and more individuals who want to invest can take advantage of the economic growth and development that has occurred not only in developed nations, but in emerging markets as well. These investment opportunities allow an investor to potentially increase returns, as well as diversify one's portfolio, thus reducing risk. This can happen by leveraging the different economic cycle of a stock market in one country to that of another. Thus, an investor with stock on a US stock exchanges as well as an exchange in Mexico has the potential to reduce risk when the US market performs badly at one point in time, while the stock market in Mexico has good returns.

An individual who wants to engage in global investing may be looking for information for several vehicles and markets available to those who want to engage in global investing. These financial instruments include mutual funds, exchange-traded funds (ETFs), depositary receipts, direct shares, and currency trading markets. In addition to increasing the opportunity for investors to engage globally, the web has also increased the amount of information that is available for that person to learn about these and other investment vehicles. This chapter describes these specific financial instruments and the sources that can be used to find details about them.

US MUTUAL FUNDS

Value Line defines a mutual fund as "a registered investment company that pools money from multiple shareholders and invests it in a predetermined range of stocks, bonds, money market securities or other assets, according to its stated investment objectives."[1] Mutual funds are bought and sold at the end of the day using their net asset value (NAV). According to the Investment Company Institute (ICI), there were 7,637 mutual fund companies in the United States at the end of 2011.[2]Many of these US mutual funds have an international or global purpose, and consequently, an individual may want to include them as a way to diversify his or her portfolio. Mutual funds have a manager, so an investor from the United States does not have to personally identify the specific stocks to include in a portfolio or to deal with the fluctuation of currency exchange rates or transaction fees that are generated when transferring money from outside the United States into the United States. The specific funds have fees that take the latter into consideration and a fund manager that identifies the stocks to includetrading globally. The specific funds have fees that incorporate these expenses.

Mutual funds can be international or global. A global mutual fund consists of stocks from around the world, including those of the home country. An international mutual fund has stocks from other countries, excluding those of the home country. Funds can focus on stocks from a specific country or region, a specific industry, or a specific level of economic development, such as developed or emerging countries. Mutual companies label their funds with names that reflect their content and the purpose described in their prospectus. For example, consider Harbor International Investment. This fund consists of seventy international stocks, and it primarily "invests . . . in common and preferred stocks of foreign large cap companies, including those located in countries with emerging markets."[3] None of the stocks that make this fund up is from the United States, thus reflecting the "international" quality of the fund. A fund like Tweedy Brown Global Value reflects the "global" feature of its name (as well as "value"). This fund seeks "long-term growth of capital by investing throughout the world in a diversified portfolio consisting primarily of non-US marketable equity securities, although investments in US securities are permitted and will be made when opportunities in the United States appear more attractive."[4] This fund includes 7.43 percent US stocks.

Mutual funds can be open ended or closed ended. Open-end funds are consistently being bought or sold and do not have a fixed number of shares. An open-end mutual fund has a ticker symbol made up of five letters, with the fifth being an X. These open-end funds can also be load or no load; the former charges a sales fee or commission, while the latter one does not. A closed-end fund is created when an initial public offering

(IPO) is made using a fixed number of shares. "It is structured, listed, and traded like a stock on a stock exchange."[5] It is typically closed once it has raised the capital intended by the fund and there are no more shares to offer. There are, however, ways to issue more shares and raise more assets if needed.

In the United States, many employers offer mutual funds in their de-fined contribution (DC) sponsored retirement plans for their employees, such as a 401(k) or 403(b). The pool of mutual funds offered is usually based on those that have been preselected by an institution's employee retirement benefits department. Anyone who wants to invest in interna-tional or global stocks would then choose a fund that had these character-istics from the selection available. Those who are interested can also deal directly with a fund company or investment advisor that offers these services to individuals.

The basic information source available for learning about a fund is its prospectus. This document gives expenses that the participant will incur and provides several years of financial information about a fund account, as well as its investment objective, principal investment strategies, how its performance will be measured (indices), principal investment risks, indexes by which the fund is to be measured, and who would benefit by investing in the fund. The prospectus, as well as other of information, is typically available on a mutual fund provider's website. For instance, some of the documents that MFS Investment Management provides for its MFS Emerging Markets Equity Fund are a summary prospectus, the prospectus, a fact sheet and a semiannual and annual report. In the case of this fund, the prospectus covers nine share classes available to an investor, and uses the MSCI Emerging Markets Index to gauge average annual total returns for each of these groups.

Commercial databases from Morningstar, Value Line, and Standard & Poor's can be used to screen for funds with a global or international focus from multiple providers. Many academic and public libraries will have one of the databases or print sources from these providers that an indi-vidual can utilize. Lipper also provides a database for mutual funds, but its market primarily consists of fund industry professionals, financial in-stitutions, and financial advisers. These vendors have their own analysts and ranking methods that they incorporate into the reports and informa-tion they provide for mutual funds.

Morningstar is a company that was founded in 1984 and is often re-ferred to as the gold standard for providing information about mutual funds. In 2010, it provided data and analysis for "91,500 mutual funds and similar vehicles in international markets."[6] It has a proprietary sys-tem that uses risk and cost-adjusted returns to rate past performance. This is the Morningstar Rating, which is available not only via the Morn-ingstar databases, but is often see on the mutual fund section of websites such as Yahoo! Finance, and on free mutual fund databases like the Mutual Funds Investor's Center. This database identifies 3,789 funds that are international or global. The Morningstar Investment Research Center groups global mutual funds as follows:

- China region
- Diversified emerging markets
- Diversified Pacific/Asia
- Europe stock
- Foreign large blend
- Foreign large growth
- Foreign large value
- Foreign small/mid growth
- Foreign small/mid value
- India equity
- Japan stock
- Latin America stock
- Pacific/Asia (excluding Japan) stock
- World stock

The researcher can select any of these characteristics to retrieve the relevant funds.

When an individual selects a specific fund, he or she will see a Morningstar rating. The rating can range from zero to five stars.[7] Other information that is included can be found in the following categories: quote, fund analysis, performance, portfolio, and filings. The fund analysis part will provide a recent analyst report when it is available, which is a review by a Morningstar analyst of strategies taken and the performance of a fund. The performance section compares a fund to relevant benchmarks. The portfolio area allows one to identify the holdings (company stock) that make up a fund, including the percent each has in the fund, country of domicile, year-to-date return, and price/earnings ratio. An investor can also select one of these individual holdings to find specific Morningstar information about it. Links to a fund's prospectus, and annual and semiannual reports are also available.

Morningstar also provides some free information at www.morningstar.com for those who don't have access to the subscription service.

Another company that provides information about mutual funds is Value Line. It has its origins in 1931, when Arnold Bernhard founded Bernhard & Company, Inc., and then became incorporated in New York as Value Line (the "Company") in 1982.[8] Value Line Publishing LLC is one of its wholly owned subsidiaries. It has been publishing *Value Line Investment Survey* since 1965, and has added other publications covering mutual funds and other financial instruments.[9] Its Value Line Fund Advisor web-based solution allows an individual to use specific criteria to identify funds that meet them. The database has over 20,000 funds, classified by four objectives: global, foreign and two that are regional. Its global equity funds can include stocks from around the world, including the United States. Its foreign equity funds have the same parameters as global except that they don't include US stocks. There are two regional fund objectives, European equity and Pacific equity. Using Value Line's "Screener," one can identify funds that fall within any these four objectives. This database has facets for refining the results, including predefined categories such as "Top Performing Funds–Five years," and "Family," the latter referring to the name of the company issuing the funds. Information provided includes a snapshot that has a chart comparing the fund with relevant indices, its market cycle performance (bear or bull), net asset value (NAV), dividend year, a risk ranking, and the top twenty-five equity holdings in the portfolio, as well as the number of shares held of each.

The third company with mutual fund information, Standard & Poor's (S&P) formed by the merger of Standard Statistics and Poor's Publishing in 1941. S&P's NetAdvantage has a screener that allows the researcher to identify those funds that have a worldwide focus by using the "Family Fund" category and then selecting either global equity or international equity. The global equity filter identifies more than 1,400 funds and consists of companies in developed countries, including the United States. The international equity type also has companies from developed countries, but excludes the United States; it has approximately 2,400 funds. S&P categorizes the results into four groups: basic, rankings, performance, and quantitative. Selecting a group presents specific information related to it. For example, basic provides ticker symbol, the fund name, its fund family, S&P category, S&P style, name of the portfolio manager, that person's tenure, the inception date of each fund, its size, the minimum needed to invest in it, net expense ratio, maximum sales load, and maximum redemption fee load. One can also click on the fund's ticker symbol to bring up an S&P "Mutual Fund Report." This document has ranking commentary, number of holdings, average P/E, dividend yield, performance benchmarked against an index, and performance commentary.

A fourth company, Lipper, a subsidiary of Thomson Reuters, provides mutual fund information and commentary as well as a wide range of analytical tools for fund industry professionals. An investor might run into a Lipper fund fact sheet to purchase if he or she is using free websites like Reuters.com and Yahoo! Finance (finance.yahoo.com). These compact reports include a fund's investment objectives, holdings, industries and the percentages in which the fund engages, exchanges it trades on, and performance indicators, both current and historical. Lipper also provides some data for funds found through Barron's Mutual Fund Screener (online.barrons.com/fund/screener.html).

There are also free websites that provide screeners with which to identify mutual funds by certain criteria. For example, Maxfunds (www.maxfunds.com) has a tool for the user to discover funds that are categorized as international diversified, global, global balanced, emerging market, Japan Asia, and Latin America. There are quite a few funds in each category; for instance, the international diversified section has 1,388 funds. Information about a fund includes its expected twelve-month return and average annualized returns. Another source is Mutual Funds Investor's Center from the Mutual Fund Education Alliance (www.mfea.com). Its international/global category identifies 2,758 funds that can come from approximately 25 fund companies. The information provided for a mutual fund comes from Morningstar and includes a description of the fund; a Morningstar rating if available; a description of the fund's managers; and the top twenty-five holdings, their percentages, their industries, and the countries in which the funds reside.

A source for closed-end funds is the Closed-End Fund Association (CEFA) (www.cefa.com). This association provides a "Fund Selector" from which one can select funds classified under global/international equity. There are fifty-eight funds that fall into this category, which are then grouped under emerging markets funds, global funds, and Pacific, excluding Japan funds. The information provided for a fund includes ten-year, five-year, one-year, and year-to-date average annual return, its objective, top holdings, top sectors, and a link to the fund's sponsor.

Another source is CEF/Connect (www.cefconnect.com/Screener/FundScreener.aspx). Focusing on closed-end funds, its screener offers four categories for international funds, four that are global, one categorized as non-US equity, and another referred to as undefined. The international funds can be Asia equity, emerging market equity, emerging market income, and Latin American equity. Those that are global are referred to as global equity, global equity dividend, global growth and income, and global income.

In addition to those websites that offer a wide range of financial information, including Reuters.com, *Wall Street Journal's* SmartMoney (smartmoney.com), and Yahoo! Finance (finance.yahoo.com), there are screeners and information about funds at other familiar sources, including websites or newspapers, such as *Barron's* (online.barrons.com), *Financial Times* (ft.com), MSN Money (money.msn.com), and *USA Today* (funds.usatoday.com). Each provides a section in which articles about mutual funds in the news are available, as well as screeners. Bloomberg *Businessweek* (www.businessweek.com) also provides news articles related to mutual funds, and CNNMoney (money.cnn.com) provides some mutual fund-related news, as well as an overview of the biggest funds, gainers and losers, and performance of funds by type (i.e., global real estate). However, users might have to pay in order to access articles from *Barron's*, *Financial Times*, or the *Wall Street Journal*. In such cases, individuals should contact his or her library because it might have databases that provide full-text articles to these newspapers, as well as others that might be useful.

Another strategy would be to go to a mutual fund provider's or sponsor's website and find information about the funds they offer.

NON-US BASED MUTUAL FUNDS

According to the Investment Company Institute (ICI), there were 72,657 mutual funds worldwide in the fourth quarter of 2011, with 57 percent from the Americas, 30 percent from Europe, and 13 percent from Africa and Asia/Pacific.[10] This data includes funds around the world that are used to collectively pool money in order to invest and share risk. Mutual funds around the world share several characteristics, but there will also be some differences. Some common characteristics for mutual funds worldwide are that

- A group of investors contribute to a pool of funds so that it can be invested in stocks or some other type of capital and receive returns on the results
- They are available to the individual (retail) and to businesses, foundations, pension funds, government bodies, and so forth (institutional)
- They are made up of a diverse set of financial instruments such as stocks and bonds
- They have different styles, which can be based on companies in a specific country or industry, different investment strategies (i.e., growth, value, conservative), and so forth
- Each country has its own set of regulations that govern such funds in order to protect the investor.[11]

In the United States, the pooling of investors is most commonly referred to as a mutual fund. Other countries have different arrangements for this type of investment. The United Kingdom has unit trusts and open-ended investment companies (OEICs). Both are open-ended funds, whereby shares can be added or removed from a particular investment instrument as the situation warrants. OEICs trade on the London Stock Exchange (LSE; www.londonstockexchange.com). One can use LSE's "Fund" selection tool and choose the "UK Unit Trusts and OEICs" option to get a list of these funds. Another source with which to identify OEICs and unit trusts is provided by Money.co.uk (www.money.co.uk). It lists 483 unit trusts and 1,520 OEICs from the United Kingdom for five asset classes that are made up of fixed interest, Individual Savings Account (ISA), ethical, equity, and performance. These funds are comparable by price, performance, and asset class. Money.co.uk collaborates with moneyspider.com, which has a more robust mechanism for comparing the performance of various OEICs and unit trusts. The individual will have to register (for free) at the site in order to get information.

Another way to potentially identify specific OEICs is by going to a fund manager's website. One can identify these managers at Money.co.uk and then use an Internet search engine to find the sponsor's website. To find the status of a "collective investment scheme," use the Financial Services Authority (FSA) Register's search interface (www.fsa.gov.uk/fsaregister/search/cis_search). The FSA is an independent organization that regulates the UK financial services market.

In the European Union this type of financial instrument is referred to as "Undertakings for Collective Investment in Transferable Securities" (UCITS). These are "investment funds that have been established in accordance with UCITS Directive (adopted in 1985)"[12]; they can be freely marketed across the European Union once they have been registered in an EU country. The investments are in transferrable securities with strong investor protection. The securities can be listed shares or bonds, and/or other liquid financial assets determined by the law "(i.e. cash deposits, other UCITS . . . and money market instruments."[13]

Around the world there are other collective schemes. *Wikipedia* has an entry for "collective investment schemes" wherein it identifies some of the different instruments worldwide that pool investor money, but it is not exhaustive. For instance, it identifies those for the UK, Canada, Ireland, the European Union, France and Luxembourg, Netherlands and Belgium, Ukraine, Greece, Switzerland, and Australia, but it does not identify any for South Africa, Hong Kong, Japan, or China. In his book, *An Introduction to Mutual Funds Worldwide*, Ray Russell identifies these types of funds not only for those identified by *Wikipedia*, but for South Africa, Hong Kong, and Japan.[14] For example, he identifies mutual funds for South Africa as being unit trusts.

Morningstar again is a source to use to find mutual funds that are from other countries, although they will be different collective schemes, such as unit trust. In the section where Morningstar is first mentioned, the discussion dealt with US mutual funds that had global or international features. The current section deals with mutual funds or collective schemes that are from other countries, such as a unit trust from Australia or an open-end fund incorporated in New Zealand. Examples of such funds are the Australian-based Platinum International Fund and New Zealand's Mercer KiwiSaver Balanced.

An individual can go to corporate.morningstar.com and freely access some information. The site provides a drop-down box from which to select sixteen countries or regions. These include Asia, Australia, Belgium/Luxembourg (Dutch and French), Canada (English and French), Chile, Denmark, France, Germany, Italy, Mexico, the Netherlands, New Zealand, Norway, Spain, the United Kingdom, and the United States. Morningstar Direct is the subscription-based platform that, in addition to covering other financial instruments, provides information and analysis for mutual funds in the US and globally.

Bloomberg (www.bloomberg.com/markets/funds/) has a page that identifies funds from almost 100 different countries. It gives the performance of a fund, such as year-to-date and one-month figures, 52-week range, and its beta. Bloomberg also provides a description and identifies the type of fund, as well as its sponsor's website, the sponsor's country, net asset value (one week late), top-ten holdings (if available), and information about the fees.

Like the mutual fund families in the United States, a non-US fund's sponsor or family website will have information about the financial instruments it offers. For example, AMP Capital's website (www.ampcapital.com.au), has information about the funds this Australian investment company manages.

This section has covered some of the basics for mutual funds worldwide. For more information, read Ray Russell's book, *An Introduction to Mutual Funds Worldwide*. There are also guides and information about mutual funds and various collective schemes on the web. For example, the UK Financial Services Authority has a guide for this on its site (www.fsa.gov.uk/pubs/foi/collguide.pdf), and the European Commission has information about UCITs on its site (ec.europa.eu/internal_market/investment/index_en.htm). The US Securities Exchange Commission provides information about mutual funds at www.sec.gov/answers/mutfund.htm. The regulatory agency for a country or region (i.e., EU) is another source that might have information about any collective schemes that exist in the area. A list of these types of agencies can be found at the Financial Regulators Gateway (www.financialregulatorsgateway.com/).

EXCHANGE-TRADED FUNDS

Another mechanism by which an investor can globalize his or her investment portfolio is with Exchange-Traded Funds (ETF). This is an "investment company, typically a mutual fund or unit investment trust, whose shares are traded intraday on stock exchanges at market-determined prices. Investors may buy or sell ETF shares through a broker just as they would the shares of any publicly traded company."[15] They are a relatively new financial tool having first been issued in the United States in 1993, and that by 2000 had attracted individual investors.[16] At the end of March 2012, ICI reported that there were a total of 1,193 ETFs, of which 34 percent (405 ETFs) represented global/international equity.[17]

Many ETFs are designed to track a specific market index, which have grown to include not only the major indexes, but many other indices that have been created to follow the market, such as those based on a specific country, region, or industry; small or large cap value; small or large cap growth, and so forth.[18] Indexes developed by companies such as MSCI are licensed by ETF families and at times more than one of these families may use a specific index. For example, MSCI ACWI, an index that comes from Morgan Stanley Capital International, is licensed by IShares and Lyxor. These types of ETFs do not require much active management as they are created to meet a particular benchmark, but there are those who have a fund manager that selects a mix of investments to meet a particular objective.

ETFs differ from mutual funds in that they are traded throughout the day on an exchange, while mutual funds can only be bought and sold at the end of the trading day. Standard & Poor's 500 Depository Receipts (SPDR) was the first US ETF, which was launched on the American Stock Exchange in January 1993 and tracked the S&P 500 index.[19] Currency-based ETFs are also traded between dealers, which tend to be banks or securities houses. Information about ETFs can be found in their prospectus.

Companies that provide information about mutual funds do so for ETFs as well. For example, *Morningstar Investment Research Center* provides ETF screeners and information about each fund. It has about 1,540 ETFs across 22 fund families, of which 207 (13 percent) are in Morningstar's international group. This database gauges performance of ETFs using relevant indices, provides the top five holdings in the fund, and enables the user to link to Morningstar information about those companies that make up the fund's portfolio. It also provides a Morningstar analyst report.

S&P's NetAdvantage provides a list of ETFs from which from which to identify those with an international or global focus using the name of the fund. The database has than 300 ETFs, each of which has an "Exchange Traded Fund Report" that gives the price, NAV, and S&P rankings for performance, risk, and cost. This report also has commentary, market perspective, key statistics, ETF peer comparisons, and the top ten holdings of the fund.

Value Line ETF Survey provides an interface to select ETFs listed in the United States and Japan, and gives data and analysis for each ETF it identifies.

In addition to the fee-based sources that have an interactive tool to identify global- or international-based ETFs, there are several free ones. For example, there is the ETF screener from Bloomberg (www.bloomberg.com/apps/data?pid=etfscreener). An individual is able to search not only for US-listed ETFs with a world view, but also those that are trading on another country's exchange. Information provided includes a snapshot that has a description, its objective, geographic focus, performance on the exchange, the top ten holdings, and a link to the sponsor's site. Bloomberg also provides a way to identify world ETFs by regions, made up of the Americas, Europe, Africa and the Middle East, and Asia-Pacific. It should be noted, however, that an ETF trading on a non-US exchange, such as the Lima Stock Exchange, may actually be US based, which may be acceptable from the Peruvian point of view, but not from the American side. Such a fund is Powershares QQQ Trust Series 1, ticker symbol QQQ, which is made up of US stocks.

A partially free source for identifying ETFs is XTF (www.xtf.com), which focuses on ETFs trading exclusively on US or Japanese exchanges. It has an "explorer" tool to identify ETFs meeting certain criteria and provides some free information, such as the top ten holdings, the most recent fund exposure, and data that includes its annual yield and net asset value to date. However, much of the content is fee based, thus requiring a subscription. For example, one of the premium features the vendor offers is a tool to identify and compare up to six ETFs.

Another website focusing on ETFs is ETFdb (etfdb.com); it describes itself as "the comprehensive & original ETF database." The free section of the website allows the user to identify US-listed ETFs that are global or international in nature and get some information about them. However, it is necessary to become a pro member to be able to use features such as Excel downloads and comparison tools. A useful link on this site provides a list to eighteen ETF screeners online (etfdb.com/2009/top-50-free-online-etf-tools/). Although last updated in November 2009, only two URLs identified at this site were unavailable.

An exchange on which an ETF is traded is another source. For example, NYSE Euronext (etp.nyx.com) provides information on ETFs trading on NYSE Arca, NYSE Amsterdam, NYSE Brussels, and NYSE Lisbon. NYSE Arca is an electronic listing and trading platform for ETFs. In order to identify any ETF listed on Arca with a global or international perspective, one will have to rely on its name. For example, one of the funds listed is Direxion Daily Latin America Bear 3X Shares, a fund focusing on the S&P Latin America 40 Index (Latin America Index). Information that Arca provides for an ETF includes a description, market data, and links to relevant SEC filings. Yet another example is the London Stock Exchange, which provides ETFs that are trading on it at www.londonstockexchange.com/specialist-issuers/ETFs/issuers/issuers.htm.

Utilizing an Internet search engine and using keywords, such as "list of ETFs trading worldwide" (without quotes), can find websites such as Stock-Encyclopedia.com (stock-encyclopedia.com/PAO.html). At this site the investor can find ETFs listed on the Toronto Stock Exchange and the London Stock Exchange. Of course, there is also the high probability of many false hits.

Finally, searching a sponsor's website for ETFs is another way of identifying and finding information about them. Morningstar and many of the free websites have mechanisms that allow the individual to do this.

Morningstar refers to these as "fund families," of which there are 23. The London Stock Exchange provides a list of 13 ETF "issuers."

In addition to identifying specific ETFs, the researcher may want to find more information about them. A strategy to use would be to focus on the index on which it is based, find the latter's sponsor's website, and search for information about the index there. For example, MSCI, which has many indices, provides a factsheet that defines an index, its annual performance for at least ten years, the top-ten constituents, and sector and country weights. The sector weights provide the percentage of an industry represented in an index, and the country weights show the percentages of the countries.

For those who would like a list of indices available worldwide, Bloomberg is a place to go (www.bloomberg.com/markets/indexes/) to find specific indices by letter or by the country. Clicking on a letter, for instance "S," will identify all those indices that begin with it, which, in this case, primarily consist of the S&P indices. The individual can click on an index and download a snapshot which includes the opening and closing price, day range, 52-week range, a description, and the top company gainers and the top losers.

Other sources to use are *Barron's* (online.barrons.com), *Financial Times* (ft.com), MSN Money (money.msn.com), Reuters.com, *USA Today* (www.usatoday.com/money/index), the *Wall Street Journal's* SmartMoney (smartmoney.com), and Yahoo! Finance (finance.yahoo.com).

The previous discussion focused on sources to find information about specific mutual funds or ETFs, as well as ways to identify those that meet specific criteria, such as having an international or global focus. However, a researcher might want to find information about the mutual fund and ETF industry in general. A primary source for this is the Investment Company Institute, the National Institute of Investment Companies (www.ici.org). This organization engages in research related to mutual funds as well as other types of investment instruments such as ETFs. They engage in policy, investor, and retirement research; compile worldwide statistics; and present commentary in order to educate the public about mutual funds and other types of investment companies. Each year they publish the *Investment Company Fact Book* (www.ici.org/pdf/2012_factbook.pdf). Made up of more than 260 pages, the 2012 edition includes information about mutual fund trends, exchange-traded funds, characteristics of mutual fund owners, and data tables for US and worldwide mutual funds.

ICI also deals with global policy and provides worldwide statistics on the mutual fund industry on behalf of the International Investment Funds Association (IIFA), an organization of national mutual fund associations (www.iifa.ca/). At the IIFA website one will find world industry statistics that are produced by ICI. IIFA also provides links to organizations relevant to the fund industry, including the Bank for International

Settlements, the European Finance Association, and European Securities and Markets Authority. To date IIFA has forty-one members from Africa, Asia and the Pacific, Europe, North America, and South and Central America.

There is also the Investment Management Association (IMA) from the United Kingdom (www.investmentfunds.org.uk/). This association conducts and publishes research, looks at trends, and addresses regulation facing the industry in the UK. It annually publishes the *Asset Management Survey*, a document that is based on a questionnaire to which IMA member firms have responded, as well as interviews from executives of these member firms. It has a section dealing with funds, specifically unit trusts and open-ended investment companies (OEICs). Investors in these outlets are considered to be either institutional or retail.

Another entity is the European Fund and Asset Management Association (efama; www.efama.org). This organization supports its members in the European investment management industry. Latest quarterly and monthly statistics about the industry are also released on the site, such as the "EFAMA Investment Fund Industry Fact Sheet" that provides data for UCITs and non-UCITs. The association also produces its fact book, *Trends in European Investment Funds*, annually. The publication includes trends and analysis of the industry both for Europe and outside of it, and covers the industry for each of the twenty-six European members of efama.

DEPOSITARY RECEIPTS

An individual may also globalize his or her portfolio using depositary receipts (DR). Depositary receipts are negotiable certificates managed by a major bank, representing the shares of a company not located in the country of the local exchange. One type of DR is an American Depositary Receipt (ADR), where the shares of a foreign company are represented by these negotiable certificates at a certain ratio. The investor doesn't actually own the shares, which are deposited in the home country, but by virtue of the certificate, he or she owns shares of a foreign company in a local exchange.

An example of a foreign company that has ADRs is Toyota Motor Corp. These are available through the Bank of New York/Mellon and on the New York Stock Exchange. These ADRs have a one to two ratio, meaning that one certificate is worth two Toyota shares. The certificates will trade on the NYSE in US dollars, which is based on the changing rate of exchange of the US dollar to the yen. The activity on the exchange reflects what is happening in its home exchange (NIKKEI). Unless the exchange rate between the two is one to one, the company's activity will not be the same on the two exchanges.[20] Information about the number of

DR shares Toyota has issued will be noted in the 20-F it submits to the Securities Exchange Commission. (A 20-F is similar to the 10-K, but is the form that foreign companies listing on the US exchanges use.)

DRs can be American (ADRs), global (GDRs), regional (such as European, which are referred to as EDRs), or related to a specific country (Brazilian DRs). A global DR (GDR) is "a bank certificate issued in more than one country for shares in a foreign company. The shares are held by a foreign branch of an international bank. The shares trade as domestic shares, but are offered for sale globally through the various bank branches."[21] One can find GDRs that have been issued by using J. P. Morgan's DR interface (https://www.adr.com/DRSearch/CustomDR-Search). There are 1,053 GDRs on worldwide exchanges, managed by four out of the five institutions that have DR services. More about these establishments will be presented later.

An EDR is "a negotiable security (receipt) that is issued by a European bank, and that represents securities which trade on exchanges outside of the bank's home country . . . These securities are traded on local exchanges and used by banks—and issuing companies in the United States and other countries—to attract investment capital from the European region."[22] Sometimes these are referred to as "Euro Depository Receipts," which doesn't automatically imply that the currency of the receipt is issued in euros.

Country-specific DRs are like ADRs, except that it would be a foreign company with certificates trading in that country. For example, a non-Brazilian DR would be a foreign company using the Brazilian stock market.

ADRs can be either sponsored or unsponsored. If the ADR is sponsored, this means that a company has entered into an arrangement with a specific bank (the depositary) because it wants to issue its stock in a particular country. An unsponsored ADR, with some exceptions, can only be traded on the non-NASDAQ over-the-counter (OTC) market[23] and there may be more than one depositary handling it. An example of such a company is Alibaba.com, which is using this market and has three depositaries handling it, BNY Mellon, Citibank, and Deutsche Bank. An unsponsored ADR occurs when a bank or broker determines that there is sufficient US investor interest in a foreign stock, and thus sets up a DR without any direct participation from the company.

Sponsored ADRs can be at Level I, Level II, or Level III. A characteristic of a level I DR is that it is traded in the US over-the-counter (OTC) market with prices published in the *Pink Sheets* and on some exchanges outside the United States. A company established in this way is not required to fully register or provide full disclosure with the SEC, nor does it have to use United States generally accepted accounting principles (GAAP) to report its accounts. Consequently, a company benefits from such a system because it doesn't have to follow strict regulations. Level II and Level III versions of an ADR allow a company to be listed on NAS-DAQ, the American, and the New York Euronext stock exchanges. Both require SEC registration and adherence to US GAAP. Level II Depositary Receipts are exchange-listed securities but do not involve raising new capital while Level III programs do.

Financial institutions that manage these types of financial instruments include the Bank of New York/Mellon (BNY Mellon; www.adrbnymellon.com), Citibank (www.citiadr.idmanagedsolutions.com/www/front_page.idms), Computershare (https://wwss.citissb.com/adr/common/linkpage.aspx?linkFormat=M&pageId=3&subpageid=19), Deutsche Bank (www.adr.db.com), and J. P. Morgan Chase (www.adr.com).

Each of the banks mentioned in the previous paragraph provides a freely accessible online directory and a section that explains in detail what DRs are and the different regulations that apply. Each also has an interface that allows the user to search by company name or ticker symbol. Computershare and Citibank share their systems under the Computershare's Investment Centre.

Each of these banks gives the investor the ability to identify DRs that the institution itself manages, as well as those administered by other depositaries. These directories can be searched by company, a specific country, region, industry, and DR exchange. There are as many as eighteen DR exchanges that are managed among these banks, most of which are the same, but some that are unique to the depositary as well. For example, at the time of review none of the banks had DRs trading on the Stock Exchange of Hong Kong, except J. P. Morgan, which had two. Other differences include the use of different vocabulary for categorizing an industry. For example, BNY Mellon categorizes China Telecom Corp. LTD as being in the fixed-line telecommunications industry. Citibank uses the GICS industry system and classifies it under telecommunications services. J. P. Morgan lists it under communications. Another difference is in terms of content. J. P. Morgan identifies 261 Chinese companies with DRs, while Deutsche Bank lists 78. China Telecom is not in the Deutsche Bank directory.

These online directories provide important information about the companies within them. In addition to giving the investor a way to monitor his or her investment, they also provide information useful for company research. For instance, a company record in BNY Mellon has a description, current news about it, its DR exchange/s, latest stock quote, fifty-two–week performance, institutional ownership, and NYB Mellon indices in which the company's DR is a constituent. One can then access each of these indices and compare a company's DR performance against it.

Each of the depository's portals have unique characteristics. For example, J. P. Morgan's interface can be used to identify ADRs and GDRs, whether they are sponsored or unsponsored, in addition to searching by some of the same features available in BNY Mellon's system. Deutsch Bank offers a way to sort for DRs by sponsored or nonsponsored, as well as by level. All of the directories are very robust, but those for BNY Mellon and J. P. Morgan stand out.

If an individual is interested in investing in ADRs directly, Fidelity Online provides a tool by which an investor can do so (www.stockpar.com/).

CURRENCY TRADING

Another avenue available to the investor who wants to diversify his or her portfolio globally is to engage in currency trading. International business activity involves the exchange of currencies between one country and another in order to purchase and sell goods and services between them. The cost to change one currency for another country's currency is the exchange rate. As a result of supply and demand economics, and factors such as a country's trade flows, balance of payments, investment flows, money supply, inflation, government interventions, and currency manipulation, the value of currencies, and thus, exchange rates, fluctuate, forming the markets for trading currencies. There are two types of currency markets in which an individual can invest. One is the foreign exchange market, referred to as forex or FX, and the other is the currencies futures market.

In forex trading, the investor buys a currency and then proceeds to purchase another. Trading currencies are expressed in pairs which fall into two main categories, major currency pairs and cross currency pairs. Major currency pairs are those that are traded the most and in all cases presently include the US dollar. Cross currency pairs are those that do not involve the US dollar. Each currency is expressed by three letters. For example, in the pair USD/MYR the first unit refers to the US dollar, and the second is the Malaysian ringgit. Web-based currency converters, such as the XE Universal Currency Converter (www.xe.com/ucc/) can be used to identify a country's currency and three letter assignation.

In all currency pairs, the one that is listed first is referred to as the base currency[24] and always has a value of one unit.[25] The second one is the quote/quoting currency. As a result, in the pair USD/MYR 3.1445, one US dollar equals 3.1445 ringgits. If the price changes to USD/MYR 3.1446, the dollar has gotten stronger since it is now possible to purchase more ringgits with the dollar. If the price changes to USD/MYR 3.1444, the dollar is now weaker because one dollar buys less ringgits.

A change in a currency pair is expressed as a price interest point (pip), or basis point. The Commodity Futures Trading Commission (CFTC) defines a pip as "[t]he smallest price unit of a commodity or currency."[26]

Usually a pip is one-thousandth of a currency's unit (four decimal places), except for the Japanese yen, whose pip is one-hundredth of the currency's unit (two decimal places). The change between USD/MYR 3.1445 and USD/MYR 3.1446 is one pip. The changes in pips are used to determine the price of the currencies that are trading.

Forex is open twenty-four hours, five days a week, in that there is always an economic region where currency trading is happening. One level of forex is made up of the interbank market, a system whereby central banks and financial institutions worldwide trade currencies at a certain rate and date among each other as part of their daily business transactions. They also provide these trading services to multinational corporations, governments, hedge funds, and individuals who are very well off. Trading in this market often involves sizes where the minimum base currency requirement is $1 million. These dealers use electronic platforms like those from Thomson Reuters Dealing as well as ICAP's Electronic Brokerage Services (EBS) that provide up-to-the minute data and allow traders to identify potential buyers and sellers of currency pairs, as well as place orders.

Other financial institutions that engage in forex are "smaller commercial banks, investment banks and securities houses, and in addition mutual funds, pension funds, hedge funds, currency funds, money market funds, building societies, leasing companies, insurance companies, financial subsidiaries of corporate firms and central banks."[27] There are also nonfinancial customers who are trading directly; this includes governments and corporations.

Forex trading is also made up of individuals, referred to as the retail market. In this case, an investor can engage in trading at a mini level ($10,000) or a micro level ($1,000). This lower level requirement for trading and advances in computer systems, as well as high-speed network connections and the evolution of the World Wide Web, makes it possible for the individual to engage in forex trading. In fact, the *Wall Street Journal* reported that currency brokers that cater to the retail market (referred to as retail aggregators) increased their volume level from 10 percent in 2010 to 18 percent in 2011.[28] Anyone who wants to participate in this type of trading needs only to enter the search term "fx broker" in a web search engine to obtain a list of potential dealers. Before selecting a broker, the individual should try to establish a firm's validity, expertise, and other qualitative factors. One way to do this is to go to the National Futures Association website (www.nfa.org) and use their BASIC interface to determine if a broker is in the system.

It is also possible to find retail forex brokers at websites that have selection tools for identifying them or offer ratings, such as FXstreet.com and stockbrokers.com. In addition to providing extensive news on the forex market, FXstreet.com also provides news on the market, live fx rates, and an economic calendar. StockBrokers.com rates fx brokers on different criteria, such as forex trades (estimate of broker commission), clearing method (i.e., registration with an oversight agency such as the NFA), minimum contract, and minimum deposit. They are also judged by the trade platforms they offer and overall quality. Below are some retail firms ranked at the top by StockBroker.com in 2012. They have been selected here because a researcher can get forex information from their sites. They are presented alphabetically and not by the rank they received. Notes on the type of exchange trading they deal with, including futures, which will be discussed later, where they trade, and whether they have an economic calendar are included. Each of these brokers presents a calendar with the relevant economic releases and the dates for each country that a currency represents. The economic calendar will be dealt with later in the chapter.

- AvaFx — www.avafx.com (forex) has an economic calendar.
- Dukascopy — www.dukascopy.com (forex) (Switzerland) has currency quotes, market news, economic research, Dukascopy sentiment index, expert commentary, and an economic calendar. Also has a currency converter.
- FXCM — www.fxcm.com (forex) has fx market news, live charts for ten currency pairs rates, and an economic calendar.
- FxPro — www.fxpro.com (forex) has an economic calendar, forex news, and calculators to determine how much to invest using margins or pips, and a currency converter. [29]

Information about the fx market can be found in specific trade magazines like *Futures* (published by Summit Business Media) (www.futuresmag.com/) and those listed here:

- *MoneyAM* — moneyam.com
- *FX Week* — www.fxweek.com
- *FX Traders* — www.fxtraders.eu
- *Profit and Loss Magazine* — www.profit-loss.com. This will require a subscription to access the issues.

There are also industry associations that have information. For example, the Foreign Exchange Committee sponsored by the Federal Reserve Bank of New York provides statistics on the volume, types of dealers, and the instruments involved in foreign exchange activity in North America (www.newyorkfed.org/FXC/index.html). It also includes data for US currency pairs (i.e., US dollar to Euro; US dollar to Mexican peso), and reports that provide guidance for fx trading, regulatory actions that have taken place worldwide, and other forex topics.

A list of other foreign exchange committees is at the Bank of England's website (www.bankofengland.co.uk/markets/Pages/forex/fxjsc/links.aspx).

An individual who wants to engage in forex trading may be looking for macroeconomic data and other information that can affect the value of any given currency, and thus the relationship that exists between currency pairs. The person may be looking for interest rates, monetary policies, country's trade flows, balance of payments, investment flows, a country's money supply, inflation, government interventions and currency manipulation, the value of currencies trade flows, economic growth and policies, geopolitical risks, and consumer sentiment. A useful tool by which to obtain some of this data comes in the form of economic calendars that are provided on the FX websites noted earlier. These calendars identify economic reports and their release dates relevant to each country's currency. Some also provide the actual data if the event has already occurred. An advantage in having these calendars available at forex or other financial websites is that one has the information readily at hand.

It is important for the investor to understand the foundation underlying such statistics in order to be able to interpret how changes to them can affect currencies. For instance, the interest-rate parity theory explains changes in currency using supply and demand economics as follows:

1. Demand for a country's bonds increases as a result of high interest rates.
2. Bonds and other assets purchased in a country must be paid in its currency.
3. As a result of increased demand for bonds and other assets, the demand for local currency also increases. This in turn increases the value of the currency.[30]

Books about currency trading can provide insight on how to interpret and relate macroeconomic data and other types of data to changes in currencies. Such a book is *All About Forex Trading* by John Jagerson and S. Wade Hansen. In it the authors identify the economic data that a trader should be aware of for countries in the Americas, Western Europe, Asia, Oceania and Africa, and Eastern Europe. They also demonstrate how the economic data that is released (reflected in economic calendars) affect currency. The statistics they cover are those relating to interest rates, employment, inflation, gross domestic product (GDP), foreign investment, trade balance, consumer confidence, retail sales, business confidence, manufacturing, and housing.

The other currency market available to the investor is the currency futures market. These are "contracts that allow a trader and buyer to buy or sell a set amount of foreign currency at a specific price on a specific date in the future (expiration date)."[31] Currency futures markets are organized and regulated by the Commodity Futures Trading Commission (CFTC) (www.cftc.gov). The US Commodity Exchange Act provides the statutory framework under which CFTC functions. Consequently, anyone who wants to engage as a futures' professional in the US must register with the National Futures Association (www.nfa.futures.org). These professionals may deal with any of the futures markets available, from currencies to grains to metals. NFA is a self-regulating organization in the US for the futures industry and helps its members meet their regulatory requirements. It is made up of 4,200 firms and 55,000 associates. The website provides a tool called Background Affiliation Status Information Center (BASIC) whereby potential investors can find the status; any regulatory actions applied by the NFA, CFTC, or the exchanges; and CFTC reparation cases of a dealer engaged in futures trading. If the individual or firm is not in the system, then legally it should not be engaged in futures' trading and, at some point in time, if not already, may face legal actions from the CFTC.

Currency futures are traded on recognized futures exchanges located around the world, including the Chicago Mercantile Exchange (CME) (www.cmegroup.com), the Singapore Mercantile Exchange (SMX) (www.smx.com.sg), the NYSE Liffe (formerly the London International Financial Futures Exchange or LIFFE; https://globalderivatives.nyx.com), and the US ICE (Intercontinental Exchange) Futures exchange (www.theice.com). The dollar index, which is a futures contract made up of the average of the value of the dollar against six component currencies (euro, Japanese yen, British pound, Canadian dollar, Swedish krona, and Swiss franc) is listed on ICE. Futures can also be bought and sold in the interbank market, which does not include retail customers or individuals.[32]

Sources for information about currency futures are the commodity exchanges on which they trade. Other resources include

- Bank of International Settlements (www.bis.org)—This organization is sometimes referred to as the central bank of central banks. It conducts research on international financial markets and the global economy and produces a series of publications, including *BIS Papers* and *Working Papers*. One of its key products is the *Triennial Central Bank Survey of Foreign Exchange and Derivatives Market Activity*. This global bank survey is conducted every three years to determine the size and structure of the foreign exchange market, which includes futures contracts, referred to as outright forwards. Data in this publication include turnover in global exchange markets by instrument, currency, and currency pair. It also produces annual and quarterly reports on the state of the global economy and financial markets, focusing on key highlights in the quarterly publications. The annual report is available online from 1997 to the present, and the *BIS Quarterly Review* is available online from August 1996 to the present. Through the triennial report one can identify the top currency pairs for the period covered.

- CFTC—This agency provides a number of reports, such as the weekly *Commitments of Trader (COT) Reports* and *This Month in Futures Market Reports* as well as press releases that contain actions it has taken in the commodities markets. A *COT Report* provides data on futures contracts (known as *long positions*) that are held by US traders in commodities markets. It also provides statistics on "contracts that have been sold without the seller owning an underlying contract,"[33] known as *short positions*. Traders look at these reports for any signs of the market moving up or down. The website also has an international section that provides the regulations that pertain to foreign boards that want to sell their products in the United States.
- NFA—This trade organization provides investor alerts related to the foreign exchange market and is the self-regulatory organization for the industry. It was discussed earlier.
- TradingCharts.com—This site provides charts for stocks and commodities, including currency futures. The individual can find price data and charts for numerous currency pairs, including ten major currency pairs, fifteen major cross rates, and the euro and seven major currencies. An economic calendar that has the release dates for relevant economic reports is provided. This site also has information for forex. Included are news feeds from RTTNews.com (a global financial wire service), a list of twenty-five forex brokers, with information such as the agency that regulates the broker, minimum deposit required in order to trade with that dealer, and the trading platform used.
- Barchart.com—This site features information and data for the futures and forex markets, as well as for other types of financial vehicles. Included are price quotes and contract names for twenty currency pairs, as well as for the dollar index. Charts based on *Commitment of Traders Reports* are also provided. News and commentary on general futures is also given.
- Other sources of information include the familiar financial websites that have been identified earlier in this chapter. This includes *Barron's*, Bloomberg *Businessweek*, *Reuters.com*, *Financial Times*, CNN Money, and the *Wall Street Journal's* Smartmoney.com. These sites also provide currency performance charts.

Individuals should also search for articles from trade and newspaper publications in databases like ABI/Inform, Business Source Premier, Business Source Complete, Business Insights: Essentials, Factiva, LexisNexis Academic, and ProQuest Central. Searching for a specific topic in these databases should retrieve relevant articles from several trade magazines, and often will produce the full-text for them.

For those not engaged in currency trading requiring real-time currency rates, but want to know the value of exchange rates, the following sources can help with this:

- Bloomberg Currency Converter: www.bloomberg.com/personal-finance/calculators/currency-converter/
- CNN Money: money.cnn.com/data/currencies/
- *Financial Times*, Currencies: markets.ft.com/research/Markets/Currencies.
- Reuters: www.reuters.com/finance/currencies
- WSJ Markets Data Center: online.wsj.com/mdc/public/page/mdc_currencies.html
- XE Universal Currency Converter (www.xe.com/ucc/): This tool also allows one to obtain exchange rates back to 1995 for ninety-five currencies.
- Oanda (www.oanda.com/currency/converter/): This site has exchange rates going back five years.
- Federal Reserve Bank of New York (www.federalreserve.gov/releases/h10/hist/): This website provides exchange rates back to the 1970s.

DIRECT INVESTMENT

Investing directly in stocks trading in foreign financial markets is another way to diversify a portfolio. Before the Internet was available to the public, and even in the early days of the World Wide Web, it was cumbersome to find information for companies trading in a foreign stock exchange unless an investor had access to online services like Dialog, which provided several databases with company data. Although librarians who had access to Dialog could retrieve this type of information for a patron, costs that were generated while a search was being conducted, as well as those of the final document, had to be taken into consideration. Another concern was having to wait for the most current edition of a newspaper like the *Wall Street Journal* or *Financial Times* to arrive in order to review stock quotes. In addition, news of economic, political, and other events in a country and around the world that had an impact on the markets could be delayed. Consequently, anyone interested in investing in foreign financial markets may have been discouraged from doing so because of the barriers that existed for finding information, particularly that which was current.

The World Wide Web as well as powerful search engines, have dramatically reduced these specific barriers. For example, a tremendous amount of information that is available to an investor, even free information. Finding the annual report of a listed company in another country may be a matter of going to its website and downloading it. There are also many sites that have solutions to help an investor, many of which are from traditional aggregators and disseminators of data (i.e., stock quotes) like the *Wall Street Journal* and *Financial Times*. This proliferation and availability of information, as well as advertising that invites the individual to make a lot of money by investing in emerging markets and other similar sound bites, can tempt someone to invest in global financial markets even if he or she does not have the skills to do so.

Today, if an individual decides to invest directly in companies trading in foreign stock exchanges, there are many ways of getting information. For example, chapter 5, which covered company research, identified several databases, including BvD's Mint Global, Hoovers Online, Mergent Online, and InfoGroup's OneSource, that can be used. These databases have interfaces wherein the individual can obtain years of data for one or more companies using criteria such as dividend yield, earnings per share (EPS), and price earnings (P/E) ratios. In addition, investment analyst reports are available via Thomson One that can be used to evaluate companies. That chapter also identified strategies for locating annual reports of listed companies, how to identify stock exchanges, and where to find company news. The same sources to search for articles about companies can be used for locating news about political, economic, and other current events that are occurring in a country. These include ABI/Inform Complete, Business Source Premier/Complete, Business Insights: Essentials, Factiva, and LexisNexis Academic.

The investor can also use many of the sources mentioned earlier to find information about listed companies worldwide. These include Barron's (online.barrons.com), Financial Times (ft.com), MSN Money (money.msn.com), Reuters.com, *USA Today* (www.usatoday.com/money/index), *Wall Street Journal*'s SmartMoney (smartmoney.com), and Yahoo! Finance (finance.yahoo.com). Not only are individuals able to find stock performance data for companies from all over the world at any of these sites, but there will also be news links to relevant information about business and stock markets, as well as to worldwide events that have an impact on the global economy. The serious investor will probably have to subscribe to some of the premium products available at these websites.

For the investor who wants to find information about indices, there are companies that provide definitions and other data about the international and global equity indices that they offer. This includes Morgan Stanley Capital International (MSCI) (www.msci.com/) and S&P (us.spindices.com/). Many world stock indices are identified at the Bloomberg site (www.bloomberg.com/markets/stocks/world-indexes/).

CONCLUSION

This chapter has dealt with a select list of investment options available to someone who wants to create an investment portfolio with an international or global focus. In addition to covering mutual funds, ETFs, depositary receipts, currency trading, and direct investment, sources for each type were identified. This included subscription-based databases and free websites.

Company information is a valuable commodity, and many academic and public libraries will probably have one or more databases that provide extensive company and other invesment-related information from around the world. Therefore, contacting a local academic or public library or scrutinizing its website may reveal that they it has databases from commercial publishers previously mentioned, or others that have similar content.

Investing, global or domestic, is an area in which these same institutions would likely provide not only databases, but books. For instance, a wide range of electronic and print books are published on the many instruments that are available for financial investment. Academic and public libraries provide these in both formats to their patrons. If an individual finds that navigating databases or downloading an electronic book is complicated, he or she should seek the assistance of a librarian. An individual who is trying to learn more about a topic or find information about it should leverage all the tools available, from the World Wide Web to a library's print and digital collection.

LIST OF SOURCES

Databases

This is an alphabetical list of the fee-based databases suggested as resources for this chapter.

Lipper (Thomson Reuters), www.lipperweb.com/default.aspx.
Morningstar Investment Research Center (Chicago, IL: Morningstar, 2002–), library.morningstar.com.
Standard & Poor's NetAdvantage (New York: Standard & Poor's, 2001–), www.netadvantage.standardandpoors.com/.
Value Line Fund Investor (New York: Value Line Pub., 2009–), www.valueline.com.

Websites

This is an alphabetical list of publicly available websites from associations, governments, organizations, and publishers referred to in this chapter.

AvaFx, www.avafx.com (26 June 2012).

Bank of England, "Other Foreign Exchange Committees," www.bankofengland.co.uk/markets/Pages/forex/fxjsc/links.aspx (27 June 2012).

Bank of International Settlements, www.bis.org (27 June 2012).

Bank of New York/Mellon Depositary Receipts, www.adrbnymellon.com (26 June 2012).

Barchart.com (26 June 2012).

Barron's Mutual Fund Screener, online.barrons.com/fund/screener.html (26 June 2012).

Bloomberg Businessweek, Markets & Finance, Mutual Funds & ETFs, www.businessweek.com/markets-and-finance/mutual-funds-and-etfs (26 June 2012).

Bloomberg, Market Data, Browse Funds, www.bloomberg.com/markets/funds/ (26 June 2012).

Bloomberg, Market Data, Browse Indexes, www.bloomberg.com/markets/indexes/ (26 June 2012).

Bloomberg, Market Data, ETF Screener, www.bloomberg.com/apps/data?pid=etfscreener (26 June 2012).

CEF/Connect, www.cefconnect.com/Screener/FundScreener.aspx (26 June 2012).

Citibank, https://wwss.citissb.com/adr/guides/uig.aspx?pageId=3&subpageID=34 (26 June 2012).

Closed-End Fund Association (CEFA), www.cefa.com (26 June 2012).

CNNMoney, Mutual Fund Center, money.cnn.com/data/funds/ (26 June 2012).

CNNMoney, World Currencies, money.cnn.com/data/currencies/ (26 June 2012).

Commodity Futures Trading Commission (CFTC), www.cftc.gov (27 June 2012).

Computershare's Investment Centre, https://wwss.citissb.com/adr/common/linkpage.aspx?linkFormat=M&pageId=3&subpageid=19 (26 June 2012).

Deutsche Bank Depositary Receipt Services, www.adr.db.com (26 June 2012).

Dukascopy, www.dukascopy.com (26 June 2012).

ETFdb, Top-50 Free Online ETF Tools, etfdb.com/2009/top-50-free-online-etf-tools/ (26 June 2012).

European Commission, Investment Funds, ec.europa.eu/internal_market/investment/index_en.htm (26 June 2012).

European Fund and Asset Management Association, www.efama.org (26 June 2012).

Fidelity Online, www.stockpar.com/ (26 June 2012).

Financial Regulators Gateway, www.financialregulatorsgateway.com/ (26 June 2012).

Financial Services Authority, Collective Investment Scheme Information Guide, www.fsa.gov.uk/pubs/foi/collguide.pdf (26 June 2012).

Financial Services Authority (FSA) Register, www.fsa.gov.uk/fsaregister/search/cis_search) (26 June 2012).

Financial Times, Funds and ETFs, funds.ft.com/uk/ (26 June 2012).

Futures, www.futuresmag.com (26 June 2012).

FX Week, www.fxweek.com (27 June 2012).

FX Traders, www.fxtraders.eu (27 June 2012).

FXCM, www.fxcm.com (27 June 2012).

FxPro, www.fxpro.com (27 June 2012).

Federal Reserve Bank of New York, www.newyorkfed.org/fxc/volumesurvey/dealers.html (27 June 2012).

FXstreet.com (26 June 2012).

International Investment Funds Association, www.iifa.ca/ (26 June 2012).

Investment Company Institute, *Investment Company Fact Book*, www.ici.org/pdf/2012_factbook.pdf (26 June 2012).

Investment Management Association, www.investmentfunds.org.uk (26 June 2012).

J. P. Morgan Chase Depositary Receipts (DR), www.adr.com (26 June 2012).

London Stock Exchange, ETFs search, www.londonstockexchange.com/exchange/prices-and-markets/ETFs/ETFs.html (26 June 2012).

London Stock Exchange (LSE), Fund Search, www.londonstockexchange.com/exchange/prices-and-markets/funds/funds.html (26 June 2012).
Maxfunds, www.maxfunds.com (26 June 2012).
MoneyAM, moneyam.com (26 June 2012).
Money.co.uk, www.money.co.uk (26 June 2012).
Morningstar, www.morningstar.com (26 June 2012).
MSCI, Indices, www.msci.com (26 June 2012).
MSN Money, Investing, mutual funds, money.msn.com/mutual-fund/ (26 June 2012).
MSN Money, Investing, ETFs, money.msn.com/exchange-traded-fund/ (26 June 2012).
Mutual Funds Investor's Center, www.mfea.com (26 June 2012).
National Futures Association, www.nfa.org (26 June 2012).
NYSE Euronext, etp.nyx.com (26 June 2012).
Reuters, Markets, Mutual Fund Center, www.reuters.com/finance/fundsReuters.com (26 June 2012).
RTTNews.com (26 June 2012).
S&P Dow Jones Indices, us.spindices.com (20 Oct. 2012).
SmartMoney, Invest, Mutual Funds, www.smartmoney.com/invest/fund/ ?link=SM_topnav_invest (26 June 2012).
StockBrokers.com (26 June 2012).
TradingCharts.com (27 June 2012).
US Securities Exchange Commission, Mutual Funds, www.sec.gov/answers/mutfund.htm (26 June 2012).
USA Today, funds.usatoday.com (26 June 2012).
XE Universal Currency Converter, www.xe.com/ucc/ (26 June 2012).
Yahoo! Finance, Mutual Funds Center, finance.yahoo.com/funds (26 June 2012).

NOTES

1. Value Line, "The Value Line Fund Advisor," 2012, http://www.valueline.com/Products/Mutual_Fund_Products/The_Value_Line_Fund_Advisor.aspx (20 Mar. 2012).
2. Investment Company Institute, "2012 Investment Company Handbook," www.ici.org/pdf/2012_factbook.pdf (16 May. 2012), 194.
3. Harbor Funds, "Harbor Funds International. Overview," 2012, www.harborfunds.com/overview-2411.htm (20 Mar. 2012).
4. Tweedy, Browne Fund, Inc., "Tweedy, Browne Global Value Fund," 2012, www.tweedy.com/resources/gvf/FactsTBGVF022912.pdf (20 Mar. 2012).
5. Investopedia, "Closed-End Fund," 2012, www.investopedia.com/terms/c/closed-endinvestment.asp#axzz1pg7g1RuT (20 Mar. 2012).
6. Morningstar, Inc. "10-K," (2011), www.shareholder.com/common/edgar/1289419/1289419-12-63/12-00.pdf (26 Mar. 2012), 4.
7. Many mutual fund companies incorporate Morningstar ratings when presenting performance information on a specific fund.
8. Value Line, "History—Arnold Bernhard," www.valueline.com/About/History.aspx (25 April 2012).
9. Value Line, "About Value Line," www.valueline.com/About/ (25 April 2012).
10. Investment Company Institute, "Worldwide Mutual Fund Assets and Flows Fourth Quarter 2011," April 12, 2012, www.ici.org/research/stats/worldwide/ww_12_11 (6 May 2012).
11. Mary Brown, "How Mutual Funds Differ Around the World," Jan. 14, 2012, www.investopedia.com/articles/mutualfund/08/foreign-mutual-funds.asp#axzz1v40PNSVT (16 May 2012).
12. European Commission, "Investment Funds," ec.europa.eu/internal_market/investment/index_en.htm (1 May 2012).

13. Deloitte, "Undertakings for Collective Investment in Transferable Securities (UCITS) Whitepaper, 2010," https://www.deloitte.com/assets/Dcom-Luxembourg/Local%20Assets/Documents/Whitepapers/2010/lu_wp_luxvehiclesucits_28042010.pdf (1 May 2012).

14. Ray Russell, *An Introduction to Mutual Funds Worldwide* (Chichester, England; Hoboken, NJ: Wiley, 2007), 5.

15. Investment Company Institute, "2012 Investment Company Handbook," 224.

16. Martha Maeda, *The Complete Guide to Investing in Exchange Traded Funds: How to Earn High Rates of Return—Safely* (Ocala, FL: Atlantic Publishing Group, Inc., 2009), 21–24.

17. Investment Company Institute, "Exchange Traded Fund Assets, March 2012," www.ici.org/research/stats/etf/etfs_03_12 (12 May 2012).

18. Harry Domash, *Exchange-Traded Fund (ETF) Investing: What You Need to Know* (Upper Saddle River, NJ: FT Press, 2011), proquest.safaribooksonline.com (27 Mar. 2012).

19. Maeda, *The Complete Guide to Investing in Exchange Traded Funds*, 21–22.

20. John A. Prestbo and Douglas R. Sease, *The Wall Street Journal Book of International Investing* (New York: Hyperion, 1997), 80–81.

21. Investopedia, "Global Depositary Receipt," 2012, www.investopedia.com/terms/g/gdr.asp#ixzz1ov93RRTa (12 Mar. 2012).

22. Investopedia, "European Depositary Receipt," 2012, www.investopedia.com/terms/e/european_depository_receipt.asp#ixzz1ov8cCSGp (12 Mar. 2012).

23. Prestbo and Sease, *The Wall Street Journal Book of International Investing*, 81–82.

24. Sometimes it is also referred to as transaction or reference currency.

25. The order of the currency pairs is established by the International Standard Organization (www.iso.org).

26. CFTC Glossary, "pip," www.cftc.gov/ConsumerProtection/EducationCenter/CFTCGlossary/glossary_p (23 May 2012).

27. Bank for International Settlements, *Triennial Central Bank Survey, Report on Global Foreign Exchange Market Activity* (Dec. 2010), 33, www.bis.org/publ/rpfx10.htm (27 June 2012).

28. Jessica Mead and Katie Martin, "Moving the Market: Retail Forex Trading Surges," *Wall Street Journal, US Edition*, April 16, 2012, online.wsj.com (24 May 24 2012).

29. Stockbrokers.com, "Best Forex Brokers 2012," www.stockbrokers.com/reviews/beststockbrokers (25 June 2012).

30. John Jagerson and S. Wade Hansen, *All About Forex Trading* (New York: McGraw-Hill, 2011), 32–33.

31. Jagerson and Hansen, *All About Forex Trading*, 237–38.

32. Securities Exchange Commission. "Forex—Foreign Currency Transactions," www.sec.gov/answers/forcurr.htm (24 May 2012).

33. *Webster's New World Finance and Investment Dictionary*, s.v. "commitment of traders report," accessed June 27, 2012, www.credoreference.com/entry/wileynwfid/commitment_of_traders_report (27 June 2012).

Index

About the Authors

Esther L. Gil has been a business and economics reference librarian since 1997 at the University of Denver, Penrose Library. As both a reference librarian and selector for business, she is familiar with the types of sources that can meet the needs for international business research. She wrote the chapter "Business Research" for the book *Research within the Disciplines: Foundations for Reference and Library Instruction* (Scarecrow, 2007).

Awilda Reyes has worked as a business librarian for the University of Puerto Rico and Colorado State University. She is presently a librarian at West Chester University of Pennsylvania. Awilda travels to lecture in other countries, such as Argentina, Chile, and Peru.

Each of the authors has also written articles published in various scholarly journals and magazines.